Sex crime in the news

Newspaper reports of sex crimes have become increasingly sensationalist in recent years. Based on 5,000 newspapers from forty years of newspaper coverage, *Sex Crime in the News* is the first systematic study of such reporting. It reveals the misleading and trivialising nature of much of this coverage, with serious research reports on rape and discussions on law reform being given short shrift.

The number of sex crimes, especially rape, reported to the police has risen dramatically over the last few years, and there is much public and political concern about the issue, both from feminists and from the law-and-order lobby. Yet, as the authors show, the media typically ignore the wider issues which these groups raise, preferring to highlight a few unusual cases. Keith Soothill and Sylvia Walby examine the increasing gap between the reality of sexual abuse and the coverage it is given in the press, and they set their detailed empirical work within a context of broader concerns about the relationship between the media, the individual and the state.

Critical though it is of the press, *Sex Crime in the News* will be of special interest to people working in the media, and to legislators involved in debates about the press. It will also be of value to students on courses in women's studies, cultural and media studies, and deviancy.

Keith Soothill is Professor of Social Research in the Department of Applied Social Science at Lancaster University. **Sylvia Walby** is Lecturer in Sociology at the London School of Economics. They have both written widely on sex crimes and the related issues of gender relations and deviancy.

Sex crime in the news

Keith Soothill and Sylvia Walby

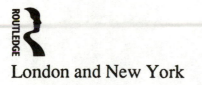

London and New York

First published in 1991
by Routledge
11 New Fetter Lane, London EC4P 4EE

Simultaneously published in the USA and Canada
by Routledge
a division of Routledge, Chapman and Hall Inc.
29 West 35th Street, New York, NY 10001

© 1991 Keith Soothill and Sylvia Walby

Typeset by LaserScript Limited, Mitcham, Surrey
Printed and bound in Great Britain by Mackays of Chatham PLC, Kent

British Library Cataloguing in Publication Data
Soothill, Keith, *1941–*
Sex crime in the news.
1. Great Britain. Crimes. Rape. Social aspects
I. Title II. Walby, Sylvia
364.15320941

Library of Congress Cataloging in Publication Data
Soothill, Keith.
Sex crime in the news/Keith Soothill and Sylvia Walby.
    p. cm.
Includes bibliographical references and index.
1. Sex crimes in the press—Great Britain. 2. Freedom of the
press—Great Britain. 3. Privacy, Right of—Great Britain. 4. Sex
crimes—Great Britain. 5. Crime journalism—Great Britain.
I. Walby, Sylvia. II. Title.
PN5124.S47S66   1990
070.4'49364153'0941—dc20   90–38051
                                                  CIP

ISBN 0-415-01815-3
        0-415-05801-5 (pbk)

ACQ8804

Contents

Illustrations

Tables

Acknowledgements

We would like to thank the Nuffield Foundation for the grant which made the empirical work for this project possible; Sue Penna and Brenda Penn for help in carrying out some of the fieldwork; Chris Quinn for help in the preparation of the manuscript; the Department of Sociology at the University of Lancaster, where the project was originally based; and one of us would like to thank loved ones at home for allowing mountains of newsprint to remain around.

Chapter one

Introduction

It is a paradox that while sex crimes are popularly abhorred little action is taken against the majority of offenders. We know that the majority of women who are raped do not approach the police for fear of the judicial procedure they may face and the publicity they may have to endure. We know that in 1987 only 18 per cent of these complaints ended in the conviction of a rapist.[1] Yet simultaneously rapists, and indeed all men who commit violent sexual offences, are regarded as particularly villainous by the majority of the population, and these crimes have a high priority in the public's demand for law and order. Why is such a hated crime dealt with so ineffectively?

One of the themes of the book is to explore how this contradiction is negotiated in popular discourse via an examination of newspapers. What is the image of sex crime which is portrayed in the press? Why does most of the coverage focus on the very few disturbed serial rapists, rather than typical rape? How is it that the majority of people are given such a highly distorted overall picture of the nature and incidence of sexual violence? How does the manner and level of reporting affect women's fear of crime?

There have been major changes in both the interface of the police and raped women and in the media coverage. Firstly, we are seeing a dramatically increased number of rapes being processed by the police and courts. Secondly, there have been major changes in the amount of rape reported in the press.

A second major theme is with the viability of a variety of policy options to control the negative aspects of press reporting of sex crimes, especially rape. This practical reference frames our discussion of the newspaper reporting. Hence we examine the issues surrounding the development of legislative and other means of intervening in the press.

Changes in reporting of crimes of sexual violence to the police

There has been a significant increase in the amount of sexual violence reported to the police. The number of rapes reported to the police increased from 1,015 in 1977 to 2,471 in 1987, an increase of 143 per cent.[2]

However, since the majority of rapes are not reported to the police, it is difficult to interpret these figures. On the one hand they could indicate a large increase in the level of rape. On the other they could indicate that more women are reporting the crime. If the former is correct then we are seeing an enormous increase in the use of violence against women. If the latter then perhaps we are seeing a reduction in the distrust women have for the police in relation to their handling of rape, or maybe the greater ability of women to withstand the trauma of carrying through a complaint of rape.

However, while the increase in the rate of rape reporting has increased, the rate of conviction has declined. In 1977 32 per cent of rape complaints were concluded by conviction of the rapist, while in 1987 only 18 per cent were similarly convicted.[3] The rate of increase of convicted rapists is 39 per cent as against an increase in rape reports of 143 per cent. If we take the former interpretation of the increase in rape reporting then this would mean that not only are more men raping, but also the judiciary is increasingly allowing them to get away with it. If it is the latter, then we are seeing a constant rate of rape over the last decade but where women are more willing to make legal complaints and the police and courts not willing to convict other than a very small increase in the number.

A similar but less marked pattern is to be found in other cases of sexual violence. The reported cases of indecent or sexual assault increased by 21 per cent over the 1977–87 decade, while the number of men convicted rose by only 2 per cent, a decline in the conviction rate from 31 per cent to 26 per cent.[4] In the same decade reports of incest increased by 73 per cent, while the number of those convicted rose by 55 per cent, a decline in the conviction rate from 53 per cent to 48 per cent.[5]

Whichever way we look at these figures, whether we believe they represent a real increase in the rate of sexual violence or not, the decreasing conviction rate indicates that the state has not effectively responded to demands that sex crimes be treated more seriously. Yet there has been sustained pressure from two political directions to do so. The first is that of feminist campaigners based, not only in rape crisis centres and refuges, but also in specialist lobby groups such as Women Against Rape and Women Against Violence Against Women. The second is the law and order lobby of the right, which is also picking up on demands that the law be tougher with rapists and other violent criminals. So why has it not led to a rise in conviction rates?

The optimistic reading is that we have been successful, in that the number of men convicted of rape has increased over the last decade by 39 per cent in the case of rape, 2 per cent in the case of sexual assault, and 55 per cent in the case of incest. The pessimistic view is evidenced by the fact that the rate of conviction stemming from reported rapes has declined by 44 per cent in the case of rape, 16 per cent in the case of sexual assault and 9 per cent in the case of incest. Whether the increase in reported rates of sexual violence are positive or negative depends on whether they are considered to be real increases or higher rates of reporting.

Changes in press coverage

There have been major increases in the amount of reporting of rape and other sex crimes in the media. The popular daily newspapers are much more likely to carry such stories today than twenty years ago. However, the reports are typically sensational and titillating, rather than serious accounts of these crimes. All manner of sexual detail is squeezed into these reports, anything from the previous sex life of a convicted rapist ('the savage between the sheets') to the newspapers' reading of the sexual history of the raped woman 'Para case girl was "sex maniac" '.[6]

This sort of press coverage is problematic for all manner of people. Firstly, the woman or girl who has suffered a sexual assault is made to suffer again by having sensationalist accounts of their ordeal blazoned to the entire nation, defeating attempts to forget. Secondly, the lives of others may be dragged through the media if they have been associated with a notorious rapist. Thirdly, the image of rape portrayed is misleading and may encourage mistaken beliefs by judges and juries, so that they do not convict in cases which fall outside this narrow stereotype.[7]

What do we think about this increased reporting? Is it good that rape is now reported, and its existence no longer denied? Is this coming into the open of crimes against women useful in assisting reforms in this area? Or are the stereotypes of rape portrayed by the press so narrow and unusual that they hinder the process of effective intervention by the state and others. Does the reporting raise women's fear of crime?[8] In a society where many women are afraid to walk alone at night does this increase in reporting increase women's fear still further? Do the rape reports encourage further rapes, by providing information to potential rapists? Does the pornographic nature of some of the reports encourage attitudes which facilitate rape?[9] Given that we have so little information about rape, does the increased press reporting, given its restricted nature, hinder the chance of a raped woman getting a fair 'trial'? Are juries

legislative

increasingly inhibited from convicting men who are different from this stereotype? Does the press narrow popular conceptions of rape and make it more difficult for raped women to obtain justice? If the reports do contribute negatively, what should be done about it? Should they be compulsorily edited so as to be accurate and balanced, that is censored? Or is this going too far and risks losing more, in terms of freedom of speech, than we would gain?

These questions demonstrate the complexity of the freedom and control issue which are implicitly in discussion in many parts of the world.

National differences

The balance between press freedom and control over problematic reportage varies between different countries. In the USA press freedom is held up as sovereign. The First Amendment of the Constitution about freedom of speech and the press not only symbolises this commitment, but also is used to defend this position in the courts,[10] though even here there are some limits. In Scandinavia the interests of the victim of sexual attack are given highest priority. In Sweden the press engages in comparatively little coverage of sex crimes, with the exception of the most popular evening papers.[11] Britain is in between with more constraints upon the media than happens in the USA, but more press reporting than in many Scandinavian countries. The British 'compromise' is in practice closer to the American than Scandinavian model.

British legislation

In 1976 Britain, or more strictly England and Wales, introduced legislation which sought to control the worst excesses of the press and the courts in relation to rape. The press was banned from publishing the name of the raped woman and the courts were prohibited from enquiring into her previous sexual history except at the discretion of the judge.

This legislation has had a limited effect, as we shall show. We evaluated the effect of the 1976 legislation on the issue of the anonymity of the rape survivor; on the basis of press reporting in 1978, we found that she was now most unlikely to be named, but identifying detail was still published.[12] Adler's study of eighty rape trials examined actual court procedure in detail, providing evidence on what actually happens rather than what should.[13] Adler found that despite the legislation a woman's sexual history was routinely introduced during a rape trial. This usually occurred indirectly, but none the less effectively introducing this information which Parliament had tried to rule out as admissible evidence. This practice did not strictly contravene the legislation since

4

there is a loophole which allowed the introduction of this line of questioning at the discretion of the judge, if the judge thought it was essential. It is this discretion that has been used routinely to allow questioning which Parliament had intended should be exceptional. This questioning is of direct relevance to press coverage because reporters use the courtroom as a major source of their information for their writing. When the judges allow the woman's sexual history to be heard in court, they allow it to be reported in the press.

Policy instruments

The three main forms of regulation of press reporting of sexual offences are, firstly, that embodied in the Sexual Offences Amendment Act 1976, secondly, the Press Council administered Code of Practice, and thirdly, the libel laws. In the first the press is expressly refused permission to print the name of the raped woman. The Act also sought to restrict the extent to which a woman's prior sexual history could be used as admissible evidence in court, thus indirectly affecting the material available to the press to publish. In the second the press is restrained by its own professional Code of Practice not to misrepresent or mislead the public. In the third, the press faces financial penalties if anyone successfully sues the paper through the civil courts for defamation of character.

Studies of sexual violence

Why do men rape and sexually assault women and girls? It is important to discuss the various explanations briefly, if only because these surface in the press in a variety of forms.

Classically these crimes have been seen as a result of a few mentally deranged men. They have had unfortunate childhoods in which they have been neglected and brutalised. They grow up unbalanced, and need only minor frustrations or the stimulus of pornography to tip them into an orgy of violence against women and girls. There are occasional academic studies which appear at first glance to support such interpretations, such as that of West, Roy and Nichols.[14] But on closer examination it can usually be found that they have used very selected samples that are not representative of sexual offenders as a whole. For instance, the West, Roy and Nichols study looked at the cases of men who had already been incarcerated in an institution for mentally ill offenders – they were not a random sample of even those few rapists who are convicted.

A second explanation is in terms of the frustrations that men of the disadvantaged classes and ethnic groups suffer in a class-based and racist society.[15] These socially and economically deprived men are considered to develop alternative social values in consequence of being excluded from the possibility of success in terms of the mainstream society. These values include a macho version of masculinity and an embracing of violence. Women suffer from the resulting behaviour. The problem with this type of explanation is that it fails to explain why women, who are surely more deprived than men, do not also engage in violent acts. In fact women are significantly less violent than men, suggesting that frustration with socio-economic deprivation is not a sufficient explanation.

Both these explanations fail to deal with the generalised nature of aggressive actions by men towards women. There is a wide range of sexually aggressive actions from men to women which form a continuum from sex murders through rape and sexual assault to sexual harassment and flashing to wolf whistling.[16] To understand this we must turn to explanations at the level of social relations in a sexist society. These acts can be traced to a plethora of practices which encourage sexually aggressive behaviour in men and boys, in a context in which there are few effective sanctions.[17] Not only pornography, but also the general denigration of women, has been implicated in the construction of male sexual scripts in which aggression is seen as a positive masculine quality. Further, the failure of the police and courts to prosecute and convict more than a small proportion of rapists means that there is little effective legal deterrent. Recent feminist work has focused not only on the continuum of male sexual violence,[18] but also on the serial rapists[19] and sex murderers.[20]

The politicisation of crimes of sexual violence

Sex crimes against women have emerged on to the political agenda over the last twenty years. This can be traced to two, radically different, political forces. Firstly, feminism; secondly, the right wing law and order lobby.

Feminists have launched major political campaigns about male violence and backed these up with the establishment of national networks of centres to help those who have suffered male violence.[21] The 1970s and 1980s saw the setting up of rape crisis centres, refuges for battered women, groups for incest survivors, and a host of local and national campaigning groups including Women Against Rape, Women Against Violence Against Women, and the Women's Aid Federation. They have extended their protests to the legal process and judges' behaviour in court. Feminist debates on the control of representations of sexual violence are examined below.

The law and order lobby has grown in strength during the Conservative ascendancy. While it is closely associated with the Conservatives, it is not to be simply equated with the Conservative Party, and indeed, sometimes acts as a lobby within that party for stronger intervention against crime. For instance, the Home Secretary is regularly criticised for leniency on such issues from this lobby at the Conservative Party conferences.[22] The place of 'Thatcherism' in these issues is discussed below.

Interestingly women form a disproportionately large section of the law and order lobby. Campbell[23] suggests that this is due to their own recognition, as vulnerable women, of the problem of male violence and thus wish to have it controlled. Hence, it is women in particular, though not alone, who have raised the issue of criminal violence, but with radically different policy proposals. Feminists tend to start by asking the survivors of this violence what they want and need, and hence have focused their efforts on assisting these women, often with considerable amounts of voluntary labour. The law and order lobby, in contrast, focuses on deterring the offender with ever harsher punishments.

A brief history of recent reforms

The recent changes in police practice and courtroom procedure stem from this politicisation of sexual assault in the 1970s and 1980s. The first set of changes in this period led to the Sexual Offences Amendment Act in 1976; the second led to Home Office guidelines on revised police procedures in 1983 (and later 1986).

While there had been a lot of activity by feminists regarding questions of rape in the early 1970s, it was the Morgan case[24] which was the focus of the mainstream public debate prior to the 1976 Act. In this way, some of the concerns of the women's movement gained a more public stage. The Morgan case created a legal debate which produced some contortions of legal reasoning. In this case the judge held that a man is not guilty of rape if he has sexual intercourse with a woman who does not consent to it if he believes she does consent, whether his belief is based on reasonable grounds or not. That is, the woman's experience of rape was deemed irrelevant to the question as to whether she was legally raped, since this depends upon the man's state of mind. It was this statement of the law which led to outcries that it was a 'Rapist's Charter'.[25] Eventually, however, all four men were convicted, but this did not settle the legal issue at stake.

The Morgan case was one of several which generated controversy. For example, in the Stapleton case in 1975 the defendant was acquitted of rape despite the fact that even the judge in passing sentence had said: 'I have no doubt you instilled terror into this woman when you went into that room and made your intentions quite clear'.[26] Another controversy was caused by Justice Stevenson effectively blaming the woman for getting raped because she had hitched a lift, giving the rapist only a suspended sentence, and summing up thus – "It was, as rape goes, a pretty anaemic affair. The man has made a fool of himself, but the girl was almost equally stupid. This practice of hitch-hiking must be stopped".[27]

Following the Morgan controversy the Home Secretary appointed an Advisory Group chaired by Justice Rose Heilbron to consider the law of rape in June 1975.[28] This led to the Sexual Offences (Amendment) Act in 1976.

One of the issues in the passage of this legislation was that of the anonymity of raped women and girls, although the nearly all-male Parliament was also concerned about anonymity for the accused men. In the summer of 1974 there had been several questions regarding the possibility of anonymity in rape cases.[29] In answer to questions the Home Secretary at this time had stated that this was an issue for individual courts to make requests of the press, not a matter for legislation. However, there were attempts at a private member's bill: the Rape (Anonymity of Victims) Bill was introduced by Mr F.P. Crowder,[30] and there was another in 1975 by Jack Ashley, stemming from concern that raped women were not reporting the crime because of fear of press publicity. This potential increase of reporting rape incidents became the main rationale for seeking anonymity for the victim.

The Heilbron Advisory Group confirmed these fears and maintained that "disclosure of a rape victim's name caused her great distress and also tended to discourage women from reporting alleged rape".[31] Specifically the Heilbron Report did not recommend similar anonymity for defendants in rape cases. However, the Heilbron Report made no proposals to change the law on the issue which had been at stake in the Morgan case – that a man could escape a rape conviction if he thought that the woman was consenting whether she was or not. Thus while the original concern was not dealt with, other issues which had been raised earlier were.

During the parliamentary debates, the main feature was the male MPs' interest in the "equality" issue. Mr Rees-Davies suggested that "surely . . . if anonymity is to be given during a trial to the complainant, it should also be given to the accused".[32] Others maintained that the ordeal of publicity was essential to "effectively test the veracity of a witness".[33] The official Conservative Opposition was unenthusiastic about the Bill.[34] A specific interest of the almost entirely male chamber was to focus on the defendant. The tale of the prospective parliamentary candidate who, a few months before a General Election, was charged with a rape offence, and acquitted, haunted the debate and it was alleged that his whole prospective parliamentary career had been unnecessarily ruined. This account helped the inclusion of anonymity for the rape defendant as well.

The Act also attempted to deal with the problem of the tendency of defence lawyers to pillory a woman if she had had any non-marital sexual experience.[35] This could in turn receive extensive media coverage. The Act thus attempted to control the admissibility of such evidence in the courtroom for reasons not only for its biasing effects upon a jury, but also for subsequent press coverage, which is often based on courtroom interaction. Further, it was hoped that if nothing happened during the trial which newspapers could turn into titillating copy for their readers, then there would be less incentive for the papers to give widespread coverage. Indeed, in the absence of titillating and embarrassing revelations, the need for anonymity becomes less pressing.

So why the demand for anonymity? The reformers were not merely considering the desire of actual rape victims to avoid publicity. In fact, how the rape survivor feels about her experience in the criminal justice process is more likely to be affected by what happens in the police station and then in the courtroom than how it is reported in the press. For the rape survivor the experience of the court interaction is likely to be primary and the media coverage is secondary; thus for such women and girls, anonymity in the media may be a minor reform compared to others in which they have an interest. However, the portrayal of raped women in the press may be considered likely to deter women from reporting rape to the police. Most women gain most of their knowledge of the criminal justice process from the media since few will have attended actual court cases or learnt from friends of what actually happens in the criminal justice system. The significance of the anonymity issue for many of the legal experts lies more with their own concern with getting more women to report rape, than with raped women's own priorities for legal change.

Reforms of police practice

In the 1980s the focus of reform shifted from the press and courtroom to police practices. In 1982 a series of events highlighted the appalling treatment that raped women suffered at the hands of the police, leading to a public outcry and revised procedures.[36] The police handling of rape complaints was shown in a documentary on Thames television, with the approval of the police, suggesting that they saw no problem in this. Millions of viewers saw the vicious and disbelieving interrogation of a woman who went to the police saying she had been raped. This produced widespread and lasting protest. Police mishandling of the case of the 'Yorkshire Ripper', who was not caught despite the evidence available, was subject to scrutiny and complaints. Public protest followed a judge who fined a rapist £2,000 after asserting that the woman had been guilty of contributory negligence by hitch-hiking. Prosecution decisions were criticised in the case of the 'Glasgow razor rape' case in which the authorities had refused to prosecute; the woman herself then success-fully undertook a private prosecution.

Each of these incidents provoked widespread protest, not confined to the feminist groups which focused on issues of sexual violence. In this context of public protest the Home Office issued guidelines on how the police should behave in cases of rape complaints. The protest had succeeded in forcing a change in police policy.[37]

A number of changes have taken place, and a number of experimental schemes introduced. These include the setting up in some areas of special rooms and facilities where cases of sexual assault can be dealt with, the training of police by Rape Crisis groups, and some specialist police units.[38] The first of these has involved the so-called 'rape suites', a set of rooms away from the main police station, often including shower, examination room, waiting-room and kitchen. Sometimes they are purpose built (Wiltshire and London), sometimes specially furnished rooms in police stations (Northamptonshire), sometimes separate rooms in hospitals (Hampshire). In Manchester there has been a major development of a Sexual Assault Referral Centre, jointly funded by the police and hospital authorities. This has all the facilities men-tioned above, and in addition uses a medical model of the treatment of rape.[39] It offers counselling as well as physical medical support. Special police units have been set up in some areas, usually but not always staffed by women police officers. These exist in Glasgow, Leeds and Bradford, Huddersfield, and Worthing.[40] Furthermore, many police forces now receive specialist training in dealing with victims of sexual assault, often provided by members of Rape Crisis Lines. Victim-support services for the victims of all crimes are now being set up and funded by the Home Office.[41] This involves talking to those who have suffered crimes recently, including sexual assault.

Most of these developments have bypassed the work of the estab-lished Rape Crisis Lines, which have been developing expertise in the counselling of women who have suffered sexual assault. These Rape Crisis groups usually draw extensively on the experience and sense of priorities of women who have been raped. This bypassing of these groups leads to a worrying loss of expertise, for what appears to be political reasons, namely, that the Rape Crisis Lines have radical politics.

Feminism, censorship and the state

The control of rape reporting by the state raises some of the same issues as that concerning the control of pornography. That is, the debates raise difficult issues on censorship. There are parallels with the 'porn the theory, rape the practice' debate, and the censorship debate in feminism.[42] Newspaper reports of rape are not usually thought of as pornography, though sometimes they are in effect. Should the same debates apply to this? Many of the writers within this debate assume that there is a choice between censorship and freedom of speech. In relation to the material we are discussing there are already forms of legal restriction over the material which constitute regulation, though this is not usually called censorship. If pornography were to be restricted legally the mechanisms would likely to be similar to those which already affect rape reporting, so their use is relevant to both issues.

The feminist debate on censorship, as for instance caught in the collection edited by Chester and Dickey, involves many complex issues of the relationship between representations and practice.[43]

Does the portrayal of sexual violence have the effect of making it more likely? To most social scientists and policy makers this is the most important question about pornography, and is pertinent to our discussion of newspaper reports.[44] This question in relation to pornography has been central to government commissions on the availability of pornography in Britain, the USA and elsewhere. These commissions have drawn on expert opinion from the social science community, and found evidence for both sides.

On the one hand we can cite the experiments of social psychologists such as Malamuth, who state that an empirical correlation can be established between men's exposure to pornography and propensity to rape.[45] He and his colleagues performed a variety of laboratory experiments in which men's attitudes and responses to rape were tested before and after exposure to pornography. The means of measuring response varied from attitudinal statements to degree of penile tumescence. Malamuth's methods are rigorous and his analysis convincing.

On the other hand, theorists in the field of Cultural Studies caution against any simple notion that exposure of individuals to cultural representations modifies their behaviour.[46] Typically they regard such questions as untestable and, since unanswerable, not worth asking. Such scholars suggest that we should analyse pornographic representations as representations, not causes of social behaviour.[47] This does not necessarily imply acceptance of these images since they may be seen as unacceptable in their own right. That is, unacceptable as representations, whether or not they have effects on sexually violent behaviour. Kappeller[48] argues that pornography should be analysed as representation, and that it is degrading to women. And that is sufficient to argue against it.

The feminist debate on pornography often, but not always, links it to that of censorship.[49] The question appears at first in terms of whether the suppression of pornography by censorship is worth the price in terms of loss of freedom of expression. Initially it appears as an act of balance, with vigorous debate between those who think that censorship is never worth it, and those for whom pornography is so dangerous that censorship is not too high a price at all.

However, this debate is over-simple since it is predicated on an assumption that censorship would work, that it is possible to stop pornography by state action. The dubiousness of this is obvious when we reflect on the failure of the state to stop all manner of illicit and illegal activity. Censorship may have an impact on pornography, but is unlikely to stop it.

Further, there is the problem of the practice of censorship once introduced, as to whether it would focus on the kinds of sexual behaviour which are violent and degrading to women, or whether it would be used to ban representations of sexual behaviour that feminists found acceptable, such as non-violent gay and lesbian sex. There is a question as to who would control the censorship apparatus, and whether it would be used by reactionary rather than progressive forces once in place.

The initial apparent similarity between some feminists and some of the right on the issue of pornography is curious.[50] At first glance some strands of these otherwise opposed political forces seem to agree on the use of censorship to oppose pornography. However, on further examination it is clear that they often disagree as to what constitutes pornography, while overlapping on representations of sexual violence, they radically disagree on those of non-violent, non-marital sexual practices.

The historical reporting of rape

The use of sex crime in the media as a source of titillation has a long and inglorious past which has emerged spectacularly again in the Thatcher years.

As far back as the eighteenth century,[51] and probably before, trial reports about cases of sexual crimes, adultery and non-traditional sexual practices have been constructed as a genre of pornography. In addition, some trials of priests charged with sexual crimes provided material for pornographic and anti-religious writings.

tech. While as early as Elizabethan times crime chap-books were published to give news about recent crimes, Wagner suggests that it was only toward the end of the seventeenth century that a diverse crime literature appeared. Some sections of the reading public became enthusiastic for trial reports as bawdy 'entertainment'. By the 1740s newspapers were replacing books as the primary source of this material with an interest by middle-stratum men in the sexual misconduct of the nobility.[52] Towards the end of the century pornographic magazines, which extensively used the sexual content of cases with accompanying obscene prints, began to emerge and the number of these kinds of magazines increased appreciably after 1800.

In the nineteenth century there were a variety of sources available about criminal cases. The 1840 Preface to *The Chronicles of Crime; or The New Newgate Calendar*[53] indicates a new 'moral' tone – "Chronicles of Crime must comprise details, not only interesting to every person concerned for the welfare of society, but useful to the world in pointing out the consequences of guilt to be equally dreadful and inevitable".[54] Similarly, the broadsheets – produced in large quantities from the sixteenth to the nineteenth centuries – "were the popular journalism of the day, recording [such events], usually with a combination of a report and ballad, sometimes with a ballad alone". Goodman stresses how "the crime broadsheets, with their tut-tutting moral tone giving the excuse of a welter of gory details, are the ancestors of our mass-circulation Sunday newspapers".[55]

Clearly the *News of the World* strongly maintained the tradition of the crime broadsheets through most of the twentieth century. Today, this mode of reporting continues to be controversial. A crucial question is whether 'Thatcherism' has a distinctive position on crimes of sexual violence.

The law on the control over sexually violent images has been slightly strengthened with the introduction of legislation against the 'video nasties' and the banning of pornographic images from direct public view, although not preventing their availability.

This relates to the general issue of whether there is a consistent policy on state control of the media. Television and media have come under increasing pressure from the government not to publicise controversies about military and security matters. The press were taken to court over publication of extracts from *Spycatcher* with its details of the adventures of the 'security' forces. Film about a new spy satellite was seized from the BBC under a court order.

Yet in contradiction to these developments, which increase state control, there is also the policy of encouraging the market and decreasing the size and scope of the state. For instance, the development of satellite television which necessarily decreases government control has been welcomed and there is a policy of decreasing the regulation over existing commercial television.

Government policy over the media and its display of sexually violent images thus appears contradictory. There is some pattern in that commercial matters are given greater freedom, while issues pertaining to the military are subject to greater control. This is illuminated by Gamble in his thesis that Thatcher's policies represent simultaneous moves towards both a free economy and a strong state.[56] However, the policing of images of sexual violence appears to fall down the gap between the two, sometimes being subject to one policy, and sometimes the other. Thus on the one hand the liberal, free economy strategy is evidenced in the non-censorship of all but the most extreme pornography and the encouragement of commercial values in broadcasting, which is likely to mean decreased control over pornographic images, while on the other the strong state strategy is evidenced by that hard core pornography is not open to direct viewing by the public and by the appointment of censorious watchdogs over the BBC.

Today's newspapers

The debates on sexual violence raise a series of questions about the way that ideas on this subject are constructed and maintained. Clearly there is some discrepancy between the facts about these crimes and the ideas that many people hold.[57] Our present study was designed to examine one of the major sources of information available to people about rape and sexual assault – newspaper reports of the crimes.

There is obviously a complicated relationship between what is printed in the newspapers and what people come to believe, and we would not wish to suggest that people passively and uncritically absorb all that they read there. The meaning is formed within the relationship between the text and the reader. It is not simply pre-given on the page, ready to be absorbed.[58]

Some media studies writers have suggested that the meaning of a text is mediated via discussions people have with the friends and household about their viewing and reading. That is, it is not shaped simply by individuals, but by group interpretations. If this latter is important, then we would expect the big rape cases which get a lot of media coverage to be especially important in the formation of beliefs, since they are more likely to be common currency for discussion than the smaller cases.[59] Some Cultural Studies writers, however, despair of being able to specify this relationship at all. However, this indeterminacy of meaning should not be pushed too far. It is not realistic to suggest that any meaning is possible. Certain meanings are privileged, in the sense that they are more likely interpretations, given the context of the existing social and cultural codes.[60]

In our study a sample of newspapers was examined for all their stories about rape and sexual crime more generally. This book focuses upon 1985, a mid-way point in the Thatcher years, but places it in the context of the changing reporting which we have studied in the years 1951, 1961, 1971, 1978 as well as 1985.

14

gathering:

The material for the newspaper reports can be gathered in four main ways. Firstly, it can be taken from court proceedings. Many of the small reports are produced from such a data source. Because of this, many of the reports are structured by the courtroom discourse. Secondly, they can be a result of wider journalistic efforts either from contacts with the police, or from interviewing people associated with the rape in some indirect way, either near the time of the offence, or the trial, or even, in a few cases, some time later. Newspapers seldom initiate reports about specific sexual assaults themselves, but depend upon the police and courts. Thirdly, newspapers report on parliamentary proceedings discussing changes in the law. From these three major sources it can be seen that rape and sexual assault are very rarely the subject of investigative journalism outside of some judicial context. Hence newspapers and the judiciary are more intimately interconnected on this topic than on many others which are the subject of journalistic interest. The fourth type of information about sexual assault and rape, which is the only major source outside of a judicial context, is that of research by academics and activists. As we shall see later these sources often receive short shrift in many of the papers.

The changing reporting of crimes of sexual violence

It is important to note that sexual violence, including rape, has a wider range of forms than is typically reported upon in the press or recognised as a crime. The growing concern about marital rape exemplifies how some forms of serious sexual violence can be excluded from both the law and media coverage. The media, in fact, are highly selective in their focus upon sexual violence.

The context of this book is the increase in the *official* reports of rape and other crimes of sexual violence and an increase in the newspaper reporting of such crimes. In these circumstances we are interested in how the press reports these crimes and how this has been changing. Are there any links between the increases in the two types of reporting? What does it mean when rape and sexual violence are no longer quite so hidden away from the public view? Will there be an increase in public debate which helps to reduce the rate of sex crimes? Or does it simply increase women's fear of crime? In policy terms we are interested in the regulation of the press reporting, how and why this has been done, and its effects, if any.

Chapter two

The newspaper studies

The newspapers

We have studied the reporting of rape and other crimes of sexual violence since 1951[1] and have samples of newspapers for 1951, 1961, 1971, 1978 and 1985. This book will focus on the most recent set, that for 1985, mid-way through the Thatcher term. However, we shall also discuss the changes which have occurred over these three and a half decades.

In all years they included a series of national newspapers; the *Daily Mirror*, *The Times*, the *News of the World*, the *Sunday People*, and one local, the *London Evening Standard*. In 1971 the *Sun* was added. In 1985 the *Star*, *Guardian*, *Observer*, *Mail on Sunday*, *Sunday Mirror*, *Coventry Evening Telegraph*, *Lancashire Evening Post*, *Lancaster Guardian* and *Middlesex Chronicle* were added to the sample. They fall into four main categories: popular dailies, quality dailies, national Sundays, and local papers. The 1985 study was based on a reading of 3,015 newspapers.

For one complete year (1985) every item relating to sex crime was identified in the sixteen newspapers – four popular dailies, two 'quality' dailies, five national Sundays, three local evenings, and two local weeklies.[2]

In order to engage in comparisons over time we were faced with a dilemma stemming from the change in the range of newspapers over this period. In particular there has been a significant expansion of the 'down-market' dailies. If we used only the same newspapers then we would miss new developments which added to the range, while if we did add to the sample then we were not comparing like with like. In order to deal with this we have done both, that is not only compared a strictly identical sample of newspapers, but also provided the full range of the newspaper selection for each sample year.

This chapter will examine the range of reporting for different types of sex crimes in different types of newspapers. It will also examine changes in the reporting of rape over three and a half decades.

The range and structure of newspaper reporting

There are several different moments in the judicial processing of sex crime that may be the subject of newspaper reports. Each of the phases has a different type of coverage:

1 *The search* – the police hunt for an attacker will occur only under certain circumstances, when the police really believe that a crime was committed and, usually, that he is unknown to the victim. In this type of reporting the newspapers typically focus upon the criminal and deviant character of the man.
2 *The courtroom* – there are three types of courtroom action:
   The committal – this is a preliminary hearing in a magistrates' court and little information usually emerges at this stage.
   The trial – if there is a contested case it will be heard before a jury. In this stage the focus often shifts on to the victim and her conduct, since a typical defence of the accused man is that the woman consented.
   Sentencing – here attention is both on the level of the sentence, whether it is considered lenient or harsh, and also sometimes on the judge's comments on the case.
3 *Post-conviction* – a few particularly notorious sex offenders will be reported in the press after imprisonment. These are the most unusual and sensational cases.

Our study also examined press reporting of discussion about sex crimes, for instance around official reports and attempts to change the law. These gave an opportunity to consider media reporting of sex crime outside the immediate context of sensational cases.

In our previous studies we focused on press reporting of rapes. While that remains a central concern, in this book we have broadened our concern to include murders where there is a clear sexual element, and some other forms of sexual assault and crime. In our comparisons over time we necessarily are restricted to press reporting of rape trials, but in the analysis of the mid-1980s the study is much broader.

In fact, at each stage of the criminal justice process, there are only a few cases which get both widespread and sustained coverage in both the national and local press. At each stage there are only around half a dozen cases in any one year which are the focus of major interest which impinges upon the national press in a sustained manner.

17

Changes in rape trial reporting

From 1951 to 1985

There has been a massive increase in the reporting of sex crime in the national press during the post-war period, as Table 2.1 shows.

Table 2.1   Coverage of rape cases by six newspapers, 1951–85

	1951	1961	1971	1978	1985
Sun	n/a	n/a	10	32	49
Daily Mirror	1	5	8	26	45
The Times	0	6	3	21	19
News of the World	22	46	62	72	2
Sunday People	1	5	2	1	3
Evening Standard	5	9	8	10	15

Not only has the popular daily press, represented by the *Daily Mirror* and the *Sun*, shown a rapidly increasing interest in printing rape cases, but so has the "quality paper", *The Times*. During the early post-war period, the twenty-year period from 1951 to 1971, as evidenced by the years 1951, 1961 and 1971, there was little reporting of rape outside of the *News of the World*. After the mid-1970s, however, there has been a growing surge of interest. The most dramatic shift is between the years 1971 and 1978. Now in the popular dailies there is, on average, a case a week.

Until recently the bulk of rape reports were, however, only to be found in the *News of the World*. In the last few years this pattern has ceased as most papers carry these reports and, curiously, the *News of the World* has nearly stopped. The change is dramatic, from seventy-two cases in 1978 to only two in 1985. In the first twenty-year period, 1951 to 1971, the *News of the World* had carried the vast majority of the rape cases which were reported anywhere in the national press (despite being only a weekly paper). This change can only be a result of conscious policy.

The type of reporting has also shifted. In the earlier period the reports were much less explicit than now. For instance, they rarely used the word 'rape' in 1951, only the horrible euphemism – 'carnal knowledge' of a woman.

Between 1951 and 1971 the likelihood of the court reports of rape cases gaining publicity in the national press largely rested on whether the case was reported in the *News of the World*.[3] In 1951 in four widely read newspapers – two national dailies (*Daily Mirror* and *The Times*), one national Sunday (*Sunday People*) and one evening paper (the London *Evening Standard*) – there were only two cases reported which were not also covered by the *News of the World*. Similarly for 1961, there were only five cases, and for 1971, seven cases. In contrast, the *News of the World* itself covered eighteen cases in 1951, thirty-five in 1961 and fifty-eight in 1971 which were not reported in the other four.

The *News of the World* had developed a distinctively titillating style of reporting rape which was matched only by the arrival of the restructured *Sun*, which began to develop its present style in the early 1970s. From the outset the *Sun* was equally titillating but with a different style from the *News of the World*. The *Sun* made less use of the *News of the World* style of long reports which unfolded the plot of a sex crime in a 'racy' style, like a novelette. However, in terms of increasing the chances of publicity in the national press, the rising of the *Sun* did not significantly alter the general picture. It covered ten rape cases in 1971, but reported only three cases not covered in the other five newspapers. What it did do, however, was to herald the potential use of sex crime allied to other explicitly sexual gossip, photographs of topless models and so on to become close to a 'soft porn package' which was its strategy in the ensuing circulation warfare.

This research by Soothill and Jack masked the amount of sex crime being reported in newspapers, for by concentrating entirely on cases which would appear as rape in the *Criminal Statistics* for the relevant year, this provided a narrow definition of sex crime. Indeed, even cases of rape in the *News of the World* was a serious underestimate, for this popular Sunday lived up to its name and rape cases were reported from all parts of the globe.

Each year there were a few sex crime trials which got particularly extensive publicity. These were not necessarily rape trials. Indeed, those reports with a murder together with explicit sexual activities, perhaps involving some sort of celebrity, would be the 'ideal' ingredients to produce a national soap opera. However, this research was specifically conducted in the mid-1970s with the then current concern about rape in mind, so other types of sex crimes were neglected.

The emphasis of the research mainly focused on the press reporting of the rape victim. It was argued that when the woman was "named in a press report, this obviously dramatically widens the number who may point an accusing finger at the unfortunate victim – or at least the victim believes it will."[4] In both 1951 and 1971, the same proportion (54 per cent) of the press reports actually named the victim. Further, there was no invariable respect or reticence for age, whether young or old. In 1951 the names of a 12-year-old girl as well as that of a 55-year-old woman were stated. In 1961, there was a more restricted age-range of named victims, from 15 to 34 years; in 1971, from 12 to 60 years.

There was evidence that some had their names withheld due to a specific request by a magistrate, judge or, in one instance, by the victim's husband. There were other cases where the name of the rape survivor was not disclosed in the first press report but a few weeks later, the name would suddenly appear in front of several million readers. One report of committal proceedings noted that "the magistrate asked that the girl's name should not be disclosed". But at the trial at the assizes a few months later, the name and address of the girl were both disclosed.

Anonymity became one of the major issues of the 1970s legislation, but there is no doubt that the detail of much of the reporting of rape cases in the early 1970s became – and we would argue, has continued to be – deliberately titillating. It is difficult to estimate what kinds of discrediting remarks are likely to most upset rape survivors and deter others from reporting rape. Indeed, this is likely to vary over time with changing social context. Writing in the mid-1970s we suggested that "one suspects that, in 1951, it would be potentially more disturbing for the victim if the world knew she had been "intimate" with her boyfriend than it would today. By 1971, virginity was much less expected."[5] So questions of prior sexual experience take on a different meaning and emphasis over time. However, the theme of attempting to discredit the woman in the witness box continues. For instance, in one case the defence counsel tried to establish their client's case thus – '[The defendant] said: "She was not raped at all. She was an old scrubber. She loved it. When we got to the caravan, she jumped on the bed and said something like: 'Come on then, who is going to satisfy me tonight?' She seemed to enjoy it." '[6] Any woman in the early 1970s did not need to be very observant to notice that there were serious dangers of being discredited by name in the media.

From 1971 to 1978

The changes in the period 1971 to 1978 are particularly important since the sample years are either side of the 1976 Act which attempted to restrain press coverage of rape. We considered the same six newspapers in both 1971 and 1978 (*Sun, Daily Mirror, The Times, News of the World, Sunday People*, and the London *Evening Standard*).[7] Surprisingly, over this period the press reporting of rape dramatically increased, despite the indirect attempts to control it. The percentage of all rape cases reported in our sample of newspapers increased from a steady 25 per cent over the two decades, 1951 to 1971, to very nearly 40 per cent in 1978. Most of the newspapers – as Table 2.2 shows – dramatically increased their reporting of rape between 1971 and 1978, but particularly the *Sun, Daily Mirror*, and, rather surprisingly, *The Times*. The *Sun* increased from ten court cases to thirty-two, *Daily Mirror* from eight cases to twenty-six, and *The Times* from three cases to twenty-one.

The nature of the shift in *The Times* was particularly striking. Not only was there little difference in the reporting of the cases compared with the popular press, but also *The Times* had become attracted to sensational headlines. Headlines like RAPIST OF 16 WAS LIKE A VULTURE GOING IN FOR THE KILL and TOMBSTONE RAPIST LIKE A VULTURE? could both come from a couple of popular dailies, but the first was from *The Times* and the second from the *Sun.*[8]

Table 2.2 Court cases compared with press cases of rape, 1951-85

	1951[a]	1961[a]	1971[a]	1978[a]	1985[a]	1985 total[b]
No. of rape offenders [c]	119	266	358	396	450[d]	450[d]
No. reported in press	28	69	91	155	101	154
% reported in press	23.5	25.9	25.4	39.2	22.4	34.2

Notes: [a] Figures refer to the constant sample of six newspapers.
[b] Figures for 1985 total refer to the total of rape court cases in the wider sample.
[c] The figures (from the *Criminal Statistics, England and Wales*) are the number of individuals in Crown courts for rape.
[d] The rape figures in the *Criminal Statistics, England and Wales 1985* (Cm. 10), London, HMSO refer only to offenders found guilty. If acquittals were included, the proportion reported would be lower.

The hope that the restriction imposed by the 1976 Act which limited defendants' rights to produce evidence in court of the rape survivor's past sexual relationships with persons other than the defendant would cause newspapers to lose interest in reporting rape cases was a hope that was totally misplaced. We found, as has Adler,[9] the loopholes that could be exploited – "to state, or allege, that the victim was a prostitute was at least to imply past sexual relationships with other men. Or the prosecution might inform the jury that 'Miss R . . . was single and having regular sexual relations with her boyfriend' ".[10] The sexual relationship between the victim and accused was on occasions the focal point of the press coverage. These loopholes remain despite the concern of some judges such as Mr Justice Boreham, who once said in judgment: "I know a little about life and even if [the accused] had had intercourse with the girl before, he does not have the prescriptive right to it thereafter. She has the right to say yea or nay, and if she says nay, that is the end of it".[11]

The character of a woman may be attacked in ways other than an explicit recounting of her past sexual relationships or, indeed, that she was having sexual relationships. For instance, *The Times* informed us that the "*unmarried office manager* . . . kept her lunchtime appointment to have a contraceptive coil fitted" (our emphasis).[12]

In strict legal terms, the letter of the 1976 law was being followed in

1978, but the Act had not produced the results in dampening down press publicity in the way that had been hoped. However, beyond pointing to the dramatic increase in rape reports, we also began to speculate on the reasons for the shift by practically all the newspapers.

The press reporting of rape can be seen as part of the sexual titillation increasingly being employed to sell newspapers in a tight market. We focused on the two newspapers owned by the same person, Rupert Murdoch, and which included the most rape reports – thirty-two in the *Sun* and seventy-two in the *News of the World* in which not one rape case in 1978 was covered by both newspapers. The possibility of this happening by chance is so remote as to defy calculation. However, when we argued "the marketing strategy is clear. The *Sun* and the *News of the World* are, in effect, being sold as a package. The reader will come to know that the rape cases he reads in his daily newspaper will not need-lessly be repeated in the Sunday newspaper",[13] this caused outrage from Sir Larry Lamb. Writing on behalf of News Group Newspapers Ltd, he denied that either the *Sun* or the *News of the World* "has anything so grand as a 'marketing strategy' – whatever that is". He argued that the markets of these two newspapers "are very different, and the circulation overlap [is] in no way significant".[14]

However, even in the late 1970s we were convinced that "many newspapers were increasingly using the soft pornography of rape reports, and reports of other sex crimes, as a mechanism to sell newspapers."[15]

Press reporting in 1985

The pattern of press reporting of rape trials is quite different in 1985 from the previous years we had studied – 1951, 1961, 1971 and 1978. There has been an increase in the number of rape trials, and hence, even if a constant proportion were reported, an increase in the absolute number of such cases being reported in the press. If we restrict the focus to the same five newspapers – *The Mirror*, *The Times*, *News of the World*, *Sunday People* and the London *Evening Standard* – and for the years 1971 and 1978 include the *Sun*, we see what appears to be a steady proportion of one-quarter of this growing number of trials reported, except for a temporary surge in 1978 to two-fifths. Thus we see an increase between 1971 and 1978 falling back in 1985 to previous levels. Table 2.2 shows a drop from 155 (in 1978) to 101 (in 1985). Even when all the other newspapers in the 1985 study are added, including the local evenings and weeklies, there are still only a total of 154 rape cases mentioned in 1985. However, since there are more rape trials today than before, the reader of newspapers would find an increase in the number of reports over the years.

The distribution of these reports across the range of newspapers is quite different from earlier years with very important consequences as to the likelihood of the 'average reader' seeing a rape report. Further, the nature of the coverage has dramatically shifted. Most coverage of rape trials now takes place in the daily popular press rather than the special interest paper of the *News of the World*. This moves the reporting from the periphery of newspaper journalism to the centre, with a consequent increase in the readership and the normalisation of these sorts of reports. In the three popular dailies, the *Sun*, the *Star* and the *Daily Mirror*, there is considerable coverage and, on average, there is approaching one rape court case reported each week in these newspapers. For the *Sun* and the *Daily Mirror*, where it is possible to compare with the numbers in 1978, both show significant increases – the *Sun* from thirty-two to forty-nine and the *Daily Mirror*, even more, from twenty-six to forty-five. In contrast there has been the almost total cessation of the reporting of rape trials by the *News of the World*, as described above (see Table 2.3).

In terms of the newspapers in the present study, the sudden stopping of the *News of the World* coverage explains the fall in the total of rape

Table 2.3 Number of cases of rape reported in the press in 1985

National dailies and Sundays	
Sun	49
Star	40
Daily Mail	31
Daily Mirror	45
Guardian	16
The Times	19
Sunday Mirror	3
Sunday People	3
Mail on Sunday	3
News of the World	2
Observer	0
Local evenings and weeklies	
Coventry Evening Telegraph	27
Evening Standard	15
Lancashire Evening Post	11
Middlesex Chronicle	3
Lancaster Guardian	0

cases covered between 1978 and 1985. However, given the larger circulation figures of the newspapers which are now reporting rape, the actual number of readers of rape reports has increased. Rape reports are no longer the diet of a specialised readership, but are now part of the 'normal', 'everyday' news for a large section of the population.

A few cases dominate this reporting, while just over one-half of the rape cases mentioned appeared only in one sample newspaper. If we had included more papers in the sample the coverage might have appeared more dense, but nevertheless it is clear that it is a minority of unusual cases which get most press exposure. Table 2.4 shows that only around a dozen cases are mentioned in more than four of the sixteen newspapers in the study. If only six national newspapers (the *Sun, Daily Mirror, Star, Daily Mail, The Times* and *Guardian*) are examined, there are just eighteen cases which get coverage in more than three of these newspapers. Not all reporting of rape is of sensational cross-examination. Some were very short descriptive items, perhaps just mentioning that a person (or persons) had appeared on a remand hearing in court. In fact, extensive detail is an exception rather than the rule but, as we shall argue, these are particularly important exceptions.

The predominance of a small minority of cases is further illustrated if we use two further measures of the extent of the coverage in addition to the gross number of reports, that of the number of days and the number of pages in which each rape case is featured. There is a high

Table 2.4 Details of rape cases in which the most newspaper space is devoted to the coverage

Case*	No. of newspapers	No. of days	No. of pages	Cumulative % of total pages
	in which the case is mentioned			
The Fox	13	10	59	12.5
Brixton Gang Rape	8	15	47	22.4
Paratroopers	10	15	46	32.1
Savage	9	5	30	38.5
Bible Beasts	8	8	15	41.6
Railway Rapist	7	3	14	44.4
Teacher	3	3	14	47.4
Evil Parents	7	3	11	49.7
Bed-sit Fiend	7	2	10	51.8

Note: *See Chapter 4 for further details of the content of these cases, the titles of which are taken from the press headlines.

correlation between the number of pages, number of days and the number of overall reports of particular cases, and these measures confirm the view that some cases predominate in the newspapers.

Three cases (out of 114) have one-third (32 per cent) of the total coverage of rape court cases in our newspapers, as Table 2.4 indicates. Nine cases have over one-half (52 per cent) of the total coverage, while the remaining 105 cases contribute the other one-half. The 'top' three cases each appear on between ten and fifteen days, while no case above the 'top' five appears on more than three days. We shall examine the nature of these accounts during the next two chapters.

Amount, range and type of coverage of sexual assaults

Rape trials have been the subject of this analysis of these changes over time so far. In our recent study of papers in the mid-1980s we broadened the focus and examined not only rape but also other forms of sexual assault and not only reporting of trials but also other stages, including the search and post-conviction. The older work, like most of the other studies in this field, focuses on the dramatic moment of the court trial and the distinctive crime of rape. However, this is a narrow selection from press reporting of sex crime and runs the risk of perhaps exaggerating the degree of sensationalism in the papers. In this study we deliberately broadened the scope of the reporting under scrutiny.

In the rest of this chapter we examine not the trial stage, but the one prior to that – the search. In later chapters we focus on reporting at other stages of the process.

During 1985 there were 17 cases of sex murder, 188 cases of sexual assault, and 29 cases of minor sexual offences included in our study. The category of sexual assault includes but is not restricted to rape. A case is defined when it is reported as one alleged offender involved in one event or series of events; also it is regarded as one case where members of the same group are involved in one event or series of events.

Sex and murder

It is not easy to identify which murder cases have a definite sexual element. Sometimes a murder enquiry will have been going on for some days before it emerges that there is a sexual element involved. The police may withhold this information for 'operational' or forensic reasons. In our sample we had seventeen cases where there was definitely a sexual element or the specific mention of the lack of such an element.

It is unusual for a sex murder case to get widespread coverage during the police investigation. There were only four such murder cases (discounting the M4 Rapist case, which we consider separately) where there was more than three days' coverage or where more than five newspapers included reports of the search. One case which involved the murder of a 3-year-old girl received massive coverage over an eight-day period and then spasmodic coverage over the next seven weeks until a 27-year-old man was arrested and charged with the child's murder. The other major case, which later separated into two, involved the murders of two boys aged 14 and 6, which obtained fairly intensive coverage over a five-day period in the popular dailies. The only other case where there was the suggestion of an explicitly sexual motive and which had more than three days' coverage was the murder of a 9-year-old boy which was reported in two national newspapers – the *Daily Mail* (on three days); the *Daily Mirror* (on one day) – and much fuller coverage in the local newspaper, the *Lancashire Evening Post*. Apart from these four cases – all involving children – the other murders where there was a sexually explicit motive were few and far between, mentioned in perhaps two or three newspapers over a couple of days at most. This was a surprising finding for it was thought – with the image of the Yorkshire Ripper search in mind – that the police investigation of major sex murders would be a prime fodder for newspapers. So apart from the M4 Rapist, there was not sustained or widespread coverage of sex murderers killing adult men or women in the sample year. Perhaps such cases do not occur with the frequency one may so readily believe or that such cases do not get reported in the national press with the frequency that one might have expected; or alternatively, perhaps the police are much more successful in capturing the so-called sex maniacs than we sometimes are led to imagine.

Sexual assault

The total of 188 cases of sexual assault means that, if you were reading all the newspapers in the study, you would have at least one new case of sexual assault, usually by an unknown assailant, to read about every other day. However, ordinary newspaper readers do not see such a vast array of newspapers and reading some newspapers rather than others gives a very different view of the extent and type of sex crimes in a nation.

There are ways of considering the coverage – its range, amount and nature. The range of coverage indicates the number of newspapers which cover a particular case, while the amount focuses especially on the number of days that a case is mentioned. The relationship between the two concepts of range and amount is perhaps more complex than one might expect, for some local cases get sustained coverage in local newspapers but not get a mention in the nationals, while, on the other hand, some events get a mention over a large number of newspapers on one particular day but never get featured again. The other issue, which is of much greater interest, is the nature of the coverage and will be considered in Chapters 3 and 4.

Table 2.5 Extent of repetition of reporting of specific sexual attacks in different newspapers

Number of papers with a report on a case	All newspapers		National newspapers only	
	N [a]	%R [b]	N [a]	%R [b]
1	138	73.4	69	58.5
2	25	13.3	24	20.3
3	9	4.8	9	7.6
4	7	3.7	7	5.9
5	0	—	0	—
6	2	1.1	2	1.7
7	0	—	0	—
8	4	2.1	4	3.4
9	1	0.5	1	0.8
10	1	0.5	1	0.8
11	0	—	0	—
12	0	—	0	—
13	1	0.5	1	0.8
Total	188	100.0	118	100.0

Notes: [a]N = number of copies.
[b]%R = Percentage of reports which are recorded in only one copy, two copies, etc.

Range of coverage in newspapers

The majority (73 per cent) of sexual assaults were reported in only one newspaper in our sample, as shown in Table 2.5. A further 13 per cent were covered by only two newspapers; 5 per cent were covered by three newspapers and 4 per cent by four newspapers. The remaining nine cases (5 per cent) which attract the attention of more than four newspapers are of particular interest. These are the cases of which every newspaper reader in the country is likely to see some mention. These are the cases which are used to illustrate 'the state of the nation'. Fewer than one in twenty of sexual assault cases in the survey are covered by more than four newspapers. Even among those cases mentioned in the media, widespread coverage of a particular sexual assault case before the offender is charged is a comparative rarity.

Every case appearing in the national press is likely to appear in some local newspaper. Although we had only a very limited range of local newspapers, half (69) of the 138 cases which appeared in only one newspaper appeared only in the local newspapers. This is a very high number of cases appearing only in local newspapers, especially because of the imbalance of our sample towards the national papers. This is shown in Table 2.6, where the *Coventry Evening Telegraph* and *Lancashire Evening Post* illustrate the pattern which emerges with regard to local newspapers.

Of the fifty reports of sexual attacks featured in the *Coventry Evening Telegraph*, thirteen refer to cases which are well outside the catchment area of the newspaper and these are also mentioned in the national press. Of the remaining thirty-seven falling within its wide catchment area, only one (3 per cent) is mentioned in a national newspaper.

Similarly, of the twenty-three reports of sexual attacks mentioned in the *Lancashire Evening Post*, six refer to cases which are well outside the catchment area and are among the cases occasioning a national interest. Of the remaining seventeen falling within its catchment area,

Table 2.6 Number of cases involving sexual attacks reported in the press

National dailies and Sundays	
Sun	65
Star	43
Daily Mail	30
Daily Mirror	29
Guardian	11
The Times	8
Sunday Mirror	7
Sunday People	6
Mail on Sunday	3
News of the World	3
Observer	1
Local evenings and weeklies	
Coventry Evening Telegraph	50
Evening Standard	34
Lancashire Evening Post	23
Middlesex Chronicle	4
Lancaster Guardian	1

only three (i.e. 18 per cent of the local cases) are mentioned in a national newspaper.

The difference between the two local evening papers in the numbers of the local cases reaching the national dailies is probably a chance fluctuation. However, combining the results suggests that approaching one in ten of local sexual attacks, which are mentioned in the local press, may also be mentioned in the national press. While this figure is likely to have a fair range of variation according to the amount of crime in the catchment area of the newspaper and the general interest of the newspaper in reporting sex crime, it still gives some idea that it is only a small minority of local cases that get featured nationally. Despite the obvious interest in the coverage by national newspapers, this puts into context where the bulk of sex crime reporting for the country as a whole actually takes place – in the local newspaper. However, for the individual readers the impact of reading of reports of sex crime in the national press is likely to be more important in moulding their view of what is happening in the nation.

Table 2.6 shows that particular newspapers are more likely to include reports of sexual attack than others. Among the nationals the *Sun* clearly predominates in mentions of attacks with over 50 per cent again as many cases as even its rival the *Star*. Among the locals, some – in this case the *Coventry Evening Telegraph* – have many more reports than other local newspapers.

The amount of sustained coverage

The length of coverage is taken to be the number of days that a case is mentioned during the search stage.[16] Sustained coverage of a particular sexual attack is a rarity. In the 118 cases mentioned in at least one national newspaper (70 were in only local papers), there were only 19 cases (16 per cent) where the coverage of the incident lasted more than one day, and only 8 where this lasted several days.

If a report appears in only one national newspaper then, as Table 2.7 shows, the incident will invariably be mentioned on one day only. There is a linear relationship between amount and length of coverage so that the more newspapers which cover an incident, the greater likelihood that coverage will continue over several days.[17] During the course of the year there were only eight cases which got widespread coverage and sustained coverage of several days. The majority of cases with sustained coverage involved young girls (including a couple of cases where the victim was under 10) who were usually alone and the focus of a single attack. In one case there were two 13-year-old girls, who had been sexually assaulted and left for dead. Attacks on adult women were featured in a sustained manner in the search stage in national newspapers only when there had been attacks on several women apparently by the same offender – for instance, a special rape squad was set up when a "sex beast" was believed to be responsible for a series of attacks on at least twenty-three women.

Local newspapers

There are significant differences between the local and national newspapers. Of the seventy cases which were reported only in the local

Table 2.7 Range of coverage (number of newspapers) and duration of coverage (number of days)

No. of newspapers	No. of cases	No. of cases over more than one day	% of cases
One	69	0	0
Two	24	5	21
Three	9	3	33
Four	7	3	43
Five	0	—	—
Six	2	1	50
Seven	0	—	—
Eight	4	4	100
Nine	1	1	100
Ten	1	1	100
. . .			
Thirteen	1	1	100
Total	118	19	16

newspapers in the sample, there were six cases (9 per cent) where the coverage lasted more than one day. Among the local cases, adult women are the majority and those living in their homes at the time of the attack particularly feature. Nevertheless, the case of a 13-year-old being raped at knife-point in a Coventry churchyard received the most sustained coverage. With artist's impressions and scores of posters aiding the hunt for the rapist, the 250 tip-offs did not lead to an arrest.

Combining both national and local newspapers, only around one in eight of sexual assault cases will be mentioned in the newspapers on more than one day prior to a charge being laid. However, there are differences between popular national and local newspapers in both the style of reporting and in the type of cases which routinely get sustained coverage.

Minor sexual offences

There is very little interest indeed in sexual offences prior to the court appearance unless they are sexual assaults or murders with a sexual component. In the 3,015 newspapers considered in the study, only 29 of these residual sexual cases were identified. Only two appeared in more than one newspaper – each appearing in both the *Sun* and the *Star*. In fact, the *Sun* (eight items) and the *Star* (six items) continue to dominate in a sparse field. The *Daily Mail*, *Daily Mirror*, and *Sunday People* each had three items, with just one item in the *Sunday Mirror*. The "quality press" – *The Times*, *Guardian* and *Observer* – had no such cases. Of the local evenings, only the London *Evening Standard* had one item. However, the number of these cases in the local weekly, *Middlesex Chronicle*, shows that there are likely to be large variations among local newspapers in the amount of coverage of these residual sexual offences.

While these miscellaneous cases feature very rarely indeed, they can vary widely in the amount of impact they make. On the one hand, the *Daily Mirror* story[18] had the important ingredient of television stars and the alleged exploitation of children in their front-page exclusive story, headlined **Stars in Child Porn Probe**, while on the other hand, more routinely, there are the very brief items in the local newspapers where the local police use the newspaper like a bulletin board to warn the local neighbourhood about a local nuisance who insists upon exposing himself. While indecent exposure is certainly the most frequent activity to be mentioned in this category, the rarity can be recognised when one notes that only ten cases were mentioned prior to a charge being laid. In fact, half the cases appeared in one newspaper – the *Middlesex Chronicle*, a local weekly – while the remainder were in the nationals. There is a dramatic contrast between reports of 'flashers' in national and local newspapers. There was some similarity among the headlines where there was almost without exception an attempt at a catch-line. The nationals (**Freezing Flasher Slips Up;**[19] **Flash Photo Freak;**[20] **Birdie that Bugged a Golfer;**[21] **Smart Anna and the Flasher;**[22] **Horse Kicks Flasher**[23]) reflected a greater effort at constructing titillating headlines than the local weekly (**Revealing Story;**[24] **Double Exposure;**[25] **Sex Pest Sought;**[26] **Indecent Man;**[27] **Serious Offence**[28]).

Porn and vice involving children

An important focus of reports of sexual assaults and sex murders tends to be on the sexual attacks upon children. On two occasions reports on porn and vice involving children were the main front-page story. One front-page exclusive in the *Daily Mirror*[29] reported that child porn photos involving two top television stars were uncovered in a police raid on a photographic studio. Allegedly the photos showed sex acts between young girls and a man, and teenage boys with two other men. Some of the girls pictured were thought to be as young as 6.

Interest in child porn video scandals was maintained with a front-page *Sunday Mirror* story,[30] headlined **Child Porn Video Shock**. In contrast to the glamour of television stars featured in the earlier story, this one focused on the alleged exploits of a family living in a council house in rural England. The message is clear. The problem is rampant at every level of society. It became explicitly used as part of a campaign against the sexual abuse of children.

Sex offences as humour

Finally, there is a miscellaneous conglomeration of sexual offences which are used as filler items in popular newspapers. The items fill one or two column inches and are meant to amuse; the sexual innuendoes abound and the implicit humour is of the seaside postcard variety. However, the apparent trivia is also serious. Cases sometimes tread uneasily between being trying to be funny and pointing to serious danger. They also raise the question as to who is supposed to find them funny.

Conclusion

This examination of the range and extent of sex crime reporting shows both how pervasive sexual violence has become as a news item, and also how only a very small number of cases are selected as being 'newsworthy'. The examination of rape coverage over time shows in particular how this topic has left the narrow audience of the *News of the World* and has entered the popular dailies on a large scale. Sex crime is both common, and yet the cases are highly selected. Even at the search stage which was the focus of much of the analysis in this chapter the cases were highly selective.

The criteria for selection will be examined in Chapters 3 and 4, which look at the content of the reporting in more detail.

The different stages of the legal processing of sex criminals give rise to different forms of press reporting, which will be considered in separate chapters. We shall start, in Chapter 3, with the hunt for an offender after a sex crime has been reported to the police. This is the stage during which the press will focus on the supposed characteristics of the offender and their fantasies have free rein since there is no man actually in custody. The court procedure gives rise to a different focus by the press, which will be considered in Chapter 4. Here the focus often, but not always, turns to the woman, since it is by attempting to discredit her that the majority of men accused of sex crimes try to save themselves. Chapter 5 examines the treatment of sex offenders after conviction. Here only a very few unusual men are retained in the public eye for prolonged periods. Finally we discuss press reporting of attempts to change the situation, firstly, in Chapter 6, by research and official reports, and then in Chapter 7, by changing the law as it pertains to the legal processing of sex criminals.

Chapter three

Seeking out the sex fiend

There is one major theme central to the way that the popular national newspapers handle the coverage of sex offences – that of the seeking out of the sex fiend. These papers show connections and links between incidents in a drive towards the search and subsequent identification of a 'sex beast'. The manifestation of the sex beast in florid form does not happen very often in the media, but the coverage is consistently geared up to sponsoring the arrival of the sex fiend on the national scene.

The national press differs substantially from the local press in this respect. The local newspapers are dealing much more closely with the reality of rape, while the national ones are often displaying the fantasy of the 'video nasty' in real life.

The search and creation of the sex beast by the popular press is not usually a gross misrepresentation but rather a selective portrayal of specific facts. The pre-occupation with the delineation of a sex beast tends to mask the general reality of sex crime.[1] This sets the tone of what the general public read about sex crime.

Certain cases dominate the coverage in the national press, and by using these cases it is possible to indicate how the images of sex beast are constantly being proferred to readers. However, there are many other cases – just mentioned once or twice by one or two newspapers – which contribute in various ways to the development of the same kind of image. In this chapter we go beyond the 'finished product' which is often portrayed in the major sexual assault searches and the cases of sex murder. Here we look more closely at some of the building blocks in the creation of the sex beast or, more accurately, the way that suitable building material is being shaped for possible use if an opportunity occurs. The interrelationship between the police investigation of a sex crime and the newspaper coverage is important here.[2]

The contrast between the national and local newspapers is a useful starting-point. While they have roughly similar numbers of reports on sex offences at the search stage, their approach is very different. National newspapers cull their stories from all over the country – often, indeed, from all over the world. In many respects they define what is of 'national' concern, while not having any specific geographical constituency to answer to. In contrast, local newspapers do have a more or less defined constituency and, in consequence, split their efforts between giving a brief commentary on topical cases occurring outside their geographical area, and providing routine and sustained coverage on local cases. The most significant difference at the search and investigation stage is that the national press will retain interest in a case only if there is scope for the construction of a sex fiend who continues to wreak havoc on a community. Their efforts tend to be directed towards the construction of such a sex fiend. In contrast, local newspapers tend to take cases much less selectively and on occasions will continue to maintain interest in a case which seems unconnected with any other.

The popular national newspapers have an interest in encouraging the notion that there are links between incidents of sexual assault. The construction of a sex fiend helps to sell newspapers, for the sex beast does attract a certain sort of interest. Further, in professional terms, the systematic focus on serious crime is probably the nearest that many of the journalists on the popular newspapers will get to what the quality press regard as investigative journalism. Investigative journalism usually implies intensive and detailed study revealing the 'dark underbelly' of a subject already in the public domain or dragging a subject which has remained conveniently hidden from view into the public domain. However, serious investigative journalism often provides a challenge to the official version of reality and the search for a major sex criminal is rarely like that. The newspaper coverage may have contributed to bringing the crime into the public domain, but essentially the press and the police are using the same repertoire of scripts. The role of the press is rarely condemnatory of the police and usually supportive of the official efforts to solve crime. Nevertheless, the press often has a role in providing new ideas, maintaining the momentum and quite simply continuing to ask the questions. It is investigative journalism of a very limited scope.

The police have an interest in the investigation of a sex crime developing in a particular way. So, similarly to the press, the police can proclaim their interest in solving the alleged crime but, if they are unsuccessful, the development of a sex fiend theme will enable the police to maintain resources in a particular area of investigation. Further, the sex fiend conforms to their view of real sex crime. It has the thrill of the chase and is really the only acceptable variant in relation to sex crime from the 'cops and robbers' scenario which in the eyes of most police officers is what policing is really about. There is, of course, a problem which must be confronted by both the police and the press if –

after a brief time has elapsed – the crime remains unsolved and no further atrocities are being committed which can, even remotely, be connected with the original outrage. The police do not maintain a highly expensive investigation, while the press – with no new dimensions emerging – consider the boredom factor of their readers. It is at this comparatively early stage that the imperatives become clear. The press's role is not to solve crime but to sell newspapers. If an investigation is failing to produce results, it is, of course, not in the best interests of either police or press to maintain a high profile in such cases. It is not helpful to either party for the image to be portrayed that the investigation in which the press and the police contributed, in both economic and emotional terms, has failed. Their interests coalesce in ensuring that they are in harness in orchestrating the general momentum of the investigation of sex crime.

The process of identifying links between incidents is enormously complicated. Some of the recent arguments in favour of involving computers in the task of investigating crime are that links or patterns which would otherwise have been missed or overlooked may be captured.[3] However, in practice, computer procedures are likely to produce as many links which are potentially misleading as links which are helpful. The extra and fruitless work which these new procedures often engender may remain worthwhile if some new but positive 'leads' are also found. But there are particular problems if the media hear of new 'leads' suggesting connections which ultimately prove to be unhelpful. The enthusiasm among the media for computer assistance in solving sex crime is understandable but worrying. The links are at a very low level of explanation. The media, for example, are very loath to consider that sex crime may be related to men's and women's position in society. The wealth of feminist literature which theorises violence in society seems of little interest to either the police or the popular press. The interest is not about violence in general, which may provide the context for individual atrocities. The interest is simply focused on the few individuals who commit several serious atrocities. Indeed, in the best of all possible media worlds, all rapes and sexual assaults would be committed by just a few sexual maniacs and the press could then help to orchestrate the national search against these declared aliens in our midst. The focus of media coverage in the popular press is implicitly working towards this chimera.

Producing the links

Considerable attention is often given to trying to make sense of an incident. In this respect the press are often one step ahead of the police in making explicit some possible connections: "Although police are keeping an open mind, it seems likely the anonymous phone caller and the darkly-clothed assailant are the same man" (*Daily Mail*).[4]

Other rape survivors may come forward and the police may quite explicitly make the links: "a second woman has told police at York that she was raped near the city's university only 200 yards from the spot where a girl student was subjected to a brutal, 90-minute sex attack" (*Daily Telegraph*).[5]

This report goes on to say that the attacks each took place at about midnight and were twenty days apart. The first woman didn't report her ordeal and immediately left the area. She heard about the second attack only on her return. It is finally stated in the report that the police believed the rapes were carried out by the same man, who is described quite fully. On this occasion the publicity or discussion in the town had had the beneficial effect that the first victim recognised the matter was being taken seriously and so reported the earlier incident. It is not unusual for publicity to generate interest and encourage witnesses and, indeed, other survivors of sexual attacks to come forward.

The police are sometimes concerned that they may not have the full information before them. Police investigating sex attacks at knife-point on a 29-year-old Filipino woman said that they "believe there may have been earlier victims – but the women have been too ashamed to report the attacks" (*Mail on Sunday*).[6]

In a crime which had front-page headlines in the *Star* on consecutive days,[7] the London *Evening Standard*[8] noted that the police were "looking into similarities with the rape of a 10-year-old girl in Hemel Hempstead five months ago". On the next day the *Star*'s extended coverage identified a probe into four other attacks in the area which "were being studied by police to see if there was a link".[9] The evening newspapers, however, noted that a suspect was being questioned about the current crime, so there was no further speculation about possible links between the various attacks. A specific sex beast had not emerged, but the assumption that the incidents had been linked remained.

Sometimes the possible link can be from much longer ago than a few months and here the memory is almost invariably an unsolved murder case. The police officer dips into a repertoire of previous cases available for connections to be tested. The front page headlines in the *Star*[10] **HUNT FOR A DRACULA FIEND: Bike ride pals are snatched** resurrected sombre memories

Police have re-opened the file on missing cyclist April Fabb, whose bicycle was found under a hedge in Norfolk 15 years ago. Her body has never been discovered. Inspector Brian Butcher said: 'It is the case that always springs to mind when children are involved'. Police will be going over the old ground to see if there is any link with this latest attack.

The above cases largely reflect police thinking. While overt conflict between the press and the police is rarely evident, it is quite apparent that the press sometimes goes beyond what the police feel is appropriate speculation in particular cases. The nuances are often quite subtle, but the following example shows how the press is trying to construct a sex maniac, while the police seem to be thinking more on the lines of an abductor without sexual assault necessarily being involved.

Under the heading **Warning to mums over sex attacks,**[11] the *Star* pointed to two sex attacks on a housing estate. It stated that "Detectives believe the attacks are linked and fear the sex fiend could strike again". In fact, the two separate incidents concerned a 3-year-old girl who was enticed into woods near her home and sexually assaulted and then soon afterwards, a 3-year-old boy who was abducted from a play area and driven off at high speed before being dumped a mile and a half away forty minutes later. A police spokesperson explicitly stated that: "There is no evidence that the boy was sexually assaulted but both incidents are very serious". The *Star* quoted this statement and yet still referred to both incidents as "sex attacks". To portray a sex fiend, the press needs sex attacks.

Connections which appear subsequently to have been falsely conceived are rarely abrogated, but are usually just conveniently forgotten. On a very few occasions, however, the police do make a point of denying links or connections which had been too easily assumed. The police do not always allow useless speculation to grow when an obvious link may be misleading. For example, in two cases the attackers pretended to be taxi-drivers, but it was stated that "police do not believe the assaults [on a 17-year-old girl and a woman aged 25] were linked" (*Daily Mail*).[12] Similarly, in the report of "a sex beast nicknamed 'The Acne Kid' " (*Star*),[13] who boasted to the victim that he had just been freed from prison and said: "I've served time for rape before", speculation about this possible link was scotched quickly. The newspaper reported that "detectives believe it was just a vicious taunt to terrify the girl". So while the search for links is pervasive in the coverage of sex attacks by popular newspapers, it is important to recognise that the demand is not totally inexorable.

Connections are established

The next stage occurs when everyone concerned with the case assumes that there are connections between various incidents even though the evidence may still be shaky. The defining agencies are no longer seriously in doubt that there is a sex fiend in our midst. There is now an expectancy effect created that any new atrocity is likely to be connected to the earlier ones.

The police often collaborate in producing an expectancy effect. Allied to the belief that more problems are on the way is the belief that sex offenders tend to escalate their activities. Whether this is generally true or not is not strictly relevant to attempts to heighten or maintain interest in a case. For example, fears of escalation expressed by the police set the tone for the *Star*[14] headline **BABY-FACED SEX BEAST 'SET TO KILL'** – "Detectives believe the same man carried out two earlier attacks and is becoming increasingly violent. Detective Inspector Jack Rogers, who is leading the hunt for the man, said: 'We must catch him before he kills someone' ". Such reports in a popular newspaper endorse a general belief in escalation.

While the blatant sex fiend image is comparatively rare in the local press, readers of the national press are fed a steady diet of established sex fiends. Under headlines such as **"Fiend's third victim"** (*Daily Mirror*)[15] and **"Terror of tape bondage rapist"** (*Sun*),[16] it was noted how "a sticky-tape sex-fiend has struck for the third time" bringing "terror to a triangle of Hampshire towns". Headlines such as **KIDNAPPING SEX BEAST STRIKES AGAIN** (*Star*)[17] and **Victim No 2 of the car park rapist** (*Sun*)[18] tell of "ugly and brutal attacks". What is striking about many of these cases is that there is rarely further mention in the national press, but the sex fiend message has been amply conveyed.

Providing a label

There is a ready use of such global terms as 'sex beast', 'sex monster', 'sex fiend', and so on, but the next stage is the accolade of a specific label. Here the unidentified sex attacker has moved into a new phase, with an identity created for him by the media, often assisted by the police. Some are not fully fledged nicknames, but simply *aides-mémoire* to assist in locating a description, so the headline **'JACKSON-STYLE' SEX BEAST HUNT** simply helps to identify a rapist described as having "a 'powerful' athletic build and Michael Jackson-style shoulder-length dark, crinkly hair" (*Star*).[19] Of course, names are not necessarily the creation of the press or the police.[20] The quality press and the *Daily Mail* do not so readily create nicknames, although they are willing to use the existing currency – "Yesterday, detectives were hunting a man locals call 'the stranger from Devil's Wood'" (*Daily Mail*).[21]

Generally, though, the media and the police seem more actively involved in proselytising a particular stereotype. The derivation of a particular label is often quite obvious. A *Sunday Mirror* exclusive[22]

39

linked to the television *Crimewatch* programme focused on a powerful attacker who was nicknamed "Muscle Man" by detectives hunting him. Others are less clear without some explanation: an attacker was known as "the Bizarre Beast" because of the strange clothing he wore, which included a gas mask and a dress (*Star*);[23] however, no explanation was needed why a sex fiend who struck near a university for the second time in four days was known as "The Balaclava Rapist" (*Sun*).[24] Similarly the headline 'ACNE KID' RAPES GIRL IN WOODS (*Star*)[25] is self-explanatory. Others, such as the sex fiend dubbed the "Shopping Bag Rapist" (*Sun*),[26] and the soft-spoken brute, known as the "Lonely Heart Rapist", believed to be a loner who regularly visited clubs for the divorced and separated in the Home Counties (*Sun*),[27] do not have nicknames which provide instant headlines. Nevertheless, there are plenty that do.

Symbolic links with previous fiends

The final accolade for the sex beast in the popular media is to be linked to earlier fiends. Some of these legendary figures may be dead, so, for instance, the Yorkshire Ripper took up a mantle laid down by the original Ripper in the last century. Others, such as Dracula, have their origins in successful stories. Dracula is the tale told in journals and letters of the vampire Hungarian, Count Dracula. The book by Bram Stoker and published at the end of the last century has sold over a million copies.[28] However, it is probably the various film versions and sequels that enable youngsters of today to make such connections. Under a massive front-page headline, HUNT FOR DRACULA FIEND (*Star*),[29] the report indicated that a 13-year-old was able to tell detectives that her attacker "had short dark hair streaked with grey and deep-set eyes that made him 'look a bit like Dracula'". Curiously this striking image was used only by the *Star*, which maintained the nickname in subsequent reports – DRACULA SEX FIEND 'STALKED HIS VICTIMS'.[30]

In other cases, the previous reign of horror may have more recently ended and the name – or rather the nickname – will still be easily recalled by readers. In the sample year (1985), Malcolm Fairley, known as 'The Fox', was sentenced at the end of February and immediately became a legendary sex beast to whom several subsequent reports explicitly referred. Indeed, three days later the Fox clones began to emerge. The three reports in the *Daily Mail* (Masked rapist attacks three women in flat);[31] the *Sun* (RAPE FIEND IN FOX 'COPY');[32] and the *Star* (BEAST HUNTED: WHITE-MASK RAPIST ATTACKS THREE GIRLS)[33] show the varying ways that such cases are presented in the popular press.

The contrast is clear. The *Daily Mail* does not make any reference to The Fox at all. The *Sun*, in the title, the photograph of "the mask of fear" and the body of the text, refers to the assaults as "a carbon copy of the brutal rapes carried out by pervert Malcolm Fairley, the so-called Fox, who was jailed for life last Tuesday". On this occasion the *Star* goes one stage further not only by stressing the similarities with The Fox but also by giving this new phenomenon an identity of his own – "police have nicknamed him The White Fox".

A week later it is evident that Fox-type gear was coming into common usage with no need to refer back to the specific case – "a teenage girl was seized by two men wearing "fox-style" balaclavas and raped at knife-point" (London *Evening Standard*).[34] The *Sun* made the connection quite explicit – "They were wearing balaclava helmets like the Fox rapist, who held the area in terror last summer, and skin-head-style Dr Marten boots". This report noted that this was the same area as terrorised by The Fox in the previous summer. Again there is no further mention of this incident in the study.

Later in the year a case which appeared only in the *Sun*[35] and *The Times*[36] was unusual in that the police suggested that they had a particular suspect in mind. Both newspapers noted that he had been nick-named 'The Teenage Fox':

SCHOOLGIRL RAPED BY YOUNG 'FOX'

A sex fiend dubbed the Teenage Fox has raped a 15-year-old girl at knife-point.

The attack is the second by the 17-year-old youth, and last night police – who believe they know his identity – warned he could strike again.

The rapist, who has been living rough in wooded, hilly countryside, grabbed his latest victim in a village near Chippenham, Wilts. He had a Golden Labrador with him.

Police have been hunting him since he raped a girl of 11 at Warminster, Wilts, three weeks ago. (*Sun*)

In the above case *The Times* mentioned that "the rapist has been leading a fox-style existence living rough in wooded countryside", but within a few months it was clear, in yet another case, that it is the nickname itself which becomes crucial rather than any particular style of existence. The opening sentence of the *Sun*[37] report – under the headline **Girl, 6, raped by 'New Fox'** – has the echo of the earlier report reproduced above – "A savage sex fiend dubbed The New Fox was being hunted by police last night . . . " The attacker committed the offence in the same area as "one of the major hunting grounds for the notorious Fox". However, there is another reason for the assailant to be christened the 'New Fox' for the 6-year-old girl "told a woman detective last night how her attacker's car was littered with empty Fox's Glacier Mint wrappers, paper and carrier bags".

This case provides the clearest indication of how the popular press may trade in deciding the appropriate nickname for a new case when the *Star* decided to focus special attention on this rape of a 6-year-old – "He's been called The Beast, The Monster, the evil sex maniac. . . . We have named him the Redway Rapist".[38]

Variations may abound until a particular title sticks. In another case around this time we can see how different newspapers use familiar but different tags to identify a particular 'sex beast'. According to the *Star*,[39] he was known as the 'Night Stalker', while the *Sunday People*[40] displays the headline, **TERROR OF THE COPYCAT FOX**.

The copycat evidence

We have focused on the evidence that demonstrates how the so-called Fox – jailed for life earlier in the year – continued to emerge in different guises during the rest of the year. Sometimes it appeared that the police and the media were christening subsequent sex beasts as variants of The Fox, while, much more rarely, on other occasions it seemed to be the offender who took up the mantle. In the next chapter on the court trials, we produce further evidence that suggests that the copycat phenomenon is a danger to which the media may be contributing. Malcolm Fairley was the major sex criminal in the previous year whose exploits got widespread coverage at the search stage. However, towards the end of the sample year there was the 'M4 Rapist', who received enormously detailed coverage about the way that he had trapped a woman driver on the motorway.

Within the same week as this report of the M4 rape, the *Sun*[41] ran the headlines **M4 COPYCAT FIEND GRABS GIRL: he attacks her like car rapist**. In the only report traced of this incident, the Sun reports that

> police said the attacker probably planned to rape [the 14-year-old schoolgirl] in his car after reading about the ordeal of the motorway monster's victims. A senior detective said: "We think it could be a copycat assault. The description of the man doesn't fit that of the person wanted for the other attacks."

Does the copycat phenomenon exist? There is little doubt that the popular newspapers and the police embrace the copycat phenomenon with enthusiasm, so they may be misleading on many occasions with the supposed examples they sometimes put on display. Sometimes, of course, there is really no link at all as we found with the 'New Fox' having a sweet tooth for Fox's Glacier Mints. However, there is on other occasions a remarkable similarity of techniques, of clothes and of weapons. How do they learn of the detail and, indeed, where do they learn the specific techniques? It would be tempting to focus on 'video nasties', which are seen by some as the ready harbinger of many of our social ills. The front-page of the *Sun*[42] confidently stressed that The Fox "based his sickening crimes on hard-core videos hired from sex shops". However, the speed with which copycat phenomena sometimes appear gives no scope for video nasties being the link. The concern about the unbalanced getting imageries for action from porn videos and television violence has not been matched by a concern that the popular newspapers may also be providing similar material. Did the squalid detail of the atrocities of The Fox which the press featured so fully have no effect on the variety of Foxes spawned and featured so prominently over the next few months in the pages of these newspapers?

The enthusiasm with which the video nasties explanation as a crucial influence is embraced by many newspapers provokes three thoughts. Firstly, attention to video nasties by the newspapers takes the attention off their own sensationalist coverage of sex offences. Secondly, the same relationship to sex offending could be posited with regard to the reporting in popular newspapers as is adjudged with the supposed link to video nasties. Thirdly, it draws attention away from more serious explanations of sex crime in terms of those aspects of social organisation and gender relations which encourage so many men to engage in sexually aggressive behaviour towards women.

The development of television coverage

While television coverage has not been monitored in the same way as the press in this study, there seems an increasing focus in television on sexual cases where there are thought to be many victims. Not only does this occur on specific crime programmes, such as *Crimewatch*, but also more routinely on the national and regional news programmes. To take one example, in November 1987 the *North-West Regional News* introduced by Stuart Hall had a long feature as their opening item:

> Good evening to you. There has been an important development in the hunt for a rapist suspected of attacking more than twenty women in the North-West. Detectives are hoping that he may be trapped through a gold bracelet found at the scene of his latest crime. Police in Cheshire and Greater Manchester have joined forces to investigate a series of attacks which span more than six years. Paul Craven has more details . . . [43]

Paul Craven noted how a series of attacks had stopped but . . .

> Operation Osprey has now been set up to tackle a fresh
> wave . . . . a team of detectives are trying to establish a concrete
> link between the cases [Craven is talking against a backcloth of
> computers]. If it is one man, then they believe he is white, aged
> between 25 and 35, well-built and may have a beard; his accent is
> that of North Manchester or South Lancashire. The code-name,
> Osprey, has been chosen with care, a bird of prey which hunts in
> the early morning . . .

The words are quite carefully chosen. The report does not insist that it is one man who has committed all the offences, but the implication is that is the case. At present, regional news broadcasts have the tone of a modified sensationalist journalism. With the increasing demand to attract larger audiences, it will be of interest whether television will shift down the road of creating the sex beast at every opportunity.

Conclusion

In this chapter we have traced the detailed mechanisms of the creation of the sex fiend in the press. There is a highly selective process by which the press places certain stories in the public eye and not others. While the local press reports many cases of sexual assualt with small factual stories, the popular national press generally pursues primarily those which fit its thesis of the sex fiend.

With the focus on the serious and the spectacular, there is a distorted picture of sexual assaults in which the spectacular multiple rapes are identified as the sum of sexual assaults. They are not. Among sexual assaults multiple rapes of strangers are almost certainly the exception rather than the rule. The notion of the sex fiend presents a particular stereotype of sex crime which hinders the full understanding of the nature and range of sex offences.

Chapter four

Sex crime in court

Introduction

During the search stage of a sex crime hunt the focus of the press is
usually on the violent man himself. When he is caught it is his trial
which is the next stage of the criminal justice system to attract media
attention. As a consequence the focus of the media's stories also
changes. Interest often shifts on to the woman, and the interaction
between the sex criminal and his victim. In order to defend the accused
man his defence lawyers will often attempt to implicate the woman as
an active participant rather than helpless victim. In a rape case the
typical defence argument is that the woman consented to intercourse,
while in sex murder the defence may be that she provoked him. In each
case it is the woman and her conduct that the man's lawyers will try to
put on trial. The press reporting at this stage is thus quite different from
that of the hunt.

The press often go beyond the courtroom to seek out other sexual
actors for their stories. Previous sexual partners of the accused man may
be interviewed about the details of their sex life with him. That is, the
sexual conduct of women not present at the trial is dragged into the
media's version of the event, the better to titillate the reader.

Sex and murder

In our study year there were forty-five murder trials reported from the
courts where some sexual component was raised as an issue, even if to
be denied. In cases of sex murder the victim is not there to defend herself
against accusations that her conduct was so dreadful as to excuse, at
least partially, the man's killing her. This is the ultimate occasion in
which a man can attack a woman's reputation and conduct with
impunity. Unlike cases of rape or indecent assault, where the survivor's
account of the episode often provides the point of departure and main
focus of attention, the victim of a murder attack is dead. It is rare that a

victim dies after giving an account of the interaction to an official authority. What took place has to be reconstructed with the principal witness for the prosecution being unavailable. The prosecution will give an account and the defence may challenge that account. However, it often seems to be the case that the prosecution and the defence move quickly towards an agreement on what happened. The interests of the prosecution to secure a conviction and the interests of the defence to ensure that the verdict is one of manslaughter rather than murder may on occasion coalesce, so that it often appears – in reading the newspapers – that consensus rather than conflict between prosecution and defence is the general order of the day. In brief, murder cases often lack the court interaction where two versions seriously clash. In murder cases the victim's account remains missing.

In the literature there has been concern expressed how the dead victim may be blamed. For example, Radford[1] presents the killing of Jane Asher in which her husband was portrayed in court as a model husband and father, with his dead wife as a 'two-timing flirt'. In that case the judge passed a six months' suspended prison sentence, allowing the defendant to walk free from the court. Lees argues that such 'provocation' is regularly used by some male defendants as a defence or mitigation for killing 'their' wives and lovers.[2]

Blaming the victim

However, the moral status of the victim is often portrayed as ambivalent in murder trials. There are a range of behaviours and relationships which provide a variety of ways of blaming the victim. Situations vary as to whether sexual relations are an expected component of the relationship. In each of these situations the dead victim's reputation is often called into question. Without chance of rebuttal, the victim both implicitly and explicitly was made to take some of the blame. It was much more often the man's account, whether alive or dead, which gained prominence in the headlines reporting the case. In the aftermath of a sensational trial, the popular papers sometimes unearthed persons not directly involved in the case to continue the titillation. The former lovers of the men were often compromised in such stories, while the former male lovers of women are never similarly exposed. We shall examine the different ways in which women can be blamed, according to the degree of intimacy and stability of the relationship they had with their killer.

Domestic murders

Domestic murders dominate and sexual aspects quite often emerge in such cases. As there were more cases of the husband killing his wife rather than vice versa, it is perhaps not surprising that his account often grabs the headlines and his wife's account is muted. So, for example, a 44-year-old man maintained that sex taunts drove him to strangle his wife, which produced the headline SEX JIBE MADE ME A KILLER (*Daily Mirror*).[3] The two newspapers reporting this case both focused on his claim that sex taunts from his 56-year-old wife over his impotency provoked him to strangle her with a flex. In contrast, the prosecution alleged that he had murdered his wife so that he could bring his 17-year-old mistress to live in his house. While the newspapers noted in the text that he was besotted with his 17-year-old mistress, the thrust of the message was that his wife was essentially to blame. Men's unfaithfulness is rarely made the focus of a condemnatory press report during the trial, while women's infidelity as the cause of trouble often becomes a major theme.

Unfaithful husbands are the norm, while unfaithful wives excite no sympathy, just blame. It is the cuckolded husband who kills who gets the sympathy. In a manslaughter case in which the dead wife had had affairs with other men, Mr Justice Leonard said '[the defendant] deserved sympathy because his life had become miserable'.[4] A man who reacted violently when he saw his wife in a car with a bus driver, after his wife had refused him sex for six years, was told by the Recorder of London, Sir James Miskin QC: "You saw this man kissing your wife and understandably felt the misery of the situation. I accept you had no intention of killing . . . . *Any man who had to endure what you endured might have reacted in the same way*" (our emphasis).[5]

There were only two cases reported where the wife killed her husband and a sexual relationship or activity was at issue. Another involved a common-law relationship. The contrast in the reporting of these cases is worth noting.

A local case which produced front-page headlines[6] – 'Vicious schemer' is jailed for life SHAM TEARS OF AN EVIL WIFE – described how a former Coventry man who had moved to become a licensee in a Yorkshire pub had been killed by his 32-year-old wife and her barman lover. Described in court as a hard and callous woman who hated her husband, in this case there was no sympathy for the killer at all. A policeman spoke of the popularity of the landlord – "[He] was very well thought of, very popular at the pub. All those we interviewed couldn't speak too highly of him". As she had pledged that she was innocent, she offered no account as to why she allegedly hated her husband. In this case the victim is totally exonerated, for he is the innocent husband being killed by his wicked or evil wife.

In the other case, where a wife killed her husband, there was widespread coverage when a judge decided not to jail a 25-year-old civil servant who had shot her husband through the heart just a week after their marriage. He put her on probation for three years on condition she remained an in-patient at a psychiatric hospital. The front-page story in the *Star*[7] – JUDGE'S MERCY: WIFE KILLED KINKY COPPER **Sordid facts of sex life kept secret** – told how the judge deliberately drew a veil over the last days of the victim, informing the court that the defendant went berserk after being subjected to "abuse, violence and sexual perversions". After reading statements in the case, the judge went on: "I could hardly accept it until I saw things found in their house". However, the judge refused to read the statements in public:

> There seems no reason to blacken anyone's name by going into details of their marriage. One doesn't want to be seen to be covering anything up. But it is encapsulated in the phrase that she was subjected to sadistic behaviour over a lengthy period of time which she accepted because she was in love with him.

On this occasion the judge was trying to protect the reputation of the female defendant, but the enthusiasm of the popular press could not so easily be quelled. The *Star*, for example, had managed to locate their wedding photographer, who claimed that the day after the wedding ceremony the couple asked him to do some pictures with the woman "posing in sexy French underwear".

After the verdict was given, the newspapers interviewed other women in the dead policeman's life who reported on his previous sexual conduct. A named 40-year-old nurse who was said to be his previous girlfriend for seven years was reported as saying about her sex life with the man: "We had a good love life. [The dead man] was a good lover. It was robust at times, but there was never anything kinky about our relationship" and that she did not think he was capable of what he had been accused.[8] The lengthy interview from a former girlfriend attempted to portray an alternative version which inevitably placed the dead man in a more favourable light.

This former lover seemed a willing participant in providing this story but of much more concern are the occasions when former associates, not directly associated with a sordid murder case, are resurrected by the press for exhibition. This occurs in cases where there is no attempt to rehabilitate the reputation of the man, whether he be killer or killed. The reputations of others who may not have been so willing to be identified are sacrificed in the quest for titillation.

A 23-year-old woman poured paraffin over her 38-year-old lover and set it alight as he lay bound hand and foot, and blindfolded, "wearing a pair of her open-crotch panties and nylon stockings" on a mattress in their living-room. The woman pleaded not guilty to his murder, but the Crown rejected her plea of guilty to manslaughter, so there was a contested trial lasting several days, which was fully reported in the popular dailies. Later the remarks of the sentencing judge perhaps indicated why the manslaughter charge was not originally accepted:

> The method of killing which you employed was terrible indeed. What you did went far beyond what can be acceptable to the rule of law. [The named man] met his death at your hands in a manner which must be considered revolting by all right thinking people.[9]

However, there was no attempt to exonerate the reputation of the dead man. Indeed, it emerged that he had been convicted of killing the child of a former girlfriend and had assaulted the defendant and her 3-year-old daughter. The sex-slave theme was maintained throughout unchallenged – **SEX SLAVE BURNED HER LOVER ALIVE**[10] and **KINKY LOVER BURNED ALIVE BY HIS BLONDE SEX SLAVE.**[11] The text related her evidence:

> I was not a woman any more. I felt inferior . . . I had pictures in my mind of all the sex fantasies we had been through . . . I do not know why I did it. I was not my normal self . . . I felt very deeply for him. I loved him . . . . He wanted me to be his slave – not the woman I am. He made me dress in erotic underwear and to dress as his sex slave.

After being sentenced the sex-slave image remains, but she has now become a wronged mother (*Daily Mail*) or mum (*Sun*). Even the *Sun* avoids the pejorative term, 'girl', for this 23-year-old woman whose reputation comes out unscathed from the media coverage – **Brute was burned alive by mother who lived in fear SEX SLAVE JAILED FOR KILLING SADIST LOVER** (*Daily Mail*);[12] **SEX-SLAVE MUM GETS 3 YEARS IN JAIL She burned kinky lover** (*Sun*).[13]
In the aftermath of the trial, the *Sun*'s report[14] mentioned that the dead man had 'boasted that he turned more than SIXTY young mums into his personal sex slaves'. The *Sun* said that the man's death

> delighted another of his victims, pretty [full name given] who suffered a three-month nightmare at his hands. The monster was jailed in 1978 for cruelty to [named person] and her son [also named] two. Jenny, now happily married, cried when she heard her torturer was dead and said: "I'm relieved I will never again feel my stomach churn when a man with his silhouette passes me in the street".

This is, of course, titillating information for its readers, but we need to remember that this woman was now said to be happily married; her child would now be aged 10 and could be quite aware of a trial which was getting widespread coverage in the popular newspapers. The *Star*[15] managed to trace many more previous victims than the solitary find of the *Sun*. The *Star* quoted "five women [who] regret the day they accepted his advances". Each woman was identified with her full name and, in three cases, the naming of the town where the women were currently living. It was stated that the 20-month-old child he killed twelve years earlier was a named woman's "illegitimate son". In contrast, despite its front-page headline – **Sixty slaves in the kinky fiend's harem** – *Daily Mirror*[16] did not identify or feature the comments of any of his previous victims. The desire for personal disclosure among the popular newspapers is not always universal.

Other sex murder trials

There were no trials where there was a steady boyfriend/girlfriend relationship, but an example of a more casual relationship indicates the extremity of the way that a girl could be held to blame for her own murder. An account which remained unchallenged in the press reports was that a girl of 12 had 'provoked' her death by failing to reveal her age prior to sex play. Headlined **Youth murdered schoolgirl in stabbing frenzy** (*Lancashire Evening Post*)[17] this involved a 17-year-old youth stabbing to death in a fit of temper a 12-year-old girl whom he knew. The youth pleaded guilty to murdering the girl. The court was told that he had killed the girl after taking part in sex play with her and then discovering that she was under age. The defence counsel said the defendant had admitted losing his temper on finding out that the girl was under age. Passing sentence, the judge said the fact that he had confessed would be a matter to be considered in his favour when consideration was given as to the time of his release back into the community.

Here the girl died, but on other occasions the message is sometimes that women's actions may have dire consequences for the fragile male, even though she herself may be unharmed. A headline in the *Sun*[18] more than hints where the blame should lie – **GIRL'S LUSTFUL TOUCHES DROVE ME TO KILLING**. Here a jilted lover is said to have "snapped when he saw his girlfriend fondling a man's bottom in a pub. He was so enraged that he blasted his love rival to death in front of the girl". The trial continued but the newspaper coverage did not. The message had been made that the woman had caused the outburst and the tragic outcome.

The implicit sympathy for the killer given in the coverage of newspapers which are routinely advocating more severe sentencing strategies might be considered contradictory. A further example of the assumption that women should be willing to provide sex for interested men seems implicit in the *Sun*[19] headline – **LANDLORD'S DEATH LUST FOR**

GIRL Lodger shunned sex. By suggesting that the 'fun-loving' woman lodger shunned or avoided sexual intercourse with the landlord begins to suggest that the "normal" occurrence is for women lodgers in such situations to allow sexual intercourse to take place. Even the prosecuting counsel seemed sympathetic – "Being so close to his desire without being able to fulfil his passion proved too much for him". 'Fun-loving' in the report becomes almost synonymous with being generally available for sex. Hence, she is considered to share the blame.

If female lodgers are regarded as 'available', it is also clear what the popular newspapers think of female hitch-hikers. The prosecution alleged that a 37-year-old man had picked up a 29-year-old woman when she was hitch-hiking from London towards Oxford, and "went berserk" when she rejected his sexual advances. The headline in the London *Evening Standard*'s[20] report – **I'm sorry, says man on murder charge** – was transformed the next day into the more familiar story of girl hitch-hiker getting herself into trouble. The focus was on the victim and not the assailant. The *Daily Mail*[21] headline – **Greenham girl's ride to death** – concentrated on the fact that this 29-year-old woman had been involved in the Greenham peace movement. The headline neatly shifted the danger to being involved with the protest group and implicitly reversing the message of the Greenham woman by suggesting that their activities produce a 'ride to death'. The *Sun*'s headline also focusing on the victim produces a different slant, for **Hitch-girl 'spurned sex'** again hints that 'hitch-girls' are normally willing partners. In the *Sun*'s[22] report, the accused was alleged to have told the police that he stripped the victim naked and cut off one of her breasts to make it look like 'the work of a madman'. There is no serious challenge to this account and the impression remains that he was not a 'madman' but a normal man who had met a hitch-hiker who unusually 'spurned sex'.

It emerged after the trial that the dead woman was the daughter of one of Britain's top psychiatrists. After the case he was asked by a reporter if he would offer advice to other hitch-hikers. He said: "People will always hitch-hike. I have given people lifts, and will continue to do so". Such a low-key comment is not what is required by the popular press at the conclusion of a traumatic trial. The father's balanced sentiment was reported only in the *Daily Mail*.[23]

We have shown that it is rare for the sex fiend image to be constructed at the trial stage. In fact, a case where the image of sex fiend has been developed at the search stage is often over quickly at the trial stage. The plea is often a guilty one. In such cases the sex beast image is maintained by press coverage after the trial.

One would expect some cases to get widespread coverage, especially when there is serious re-offending after a previous life sentence. For example, **SEX KILLER GETS LIFE . . . AGAIN** related to a case reported only in the *Daily Mail*.[24] In 1971 this offender had been given a ten-year sentence for attempting to rape a 69-year-old woman. In 1978 he was given a life sentence for attacking a 72-year-old woman after breaking into her home, but this was reduced to eight years on appeal. On the present occasion he was convicted of attempting to rape and then murdering an 81-year-old widow. This case merited only a six-inch column in one newspaper, but probably failed to get widespread coverage on several grounds: the case was held outside London (in Manchester) and the case was not contested. Nevertheless, the test of interest for the popular newspapers seems whether such a case has the potential for titillation rather than an outcry at such wickedness.

The potential for titillation regarding a freed rapist emerged in another case which had considerable coverage over a three-day period. The front-page coverage on the first day of the trial – **FREED RAPIST 'CAME BACK TO KILL'** (*Daily Mirror*)[25] – revealed that a rapist had returned from jail after being released to murder his victim. After a sex attack two years earlier he had said to the 40-year-old spinster that "If you call the police I'll kill you". He was alleged to have carried out his threat after being released on parole. He denied the charge. The prosecuting counsel said that nothing would be heard to criticise the victim's character, who was timid and nervous.

Despite the assurances of the prosecuting counsel, the next day the headlines certainly gave a different picture, although the newspapers do make it clear that it is the rapist's account – **Zoe stripped as we talked, claims rapist** (*Daily Mail*);[26] **RAPIST SAYS VICTIM ZOE STRIPPED OFF** (*Star*).[27] The accused maintained that he had gone to her home to ask if she had received a letter of apology from him for his earlier crime. He maintained they talked, and then the woman went upstairs, stripped, and lay on a bed.

When he was sentenced to life for killing his former rape victim, the main focus was on the release of the rapist: **MP's fury as revenge murderer gets life WHY WAS THIS MONSTER FREED?** (*Daily Mirror*);[28] **Revenge threat was ignored BLUNDER THAT LED RAPIST TO KILL** (on the front page of the *Daily Mirror*).[29] The blunder was the apparent failure of detectives to inform the Parole Board that he had threatened to return to kill her. The Home Office admitted that the West Yorkshire police's decision not to tell the Parole Board of his threat was 'highly regrettable'. The *Daily Mail* stressed that this failed to console the victim's distraught family, friends and workmates, her MP or the probation service, who were also not told of the killer's threat. The MP demanding an inquiry said: "I am appalled that this man was given parole. He should not have been allowed out under any circumstances. There must never be a repeat of this horrendous case". After this type of cathartic outburst, no one seemed to reflect that this offender had a determinate sentence and would be allowed out eventually. The focus was on the parole decision; the early parole date simply brought forward a situation which would not have been averted. It is only at this point that the newspaper reader learns that the rapist and the victim had been next door neighbours at the time of the original offence. Further, while the rapist was in prison, the victim had applied to the housing department for a change of flat, but after discussions with a social worker, she apparently decided to stay put. Of course, the 'blunder' banner makes an exciting headline, but there is no systematic attempt to consider where and what the blunder exactly was. It was said in the *Daily Mail* that

> the probation service held their own inquiry to see if they had made any mistakes. West Yorkshire's chief probation officer said: 'The baffling thing is, even with hindsight, we are still left wondering what more we could have done to stop this killing'.

The outrage eagerly orchestrated by the newspaper did not focus in a serious way on the needs and dangers facing rape survivors. There was no attempt to inform the public whether there was a significant risk of this happening to others. The message which most potential victims – that is, all women – would have grasped by default from this case was that threats made by a rapist may not be empty ones.

Our discussion is not exhaustive of murders which involve a sexual relationship. The revenge motive may be apparent. In one case,[30] a 36-year-old man was imprisoned for four years for the manslaughter of a 37-year-old craft teacher after he had discovered that his daughter was spending the night at the teacher's home, while an allegedly brutal husband was shot dead by the wife's father after she "fell into a nightmare of crime, violence and bizarre sex".[31] The latter case found its way on the front page of the *Sunday People* under the headline BEAUTY QUEEN'S LIFE OF CRIME Terrorised wife's story. This front page trailer of what is characterised as her "Bonnie and Clyde" ordeal was continued with a double-page spread on the inside pages. The theme of competent sexual performance is dominant, for

> despite his string of conquests [he] had one big hang-up. He was afraid of not measuring up as a lover and worried about his performance in bed. 'He had an inferiority complex when it came to love-making', [his wife revealed], 'but it never killed his great sexual appetite'.

The physical violence on herself and on their baby son was vividly described. Her account in effect exonerates her father, who was now starting a life sentence for shooting her husband. Finally, the violence reached the point where she left and stayed in a refuge for battered women. But she returned and eventually her husband was shot dead by her father. It is reported that police were satisfied that the wife acted under duress in the various crimes in which she got involved in.

Where the blame lay, in the case of the father who stabbed the teacher in a rage after discovering that his daughter was spending the night at the teacher's home, was made less clear. The girl had claimed that she had been having an affair with the teacher for some months. Later the trial judge lifted an order banning publication of the girl's claim that her father had sexually interfered with her. The *Sunday People*[32] continued in effect to challenge her claims: **LIES! LIES! LIES! A schoolgirl's 'fantasies' and the teacher who tried to help her**. The teacher's widow continued to deny that her husband had had sex with his killer's 15-year-old daughter, and the dead man's brother spoke of the 'fantasies' of the teenage schoolgirl. The teacher's brother also said: "All he was trying to do was help. He felt it was his duty to protect the girl if her claims against her father were right and just not a 15-year-old girl's fantasies." No further items were traced referring to this case and so the confusion was allowed to remain.

There were six cases where the relevance of homosexuality was evident. It may simply be used as a taunt which is deemed provocative and so portrayed as one of several triggering actions for the killing. For example, in a case[33] – **Sex slur drove man to lash out at bully who mocked him: Killer stepson's years of torment** – where a bullying stepfather was killed by the stepson he had tormented for years, one of the taunts mentioned was the mocking of his desires to get on at college, calling him a 'funny boy'. Usually the detail in such details was minimal. There was only one case where the homosexual activity leading to death was identified as part of a "kinky sex session". This case was covered only by the *Sun*, which had two reports under the headlines **Gay 'Killed with Chain'**[34] and **DOG-CHAIN SEX KILLER JAILED**.[35] In the first brief item the court heard that a 27-year-old chef had strangled a 25-year-old homosexual friend with a dog choke-chain after a 'slave and master' sex session. It was said that they had met only hours earlier. They had sniffed drugs and then the chain was used to heighten sexual excitement. Similarly, the murder of a prostitute provided the only case where lesbianism was explicitly mentioned.[36]

Child murder

At the search stage a child sex murder produced considerable coverage, but there was little or no sexual titillation employed during such trials. In the year there were seven such cases where there were trials or remand hearings of which only one concerned a parent killing a child. This latter case indicates how matters of sexual deviance can occur in newspaper reports after the trial.

The father was found guilty of the manslaughter of his baby daughter of three months. During the trial there was no evidence of sexual abuse put forward. As he began his jail sentence the *Daily Mirror*[37] revealed details of his life: **JEALOUS MONSTER WHO LIKED KINKY SEX**. It was clear from the reports that he was an insanely jealous man who, for example, "made [his wife] walk with her head down so she couldn't see the bulge in men's trousers".

Two of the remand cases had featured earlier in the year at the search stage. Newspapers sometimes appeared to be providing the rallying cry for future demonstration. For example, in the Leoni Keating case, interest was maintained by reporting fully the reaction of the crowd to the accused's first appearance in court – **CROWDS HURL EGGS AT LEONI CASE MAN: Mums scream 'Hang him'** (*Sun*);[38] **FURY OVER LEONI MAN** (*Star*);[39] **WIVES' FURY AT MAN IN LEONI CASE** (*Daily Mirror*).[40] They were described as "screaming women" or "a screaming mob of women", providing "a gauntlet of hate". However, the general focus of the *Sun* and the *Star* was to use the occasion to emphasise the demand for the return of capital punishment – "outside the hearing, mother of five, Mrs Sandra Daniels, founder of the pro-hanging CHILD organisation carried a banner reading: 'Did Leoni die in vain?' "

On the day after the funeral of 3-year-old Leoni, the popular newspapers had another case to focus upon for their front page headlines: **EVIL OLD MAN WHO KILLED KIRSTY GETS LIFE** (*Daily Mail*);[41] **60 YEARS OF EVIL Kirsty's killer, 79, led a life of crime** (*Sun*)[42]. The trial had been featured for the previous three days. The fact that the 79-year-old man was the oldest man standing trial for murder this century was an extra ingredient of interest. While most of the newspapers reported this feature, the *Sun* was the only newspaper to point out that "records show the only man older than him to face a murder charge was hanged in 1822 when he was 80". The exact nature of the sexual assaults was not described in the newspaper reports. The exception was the *Sun*, which reported that the child's sexual organs had been cut in the attack upon her. When the verdict was announced, the London *Evening Standard*[43] itemised the catalogue of the killer's violent record stretching over sixty years. The possible links with other unsolved child murders began to be explored. This was the real reminder that this was a sex beast who had been caught.

When child killers appear in court, newspapers do seem to resist from giving many of the more gruesome details of the tragedy. Certainly the child victims are not those whose reputations the newspapers would wish to question or challenge. Other themes must emerge. In the present case, the scope for widespread coverage was enhanced by linking the outcome with the demand for the death sentence. The three popular dailies took up this theme in their inside-page stories with almost identical headlines: **Woman juror hits out at child killer, 79 HOW CAN THEY LET THIS ANIMAL LIVE?** (*Daily Mirror*);[44] **HOW COULD THEY LET THIS ANIMAL LIVE? Juror slams Kirsty killer** (*Star*);[45] **TOO WICKED TO LIVE** (*Sun*).[46] Described as just one moving incident amid scenes of shock, revulsion and anger in the packed Old Bailey juryroom, this provides the focus on the sex beast and an interesting contrast. Unlike the search stage, when florid images can be portrayed, there is more difficulty in the courtroom, when the sex beast is discovered to be someone "looking like a loving old grand-father, [being] taken to the cells".[47]

'No' sexual assault

In some situations the press reports explicitly mention that there is no sexual assault or activity involved. These are interesting, for the explicit denial suggests that the scenario is one where a sexual connotation would 'normally' be expected. However, the main point is that there is sometimes a general reluctance to confront the issue. Whereas in the search stage the main task in the media reporting is the construction of the sex beast, at the trial stage – reflecting the activity within the courtroom – the delineation of the sex beast is often muted or even avoided.

There are situations where the general expectation is that sex may have been the motive for a murderous assault. However, if the prosecution does not raise it as a motive for murder the defence is unlikely to challenge this. If the sexual motive is introduced by the defence, it is to justify the defendant's action. The purpose of introducing the sexual motive is to try to lessen the enormity of the crime or to place the blame elsewhere. Where the question of a sexual motive is avoided, either the defence recognise that their client could be disadvantaged by being typed as a sex maniac and the prosecution may realise that such a line of questioning may unnecessarily complicate a case, or there may seem little scope for placing the blame elsewhere.

For everyone there is a problem in understanding the nature of the crime when no motive can be identified. In one case a

> baby-faced double killer was jailed for life ... without revealing why he murdered two pretty teenagers. Detectives puzzling over a motive say the girls were not sexually assaulted. And the former petty crook had no previous record for violence. One senior detective said: 'We'll probably never find out unless he decides to tell us' (*Sun*).[48]

The sentenced man had denied the killings, in which one victim had been strangled with her bra.

More usually, however, the denial of the sex motive is more readily accepted if there is an alternative explanation. The following case is a reflection of the desire for neat classifications – rapist, robber, etc. – in both the courtroom and the media. There is no place for mixed motives. In the following example, the motives of someone who stabs his victim many times in her genital area are not discussed in public; indeed the sexual component is dismissed with the claim that the victim had not been indecently assaulted. There is not the same desire (unlike the search stage) to portray the defendant as a sex maniac.

The headlines are reminiscent of an Agatha Christie title: **Murder on the 9.02** (London *Evening Standard*);[49] **HORROR ON THE 9.02** (*Star*).[50] The jury heard how a social worker was horrifically knifed to death on a late-night train. The prosecution claimed that the murder victim was alone in a carriage when the defendant – aged 15 years at the time – confronted her, demanding money and brandishing a knife. The situation is reconstructed but, of course, without any information being supplied by the victim:

with considerable courage, as you may think, she refused to hand over her money, whereupon there was a fight. The defendant struck with the knife into her throat on the left-hand side just near the jugular vein, with such force that it severed the spinal cord, causing almost instant paralysis. Thereafter, the defendant must have pulled down her pants and tights and stabbed her private parts a number of times.

The prosecuting counsel told the jury that there was no evidence that the victim had been indecently assaulted. Afterwards, the dead woman's body was thrown from the train after it left Northampton station. There is no further mention of the attack on her genital area in the newspapers.

This report of the prosecuting submission suggests that this was not indecent assault. It demonstrates the dangers of various interpretations of the meaning of an act. In this case the death of the victim prevents this account being challenged. Her virtue in death, however, is assured. With no sexual assault being claimed, the victim also remains inviolate. Unusually, no blame is attached to her for the outcome. Indeed her actions are applauded: "with considerable courage, as you may think, she refused to hand over her money".

So, unlike the search stage, there is not the same desire to portray the defendant as a sex maniac. It needs to be recognised that sometimes all parties (both dead and alive) may gain by avoiding the issue of whether the attack had the ingredient of a sexual assault. It is only when no sexual assault is alleged to have taken place that the victim seems clear of blame.

We have seen that in the media reporting at the stage of the trial a women's sexual conduct is often brought into question. Evidence garnered by reporters either in the courtroom or by pursuit of previous lovers produces highly sexualised stories. Typically the sexual conduct of a woman is an excuse, legitimising male violence ranging from the murder of a wife to the sexual assault of a girlfriend. Some papers seek out extra salacious background. In contrast sexual activity by men is rarely seen as problematic.

Rape

In order to understand the press reporting of rape trials we need to concentrate on the few cases which got enormous publicity in 1985. As we discussed in Chapter 2 three cases (out of 114) had one-third of the total number of pages devoted to rape cases, while nine cases had over half. We start with a brief summary of the nine cases which took most of the media coverage. They are presented in the order of the amount of space devoted to each court case and the immediate aftermath. Then we shall analyse the reasons the three most exceptional cases obtained so much coverage and the implications of this.

THE FOX'S REIGN OF TERROR ENDS IN JAIL FOR LIFE SIX TIMES[51]

A 32-year-old man dubbed The Fox pleaded guilty to thirteen offences including rape, indecent assault on both men and women, and burglary. Over a period of 150 days across five counties The Fox had preyed on women and some men in what was described as "an orgy of sex and violence". The reporting included interviews with his previous sexual partners.

BRIXTON GANG RAPE

Six teenagers who gang-raped two 16-year-old schoolgirls forty-five times contested the case and were found guilty. The youths were black, a fact made clear by the relatively unusual use of photographs by the papers; the young women were white. The youths attempted to defend themselves by claiming that the girls, who were returning from a pop concert, had consented.

13 PARATROOPERS CLEARED OF RAPING WRAC

Thirteen paratroopers were acquitted after a six-week trial for the gang rape of a 22-year-old woman soldier in their barracks. Eight of the paratroopers were found guilty of indecently assaulting the woman soldier. The men defended themselves by arguing that the woman had consented to sex frequently and had done so on this occasion also.

FIVE LIFE TERMS FOR SAVAGE RAPIST

A 39-year-old man admitted kidnapping two 13-year-old schoolgirls, raping one and indecently assaulting the other, before stabbing them with a three-foot-long ceremonial sword and leaving them for dead in the forest.

BIBLE SEX BEASTS JAILED FOR FIVE YEARS

Two men, aged 26 and 27, contested the case but were found guilty of rape and aiding and abetting each other on the sex attacks on a 21-year-old French woman, who told how the two burst into her room at a friend's flat while she was reading the Bible.

RAILWAY RAPE FIEND GETS SIX LIFE SENTENCES

A 35-year-old man pleaded guilty to the brutal rape of six women and the indecent assault of another four women in a sixteen-month period. He dubbed himself 'The Dragon', but was known as the 'Railway Rapist' as he picked his victims at random as they travelled on trains, waited on platforms or as they walked close to railway stations.

SEX CASE TEACHER IS JAILED

A 36-year-old married teacher, who admitted having unlawful sex with a 15-year-old pupil on a sailing trip, was found not guilty of raping the girl after a three-day trial. He was jailed for eighteen months for unlawful sexual intercourse. Whether the girl consented was crucial to the case.

EVIL PARENTS JAILED FOR RAPE

A man who admitted twice raping his 15-year-old daughter and indecently assaulting her teenage friend was jailed for six years. His wife, who was alleged to have aided and abetted him on the second occasion, was jailed for three years after a two-day trial.

BED-SIT RAPE FIEND GETS 16 YEARS

A 26-year-old man admitted to being the hooded rapist who terrorised women in a town's bed-sit area. He was sentenced to twelve years for the rape, a maximum two years for the indecent assault and a further two years for the burglary.

These nine cases, which comprise over one-half of the press coverage of court cases of rape during the year, cover a multitude of situations. The main charge was contested in four of the cases, while the accused admitted the offences in four others; in the remaining case, the father admitted the charge, while the mother contested the case. In all four cases where there seemed to be some knowledge of the victim before the alleged offences were committed, the cases were contested by alleging the woman's consent. These contested cases where there is considerable media coverage tend to be those where the defendant(s) can attempt a claim that the victim consented to intercourse. In cases where there were guilty pleas the defendants had almost invariably committed offences on several different occasions, and hence a defence that all the women consented would not be credible. The behaviour which characterised these latter cases would have called forth the notion of 'sex beast' or 'sex monster' at the search stage.

In two of the three cases which attracted most publicity the issue of whether the women had consented was an important component in the case, though in one of these there was an additional racial theme in the identification of the accused as black. The third case, in fact the largest, was one in which the man had been previously identified as a sex beast at the search stage. Press reporting focused as much on the reports about other women who had had sex with him as it did on the events to which he pleaded guilty. We shall examine each of these three in some detail.

The Fox

The case of Malcolm Fairley, known as 'The Fox', was the most widely reported court case of the year where the offence of rape was the main charge. An example of the extent and character of the reporting is that of the *Sun* which, on the day after the trial, had seven pages (including a special four-page pull-out)[52] devoted to the case. There were eighty-eight photos or illustrations relating to this court case and the aftermath, virtually equalling the number found for all the other rape cases in the year. The case was not contested, so the court proceedings were over in a day. Most of the coverage of the case consisted of the popular newspapers displaying their ingenuity in getting his first wife, her mother, his mother, brothers, nephews, nieces, friends, and neighbours to provide an account of the sex beast, especially his sexual habits.

It cannot be emphasised too strongly how unusual this case was. Serial rapists are rare. The statistically 'typical' rapist – the man who rapes one woman he knows – does not make it to front-page coverage, let alone fifty-nine pages across thirteen newspapers over ten days. This one case took 13 per cent of the total coverage of rape trials.

In a sense the rarity of the case is obvious. If it were not unusual, it would not be news. Most rape is not news. But anyone who gathers their information about rape only from the press would be seriously misled.

The themes in the coverage were: the number and nastiness of the attacks; how he did it in detail; his sex life; the causal effect of porno-graphic videos; the chase by the police.

The papers reported in endless detail the minutiae of the sex attacks. These attacks included sexually assaulting an elderly woman during a burglary; heterosexual rape; rape of women when their husbands, brothers or boyfriends were watching; homosexual rape (for which he got five times as long a prison sentence as for heterosexual rape); as well as burglary. The papers paid attention to the detail of the knives and sawn-off shot guns he used to threaten and wound his victims, the hood he used to disguise his appearance, his 'lair' and other related aspects of how he managed to get away with his exploits.

They reported in-depth information about his sex life that they gleaned from his first and current wives, their mothers, neighbours and any other informant. The *Sun* carried this to the extreme with a four-page pull-out about the **Savage Between the Sheets**.

It is clear from the differential sentencing that the judge considered that the rape of the men was a particularly heinous aspect of the case. He gave a ten-year prison sentence for this as opposed to two years for one of the rapes of women. The newspapers also commented on this parti-cular horror.

The letter of the law was observed in so far as none of the names of the actual raped women were mentioned. However, the preservation of a rape survivor's anonymity needs more than the exclusion of the name. A strip across the eyes of a photograph of a rape survivor and her boyfriend [53] is unlikely to deter speculation. Beyond the rape victims, the names of everybody else was disclosed, including the names of women who were indecently assaulted but not raped and the names of relatives of those whom The Fox had accosted. There will be some who may initially enjoy the appearance of their name in national and local newspapers, though even they, initially unused to the implications of media publicity, may come to regret their decision. However, others may be unhappy that their relationship with a now notorious "sex monster" should be so flagrantly exposed. In short, other lives – apart from the rape survivors themselves – may be damaged in the quest for sensational exposures.

For instance, the wife of The Fox undoubtedly suffered. The *Sun* proclaimed **Another Sun Exclusive**[54] under the headline **FOX CASE WIFE IN MENTAL HOSPITAL** and, despite the 'exclusive' tag, the *Star* ran essentially the same report on the same day under the headline **A WIFE'S AGONY IN WAIT FOR FOX CASE**.[55] The report told of how the wife of the man accused of The Fox sex crimes was being voluntarily treated in a psychiatric hospital. Her mother was reported in the *Star* as saying: "It has all been too much for her. The strain has been a terrible ordeal. She has been tormented by what has happened. No one can imagine what she and the children have gone through." It noted that the wife was in a Teesside hospital. The brother of the alleged offender said: "We all feel sorry for his wife. She has suffered more than anyone can know". The *Sun* 'exclusive' seemed to rely on 'friends' for their reports on how the wife had been 'shattered'. The *Sun* identified the exact hospital and also mentioned how the wife had been living with her mother in a named town since her husband's arrest.

The Fox's previous wife is the focus of another set of stories. Local evening papers described how he met his first wife, who is named: "pregnant, they married in a hurry".[56] His first wife was interviewed, as was her mother, who talked much more extensively. The next morning the national papers continued to dig into the background of The Fox, especially his sex life as revealed by his two wives.[57] The *Sun* had pages 1, 2, 4, 5, 15, 16, 17 and 18 given over to the story, while the others managed with only one or two pages fewer. In the *Star*[58] his two wives are purportedly writing on his sexual performance under the headline **THE SEX LIFE OF THE FOX - By his two wives**. But this is quite clearly a pastiche by two journalists desperate to match the efforts of rival newspapers. Certainly they have quotations from his first wife, which suggested that "Britain's most notorious sex fiend . . . was 'useless in bed' ". (The first wife is reported as being "happily married to a Durham miner".) For the same article the journalist evidently failed to get any juicy quotes from his present wife and despite the misleading by-line **By his two wives**, the material rests on the words of a named "neighbour in the tiny close of council houses", who incidentally provides no information on his sex life but on his lack of neighbourliness: "He was not very neighbourly – he would always try to avoid speaking . . . "

The *Sun* [59] went to more extreme lengths in their massive coverage, photographing Fairley's present wife under the caption "Georgina . . . sought psychiatric help" and providing a pot-pourri of detail of how **HORROR SENT HIS WIFE CRAZY**. Directly underneath was the tempter to move on to the special four-page pull-out section with the banner headline **SAVAGE IN MY BED**. His first wife – who is again named and identified as living happily in County Durham with her second husband and their 5-year-old daughter (both named) – is said to have "spoken bitterly last night about The Savage Between the Sheets". Intimate details about the relationship are supplemented by information from his first wife's 63-year-old mother, who is also named and photographed. She stressed what a violent man he was during this first marriage: "But, after the break-up, Joan just wanted to forget him."

The newspapers also sought out the previous victims of The Fox's sex attacks. The housewife who had been sleeping quietly after a Bank Holiday party when The Fox struck was identified by name, age and location. She had the ordeal of telling her story to both the *Star* and the *Sun*. The *Sun* reported how, after slipping quietly into her bedroom, Fairley leapt on to the bed, held a kitchen knife to her throat and attacked her.

The thirteenth victim of The Fox was photographed on a beach with her skirt hitched up, arm-in-arm with her boyfriend; their eyes were masked out on the photograph, which was captioned " . . . rebuilding their romance". The opening paragraphs reported how

the pretty girl victim . . . four months after The Fox subjected her
to a three-hour sex ordeal – and forced her brother and her
boyfriend at gunpoint to perform degrading acts with her – the girl
crawled into an airing cupboard in a bid to shut out the memories.

Across two pages her traumas are narrated in detail. The report identified how she was forced to quit her secretarial job and how she suffered a breakdown. The *Sun* noted the reality of the anonymity provision: "when the Press and TV spotlight turned on the village, the girl remained unnamed for legal reasons. But everyone in the close knit village of Edlesborough knew who she was".

The *Star*[60] and the *Daily Mail*[61] continued the search for female associates of The Fox with the headlines **THE SAD MOTHER HE BETRAYED** and **THE MOTHER WHO CANNOT BELIEVE** respectively. The full name and address of this 74-year-old woman is supplied, as is that of his brother, an invalid, who stated that "We're all ashamed of what he has done. We could sell his story but we could never make money from other people's suffering . . . "

Three days later, a front-page **EXCLUSIVE** in the *Star*[62] headlined **THE FOX'S LAIR – A COP'S HOME He lived with Pc during terror reign** is about a named police constable (with a photograph of his house on the front page of the newspaper) who "let the evil sex monster lodge at his luxury four bedroom house. But the friendly bobby never dreamed of Malcolm Fairley's true identity". The policeman's wife was Fairley's niece and the couple had put him up while Fairley was house-hunting in London. The newspaper reported that the constable faced a major Scotland Yard inquiry about his job. Apparently after weeks of anguish he had been told his job was safe. The previous day he had started back at work, to be followed by this front-page exclusive.

Other women who had been the subject of The Fox's violence were described by the press. A named and photographed woman who had apparently beaten off The Fox by biting him was a major story in one Sunday newspaper: "her courage saved her from becoming another of Fairley's rape victims".[63] (Did they mean to imply that 'courage' would have saved the other women from being raped?) A front-page EXCLU-SIVE in the *Sunday People*[64] – **A monster goes back to his lair: RETURN OF THE FOX** – in which the front-page photograph showed Fairley accompanied by police officers "back at this lair, showing police the scene of one of his evil deeds". This ritual of identification was used to preface a more titillating by-line: **MY BEDROOM BATTLE WITH THE FOX Pages 23, 24 and 25.**

The Woman's Editor had managed to unearth yet another EXCLU-SIVE under the headline **MY BATTLE WITH THE FOX: A tap on my shoulder . . . a violent struggle, then I'm stabbed with my bread-knife.** Another photographed and named victim who successfully resisted rape described her ordeal. Her account concluded with her saying that

> It's every woman's nightmare, of course, to wake up and find a
> man threatening to rape her. I suppose if you'd asked me before all
> this happened, I'd have said I'd give in, but I was so angry. I
> surprised myself how I acted.

Again the implication is that women can avoid rape through a display of courage when in reality other rather more fortuitous factors are much more important, as this woman actually recognised "Really I think it was James who saved me. God knows why he woke up that night. He never normally does . . . "

The *News of the World*[65] provided its own **EXCLUSIVE – FOX PUT HIS EVIL EYE ON ME: Niece tells of lonely lane terror in his car.** This report has the double ingredients of being about a person who was not only subject to the attentions of The Fox but also a relative. The report included his (named) niece's account that Fairley had terrified her by his sexual advances to her in a car.

The focus of much of this reporting of 'background' is sex. It in-cludes both his two wives' voluntary sexual activity, and also his sex attacks on other women. There is little serious exploration of the issues raised by the attacks. The reporting of the crime is on the one hand an excuse for sexual titillation and on the other a misleading warning to women as to the circumstances in which they will be raped and how to avoid it.

In the Fox case many people connected with the convicted man were hauled on to the national stage by the popular press. Perhaps some may have enjoyed their brief flirtation with notoriety, some may even have gained financially, but others may regret the publicity, possibly suffering from poison-pen attacks brought about by the exposure by the press of names and addresses of those who were victims of sexual attacks (but not raped) by The Fox or who were unlucky enough to be associated by birth, marriage or friendship to this man.

The most important point, however, is that this rapist, who got the most publicity, is the most unusual. The serial rapist is not common, but a simple scanning of the newspapers for matters to do with rape would give a contrary impression. Who or what is to blame for the production of this sex monster who terrorised five counties for nearly six months? All the newspapers focused on the supposed link between pornographic videos and the sex attacks. Fairley was considered to have been converted into a sex monster by viewing pornographic films. The judge, Mr Justice Caulfield, described The Fox as 'a casualty' of evil pornographers and went on to say: "I am satisfied that you are a decadent advertisement for the evil pornographers. They will want to forget you as one of their worst casualties".[66] The local evening papers, first on the streets in reporting the case, proclaimed **MONSTER BORN OUT OF BLUE VIDEOS**.[67] A senior police officer was reported as saying that "we believe he was influenced by some blue videos he had seen". More specifically, it was suggested that a scene in a video nasty gave Fairley the idea of forcing the brother and boyfriend of a 17-year-old girl to perform group sex acts with her at gunpoint. Terrified, they simulated the acts he ordered. The next day the front page of the *Sun*[68] took up the theme with enthusiasm: **PORN LUST OF THE FOX** (see Figure 4.1).

Michael Connell QC, defending, had focused on the video nasty theme, saying "This man is not completely to blame for his actions. He was subject to influences for which he could not compensate". Fairley was said to be "merely carrying out repetitive actions, trying to imitate what he had seen on the video screen". Mr Justice Caulfield, after studying the medical reports, said "All these reports emphasise the relevance of pornography – every one!" As Fairley was led from the dock of a packed courtroom, several newspapers reported how MPs were joining in condemning the growth of High Street sex shops and porn videos. Tory MP Jill Knight, chairwoman of an all-party Commons committee on family and child protection, said: "I now hope the Government will take this lesson on board and act to control the availability of pornography." Similarly Mary Whitehouse was reported as saying: "However wicked he was, he is the product of a society we have all helped to create." The *Sun*[69] focused on hard-porn videos as providing the key, under the headline How a little softie turned into sadistic sex maniac.

Figure 4.1 Front page of the *Sun*, 27 February 1985

THE Sun

Wednesday, February 27, 1985   18p   TODAY'S TV: PAGE 12

'You desecrated and defiled men and women, old and young' MR JUSTICE CAULFIELD YESTERDAY

PORN LUST OF THE FOX

FACE OF EVIL . . . The Fox rapist Malcolm Fairley copied porn videos

PORN films triggered the brutal lust of The Fox, who was given SIX life sentences yesterday for rape.

Malcolm Fairley, 32, dubbed The Fox, based his sickening crimes o nhard-core videos hired from sex-shops.

And as Fairley, an illiterate labourer, was sentenced at St Albans

By IAN HEPBURN

Crown Court, the judge Mr Justice Caulfield told him:

You have desecrated and defiled men and women, old and young in their own homes which you then pillaged.

I am satisfied that you are a decadent advertisement for the evil pornographers.

They will want to forget you as one of their worst casualties.

Fairley, of Kentish Town, North London, received the **MAXIMUM** sentence on each of 13 charges.

LIFE for three rapes and on three charges of burglary with intent to rape.

14 YEARS on each of five counts of burglary and entering homes with *Continued on Page Two*

Beast jailed for life SIX times

FULL AMAZING STORY—See Pages 4, 5, 15, 16, 17 and 18

The *Star*[70] similarly emphasised the amazing transformation of Fairley in a half-page 'think-piece' entitled **THE FOX: WHY HE DID IT Porn videos turned Fairley into a monster**. A spurious contrast effect is provided in the opening paragraph:

A QUIET, non-smoking teetotaller with a wife and three children was turned into a monster by the most disgusting hard-core pornography imaginable. Malcolm Fairley was transformed into The Fox by the perverted images of hard-porn videos.

The Times[71] made the suggested link their front-page headline – **Porn videos turned 'Fox' into rapist** – while the *Daily Mail*[72] used this theme in their editorial of the day, as part of their continuing campaign against porn videos. A few days later the *Sunday People*[73] followed up with a similar theme in the Voice of the People column, ending a long and forceful editorial with an impassioned plea:

The Government is trying to control the porn trade. Hard porn is legally banned, but still available 'under the counter'. Soft porn is being licensed but too slowly.
The victims of The Fox have suffered terribly. But from their suffering, we should all have learned how vital it is to beat the menace of video violence.

However, the newspapers themselves produce evidence which refutes this interpretation. Fairley had long been violent and sexually aggressive. An adjoining report on the same page of the *Sun* as the video hypothesis, based on an interview with the mother of Fairley's first wife under the headline **HE MADE HER LIFE HELL**, described how Fairley "was violent towards [his first wife] physically and sexually. She was always a mass of bruises. When he started going out with other women, she refused him sex. But he would just force her." The *Sun* report on **The Savage in my Bed** about his first wife also makes it clear that Fairley was violent and sexually abusive to his first wife and, indeed, that this was a major factor in why she left him. That is, Fairley was violent and sexually abusive before he established his collection of video nasties.

The notion that the video alone is the problem is not only simplistic, but also not supported by the facts of this case. Deeper social inequalities underly much of the generation of sexually aggressive macho behaviour in men, but the newspapers side-stepped any analysis of these. However, this is not to deny that pornographic videos may well have a damaging effect.

While we have stressed the aftermath of the court case when all his actual weapons and masks were displayed, the details of the case were described vividly in the previous year as the offences occurred. We have indicated in Chapter 3 how the search for the sex fiend is a source of considerable news coverage. Furthermore, the police themselves are involved in the creation of myths and legends which can help to titillate the public and no doubt excite the imagination of potential imitators. Nicknames and the sordid detail of sexual atrocities may provide the scope for imitation.

Potential rapists are as likely to read popular newspapers as to view porn videos. Three days after The Fox was jailed for life, the same judge, Mr Justice Caulfield, sentenced a 24-year-old man for raping a 19-year-old nurse. He was described as "a copycat rapist who had claimed to be the dreaded sex fiend nicknamed The Fox" (*Sun*).[74] The *Daily Mirror*[75] headline was **Fox copycat gets 10 years**, while the *Star*[76] similarly mentioned that the rapist imitated The Fox. The judge is not reported as making any speculation as to the source of this knowledge, which is obviously from the newspapers themselves. There were no hard-porn videos available on the activities of The Fox at the time this new offender was committing his offence, only the soft-porn reporting of the popular newspapers, which were describing the atrocities with such vivid detail as they occurred. This link is deliberately or unwittingly overlooked, as is the more serious and general issue of the making of rapists into exciting anti-heros and stars by the press.

The Brixton Gang Rape

In the second most reported rape trial of the year, six youths were accused of the gang rape of two schoolgirls. The case was contested, ending in the conviction of the young men, and the trial and sentencing reported at length. The main themes which appeared to make the case newsworthy were firstly, a gang rape; secondly, a racial theme, since the newspapers clearly identified the rapists as black and the girls as white in both words and pictures; thirdly, controversy over the sentencing being 'too light'; fourthly, controversy as to whether the girls could be held to have contributed to their own rape by being out at night. The first three were pulled together to create an image of rampaging black gangs raping white girls and being treated too leniently.

Again the first point has to be that the rapes were unusual. Most rape is done by individual men, not gangs, and by a man to a woman he knows, not a total stranger; most rape does not involve weapons and is intra- not inter-racial, in that black men usually rape black women and white men rape white women, while rape across racial groups is unusual. The case quite clearly pulls upon the same set of socially constructed fears that Hall and his colleagues analyse as the creation of the black mugger in *Policing the Crisis*.[77]

In the case of the Brixton gang, the prolific use of photographs of the accused after conviction seems to be to emphasise that these were black youths. Thirty-five (one-third) of the visual representations (photographs, drawings, etc.) identified in the total series of 114 rape cases referred to the Brixton gang (most of the remaining two-thirds were about The Fox). It does seem that photographs of black convicted rapists appear proportionately more often than those of white rapists. In fact, in the Brixton gang trial, the racial and class overtones of the case were often quite evident. The mother of one of the teenage victims said that "although many Press reports had treated the case as a racial attack, the court had not taken that attitude and she felt that was correct".[78]

The length of the sentences generated a related controversy which was reported extensively by the press. This 'campaign' was led by MPs (including the Labour MP Jack Ashley and the Conservative MPs Nicholas Winterton, Terry Dicks and Peter Bruinvels), the mother of one of the girls and the newspapers themselves. This issue made the front page on the *Daily Mail* as well as its editorial.[79] The woman columnist at the *Star* argued that the judge as a man had no real understanding of what the girls had suffered and had unjustifiably let the youths off lightly with seven-year and three-year prison sentences.[80] The view that rapists should be treated more severely was repeated in the editorial in the *Sunday People* under the headline GET TOUGH WITH RAPISTS.[81]

The universal outrage at the behaviour of the young men did not prevent the press publishing details of the cross-examination of the girls. The case was contested by the youths, who claimed that the girls had agreed to "leisurely sex". In court the young women were cross-examined at length and accounts of this published in the press. However, it seems most unlikely that from the media coverage any readers would have disbelieved the accounts of the two teenage girls, especially given the number of men involved. The two schoolgirls were raped at knife-point in a deserted Brixton garage forty-five times by a gang of youths, after attempting to return home by bus from a pop concert. When the victims were allowed to flee, they went straight to the police. In this context of the numbers of men, the use of weapons and the multiple attacks, it would be unlikely that a conviction would not have occurred, even without the racial theme.

The press reported in detail the ordeal which rape survivors must undergo in the court situation – GIRL WEEPS AFTER 90-MINUTE RAPE QUIZ[82] – when one of the girls broke down in court during questioning. It is a cautionary tale for all women reading this widely covered case to appreciate what is the reality of the experience, even in a case where few are likely to believe the defendants' accounts. Nevertheless, in what most people would regard as an obvious case of rape, the victims had to suffer a traumatic experience in court and have their humiliating experiences reported to millions.

Despite the hard line taken by the press about the rapists, they were not above sexualising the raped girls. One of them was repeatedly referred to as 'blonde', as a 'pretty school girl' and indeed as a 'blue-eyed blonde' in the *Sun*[83] and a 'pretty blonde' in the *Daily Mirror*[84].

A further controversy was over whether the girls could be considered to have brought the rape on themselves by being out at night. While the defence claim that the girls had consented was not taken seriously by the newspapers, the reports did often imply that the girls had behaved irresponsibly. They suggested that by being out at night the young women had contributed in some way to their own rapes, even though they were merely returning by bus to their homes. Both the prosecuting counsel and the police appeared to hold this view. Whether or not this was a reasonable position was one of the debates within the newspaper coverage. That is, the press reports were exploring the boundary of legitimate behaviour by women. Could women go out at night without courting rape? The coverage by the columnists diverged from that in the main news stories on this question. Anne Robinson, columnist of the *Daily Mirror*, forcefully made her point:[85]

DISTURBING THREAT TO LIBERTY

"It would have been much better if those girls had been tucked up at home in bed," said prosecuting counsel in the Brixton rape trial . . . .

"It was not wise for these two young girls to be out so late," said the detective inspector in charge of the case.

Well I find these comments worrying. Because, whether intentional or not, both these men come close to implying the girls were partly to blame.

And we are coming dangerously near to admitting total defeat if we lamely accept the solution to street violence is for women to forego their liberty and put themselves under virtual night-time house arrest.

The issue of anonymity necessarily resurfaces. Although the recent tightening of the anonymity provision for the rape survivor will probably curtail the practice of photographing the victim's residence, the Brixton gang case showed how difficult the problem of anonymity is. The mother of one of the victims maintained that although the girls were referred to in court only by their first names to protect them from reprisals, she was particularly worried that people in the court's public gallery knew who the girl was. She went on to say that "Everybody knows exactly who she is . . . . We are very concerned about the repercussions." It was later reported that the family had decided to leave the area.[86] Furthermore, the mothers and other relatives of the rapists had received threatening and abusive letters, including one from the National Front, and one letter threatening to rape the daughter of the rapist's mother.

The Brixton Gang Rape case produced several complaints to the Press Council which upheld most but not all of the complaints.[87]

The Paratroopers

In the Paratroopers' case thirty men were arrested and thirteen paratroopers were actually charged with the rape of a member of the Women's Royal Army Corps. The trial lasted twenty-five days, during which the 22-year-old woman stated that she was held down, raped several times and assaulted with a broom. The paratroopers claimed that she had consented to everything. The woman had been smuggled into the barracks under a coat. The court considered it was relevant to discover that she had spent the day drinking more than twelve pints of lager and cider along with two bottles of wine, and had sexual intercourse with a soldier during the afternoon. In the barracks she apparently agreed to have sex with one man but then was surrounded by paratroopers chanting: "Get them down, you Zulu warrior. Get them down you Zulu chief." She is said to have told the soldiers: "What, only three of you? I can take five." In court she said she was just being sarcastic. Afterwards she was forced to walk back to her own barracks on a freezing winter night, naked but for an anorak round her shoulders. There she told officers that she had been stripped, raped and abused by the men of the First Battalion. She said she had not complained at the paratroopers' barracks because she knew she would be in trouble for being out of bounds. Only one of the paratroopers expressed any regret, telling the police: "It started as a joke. I am ashamed of myself. We behaved like animals."[88]

The case received enormous coverage and the popular press made much use of the opportunity to reveal the titillating detail from the court interaction. The reporting of the paratroopers' case focused on events which were intrinsic to the court process. It demonstrated all the concerns which have been made by Edwards, Adler, and Temkin[89] in relation to rape trials about the bias of the proceedings against the woman. Some headlines indicate how all the newspapers made great use of the detail which was emerging during the court trial: **Jury told WRAC 'was sexually experienced'** (*Times*);[90] **The Big 'Un's sex sessions** (*Daily Mirror*);[91] **I AM THE BIG 'UN: Para 'gang-rape' girl tells of her sex urge** (*Sun*);[92] **MY ROMP WITH AN UNKNOWN SOLDIER**

(*Star*);[93] **Five to satisfy Big 'Un** (*Daily Mirror*);[94] **Paras case girl 'was sex maniac'** (*The Times*);[95] and so on.

Anyone reading of the trial would appreciate the ordeal of the rape victim in court as she "sobbed continuously as she was cross-examined by counsel for the men . . . " It is difficult to imagine a more thorough mauling in court than the WRAC experienced. Everything about her past sexual experience was brought out. No one seemed to question its relevance to the issue in hand. This twenty-five-day trial was probably the most talked about for many years. The essential question was whether or not every woman is protected by the law in every situation. Or, as the prosecuting counsel said "It is not the law . . . that if a girl crosses the threshold of the barracks she is fair game".[96]

All the paratroopers were cleared of rape. The judge, an ex-RAF flying officer brought out of retirement for the trial, told the men: "I take into account that none of this would have happened if the girl had not gone to your barracks for sex."[97] It was a "jolly joke" which went too far and ended in serious indecent assault, he said. (Some of the men were found guilty of indecent assault.) The front page of the *Daily Mirror* headlined **Judge jails six sex case Paras . . . then asks HAVE I GOT IT RIGHT? I'll do my best . . . but tomorrow half of England will think I have got it wrong.**[98] This conundrum puzzled *Daily Mirror* columnist, Marje Proops, who produced an excellent summary of the issues of sexual assault:

EVERY WOMAN'S RIGHT

I AM as confused about this horrendous case as everyone else must be.

Certainly the judge appeared to be confused. What did he mean when he said half of England will think he got it wrong?

Maybe he thought men, making up roughly half the population, would reckon that the poor, wretched girl, labelled so cruelly "The Big 'Un", got what she asked for, exactly what she deserved, when 13 soldiers indecently assaulted her.

Or perhaps Sir Peter was contemplating the reactions of the other half of the population, the female half.

Hopefully they would feel compassion for this victim of sexual abuse.

Though I wouldn't bet on women's whole-hearted support for their pathetic sister.

I've often heard women enhancing the well-known reaction to a sexually victimised woman: 'Well she asked for it, didn't she? She put herself about. She's obviously a slag, no better than she ought to be.'

I have news for men. And for those few women who parrot their words.

Sexual abuse and violation of a woman's body is unforgiveable and totally unacceptable in any civilised society.

Rape is entry into a woman's body without her consent. Whether or not she's a slag. Or a prostitute. Or she led on men. Or asked for it.

The final and ultimate privacy of her body is a woman's inalienable right.

Let every judge and every man take notice.

Little more was said about the case except that several days later, the *Sunday Mirror*[99] gave the sad outcome of the victim's ordeal: **HOSPITAL AGONY OF THE BIG 'UN**. A friend indicated that the Army had seemed at first to understand when the WRAC driver said she feared other Paratroopers would victimise her for "squealing" on their pals. However, her needs were totally ignored in that she was given a new posting to Aldershot – home of the Parachute Regiment. A hospital spokesman said she would be kept in for observation while doctors decided on the best treatment for her.

This case clearly had a traumatic effect on the victim but, just as importantly, the message from the widespread media coverage conveyed to all potential victims was essentially not a pleasant one. Whatever had been achieved by the 1976 Act, it had made little impact on this case except for the removal of her name from the media. This case covers perhaps in classic form the problematic use of a woman's previous sexual history in determining the outcome of a rape trial. Despite multiple accused, the woman's prior sexual experience is used to disqualify her claims that she was raped.

Interestingly it is precisely this issue which put the story on the front page after days and days of inside-page coverage. The issue had become one of public, political concern, not a minor issue of sensational titillating journalism.

We have focused on these three cases not because they are necessarily representative of rape cases but – because of their quite massive coverage – they set the tone of how the media reports rape. These are the cases which are known to everyone.

Indecent assault

There was a total of ninety-eight court cases which appeared in the sample newspapers during the year. Forty cases involved offences between males and fifty-eight cases of males assaulting females. As Table 4.1 shows, two-thirds of the cases of each kind of offence appeared in only one newspaper. In fact, there were only six cases which attracted the attention of more than three newspapers.

Table 4.1 Repetition of press coverage of indecent assault on women and men*

No. of newspapers	National dailies only		Local evenings/weeklies only		Both nationals and locals		Total	
	M	F	M	F	M	F	M	F
One	17	20	9	19	—	—	26	39
Two	8	6	—	1	1	4	9	11
Three	2	4	—	—	1	—	3	4
Four	—	2	—	—	1	1	1	3
Five or more	—	—	—	—	1	1	1	1
Total	27	32	9	20	4	6	40	58

Note: *The figures involving sexual offences between men unfortunately conflate the important distinction between consensual and non-consensual acts. This is because the distinction between 'gross indecency' and 'indecent assault' is not sufficiently maintained in the newspaper reports.

A similar number of both kinds of assaults appeared in the national newspapers. Twice the number of indecent assault on females were noted in the local newspapers, but this still remains a disproportionately small proportion of the total number of such offences. In fact, the chances of getting national publicity are quite low, though the likelihood of being mentioned in the local newspapers is higher.

The *Sun* covers more cases compared with the other popular dailies. Its total is almost matched by the *Star* in terms of its interest in assaults on males, while the *Daily Mirror* matches the *Star* in mentioning sexual assaults on females. Two of the local evening papers have similar numbers of cases involving assaults on males and females. In contrast, reports in the *Lancashire Evening Post* focus almost invariably on indecent assault on females (see Table 4.2). This provides the evidence for possible regional variation in the focus of particular newspapers.

It is comparatively rare for these kinds of cases to get widespread coverage across many newspapers, and even more unusual for these cases to receive sustained coverage. Among the assaults on males, it was only the two acquittal cases where the media coverage lasted more than a single day. The cases where there is the most sustained coverage are acquittals and yet obtaining an acquittal for this group of offences is a comparatively rare phenomenon, both as a proportion of cases reported in newspapers and what actually happens in the court. The low proportion with an acquittal outcome probably reflects that the vast majority of these cases involve a guilty plea.

Table 4.2 Number and percentage of indecent assault cases included in popular dailies and the local evening papers

	Indecent assault on males*		Indecent assault on females	
	No.	%	No.	%
Daily Mail	7	17.5	6	10.3
Star	16	40.0	16	27.6
Sun	18	45.0	22	37.9
Daily Mirror	7	17.5	17	29.3
Coventry Evening Tel.	7	17.5	6	10.3
Evening Standard	4	10.0	3	5.2
Lancashire Evening Post	1	2.5	13	22.4
Total no. of cases covered	40	100.0	58	100.0

Note: *The figures involving sexual offences between men unfortunately conflate the important distinction between consensual and non-consensual acts. This is because the distinction between 'gross indecency' and 'indecent assault' is not sufficiently maintained in the newspaper reports.

There is a similar distortion compared with reality among the indecent assaults against females. Just as there was a marginally higher proportion of cases against females to receive widespread coverage, a higher proportion also received sustained coverage. Eleven cases were identified where the media coverage lasted more than one day. Of these, eight involved mentions in the national newspapers, so while the number of mentions in the national press of assaults against females is similar to those against males, there is a much greater likelihood of the female assault cases getting longer media coverage. This is likely to be related to the fact that a higher proportion of these cases are contested. Indeed, four of the eleven cases which got sustained coverage resulted in an acquittal. A further four cases, mentioned on only one day, also had an acquittal outcome.

While there was no record of the outcome in eight of the cases, seventeen men received prison sentences of two years or more and one other was sent to a psychiatric hospital. Again this is a distortion of what is generally happening in the courts, where sentences are lighter than this average, so newspaper readers have contrasting images of many acquittals and many long sentences.

Sexual assaults on males

Men abusing positions of trust by sexually assaulting teenage boys in their charge was the main focus of the reports on male sexual assault of males. The assaulters' occupations produced the headlines. The following headlines are from different cases but the occupational theme remains the same: **Headmaster cuddled boys** (*Star*);[100] **Sex shame of a head** (*Daily Mirror*);[101] **SEX SHAME TEACHER IS SENT TO PRISON Assault on his boys** (*Sun*);[102] **Teacher in sex case to appeal** (*Middlesex Chronicle*);[103] **SEX SIR'S SHAME** (*Sun*);[104] **A TEACHER'S EVIL LUST He took sex snaps of kids** (*Star*);[105] **Teacher accused** (*Star*);[106] **Child sex offender given job in school** (*Daily Mail*);[107] **KIDDIES BOSS IN PORN SHAME: 15 years of sex snaps** (*Sun*);[108] **SEX SHAME OF A HOSTEL CHIEF** (*Star*);[109] **Child expert jailed for sex assaults** (*Daily Mail*);[110] **Mercy for a vicar** (*Star*);[111] **Choirmaster's shame** (*Daily Mail*);[112] **MINISTER IN SEX CASE FACES SACK** (*Star*);[113] **TV churchman's sex with sailor** (*Sun*);[114] **A vicar shamed** (*Star*);[115] **Kinky cop's secret shame** (*Daily Mirror*).[116]

Others may be in positions of trust not directly derived from full-time occupation, such as scout masters – **SCOUT LEADER'S CAMPING SHAME** (*Star*)[117] – as well as those in less formal and less-easily recognisable roles; the headline **Sex shame of 'uncle'** (*Daily Mirror*)[118] and text ("a mild-mannered clerk known by schoolboy train fans as Uncle Roland . . . took boys in the Rail Riders' Club on trips in Britain and Europe") shows how some offenders had eased into positions of trust with youngsters. In fact, around one-half of the cases can be identified solely from the headlines as persons abusing their positions of trust. Of the remainder, there are others where the abuse of trust is clearly evident but from the general text rather than the headline. For example, the art teacher who had a four-year affair with a pupil,[119] or two prison officers accused of sexual offences involving inmates.[120] Even where there was not direct evidence of a breach of trust, the occupation would suggest to the newspaper reader that this is a crime of the middle class, such as "a civil servant who admitted inciting a child to commit an act of gross indecency . . ."

The greater authority of the aggressor male perpetrator is further emphasised by the fact that, of the assaults against males, those coming to the notice of the newspapers largely concerned a much older set of defendants than the usual run of offenders coming before the courts. Indeed, there were only nine men aged under 30 and these included a group of four aircraftsmen appearing on a court martial accused of assaulting some young cadets at a summer camp.

The age of the victim was not always clear, but about one in eight of the cases involved children under the age of 10. However, the general pattern was men in their early or later middle age being charged for committing offences against teenage boys and then quite often receiving sizeable prison sentences. However, the main focus of the interest of the national popular press was on the individual tales of the downfall of the professional middle class.

The other sizeable group of offences reported on is where the case involves someone well known (e.g. **Bronski pop man fined for sex offence**)[121] or more frequently there is either fame by association (e.g. **GAY-SEX SHAME OF ESTHER'S 'BROTHER'**,[122] where the inverted commas in the headline indicate the rather more tenuous link with television star Esther Rantzen than the headline immediately suggests), or the actor who was said to make £12,000 a year from impersonating Prince Charles,[123] or someone who sounds from the headline to be well known (e.g. **CASTRATE ME SAYS GAY OPERA SINGER: He preyed on children**).[124]

The one case where a contested trial was covered by a range of newspapers indicated how the popular press focus on the potential fall of the near-famous and the introduction of gratuitous detail to titillate. The fact that it emerged he was a retired civil servant was an additional bonus. This case involved the 74-year-old "soccer superfan" known for the Union Jack waistcoat and John Bull costume he sported at international matches. He faced two charges of indecently assaulting two boys, aged 12 and 13. The *Sun*[125] reminded its readers that "it was his flag which helped cover topless streaker Erika Rowe [*sic*] after she ran on to the turf at Twickenham during a rugby international in 1982". The case opened a month later and was widely reported in both national and local newspapers. It was alleged that he touched the boys' genitals, put his arm around them and kissed them on the lips. On the second day of the trial the local evening papers could announce that **Mascot is cleared of sex charges**.[126] The court had been told that the boys made up stories after the accused had thrown them out of his home for stealing cigarettes. The newspapers had headlines which clearly gave the outcome of the case: **MR. SOCCER IS CLEARED IN SEX CASE 'Grudge boys made up story'** (*Star*);[127] **SEX CASE JOHN BULL CLEARED** (*Sun*);[128] **FOOTBALL MASCOT IS CLEARED** (*Daily Mirror*).[129]

The theme of sex fiend is very rarely evident in these cases. Largely the element of gratuitous violence is also missing. However, the violence and sex-fiend theme does emerge on a few occasions. The most serious examples were headlined **Sex fiend twice buried boy alive** (*Daily Mail*)[130] and **SCHOOLBOYS NIGHTMARE BURIED**

ALIVE by a sex-mad gravedigger (*Daily Mirror*).[131] The situation came close to manslaughter, and by its overt violence and the occupation of the assailant it is an exception. Generally indecent assault and gross indecency cases against males reported in the national press are not characterised by overt violence, but point to the dangers of the persuasive powers of people in positions of trust taking sexual advantage.

In contrast to the national newspapers, where particular themes, such as the abuse of professional trust, are usually evident, the local newspapers include cases which are much more simply the product of routine court reporting. There is a less specific focus on middle-class occupations. The following are fairly typical: **Diaries told of assaults on children**[132] (in which the court heard that "an unemployed kitchen porter from Leamington kept diaries setting out details of indecent assaults he committed on young children") or **Jail for man who lured boys to factory.**[133]

Assaults against females

In reports of assaults on women and girls there was always just one person accused. However, there was a considerable range of victims; in 40 per cent of the cases reported, more than one victim was involved. Approximately one-quarter of the cases involved girls aged under 10, one-quarter involving girls aged between 10 and 12, one-quarter involving girls as teenagers up to the age of 18 and the remaining one-quarter of the cases involved adult women. Of the cases where the outcome was known, seven resulted in acquittals. The victims' ages of these acquittal cases were 3; 11; 11 and 12; 13; 16; 21 and 27; 28; 29. So, although the numbers are small, a pattern emerges. A higher proportion of cases result in acquittal as the ages of the victims rises. This is probably a function of a higher proportion of guilty pleas being put forward when the victims are younger: something akin to plea bargaining is almost certainly taking place. The contested cases – which tend to attract more extended coverage – are very particular types of cases.

As with the indecent assaults on males, the predominant feature of these reports is that they are concerned with men abusing their positions of trust rather than being some unknown sex beasts who are assaulting victims not known to them prior to the offence. The headlines often reflect this focus on the alleged offender's occupation, but not quite to the same extent as in the attacks on males. In fact, nearly one-third of the reports identify the person's occupation in the headline. Again there is the range from formal positions of trust, particularly teachers (e.g. **TEACHER ACCUSED;**[134] **HEAD IN DOCK**[135]) and ministers of the church (e.g. **PARSON ON SEX CHARGES;**[136] **PRIEST IN SEX**

CASE[137]). The teacher may be self-employed, but still the profession rather than any other detail is what is of primary interest (**SHAME OF A KINKY SIR**[138]). The jackpot for the popular press comes when the defendant is both a teacher and a priest, although this does not come across in the headline (e.g. **SHAME OF KINKY HEAD, 55**[139]). Other professions also feature, which did not occur in the male assault cases (e.g. **DOCTOR JAILED FOR SEX ASSAULTS;**[140] **DENTIST FONDLES GIRLS**[141]). People attached to the church in a voluntary capacity are in a quasi-professional position (e.g. **SUNDAY SCHOOL BEAST'S SHAME;**[142] **PERVERT RAN CLUB FOR KIDS**[143]). Other occupations which deal directly with the public feature (e.g. **SEXY PRANKS OF A PC ON PATROL**[144]). Occupations can feature predominantly, even where the victim is not in the person's charge (e.g. **SEX OFFENCES OF FORMER MI5 MAN;**[145] **TOWN CRIER'S SEX ATTACK ON GIRL, 9;**[146] **MARINE IN BED WITH TOT, 3;**[147] **MARKET MANAGER IN INDECENCY CASE**[148]). The only front-page item in this series was headlined **ROYAL COP'S SEX WITH A GIRL 14,**[149] which again stressed the high-profile occupation. In the body of the text, it may also be revealed that the person is in some position which may give opportunities for taking advantage of children, such as a registered fosterparent, a holiday-camp entertainer, a landlord who placed ads offering single mothers a home at his seaside lodging-house, a coach-driver who took a party of thirty-four primary school children. However, the coach-driver case was an example of a case not reported directly but taken up in Paul Foot's column,[150] after the relatives of the victims had made a protest to him about the sentences and the *lack* of publicity of the case. Essentially the case involved a youth leader of the Red Cross, who admitted joining the Red Cross to bring him closer to young girls, whom he had been abusing for thirty years. It provides an example where the relatives of victims are concerned about the *lack* of publicity.

As with the indecent assaults on males, there were few headlines which dwelt on the theme of sex fiends and sex beasts. In fact, there were only five which displayed these kinds of stereotypes: e.g. **NEW ATTACK BY FREED SEX PEST;**[151] **VILLAGE IN FEAR OVER SEX BEAST;**[152] **CHILD SEX BEAST JAILED;**[153] **GIRLS' BEDROOM SEX PEST;**[154] **PERVERT RAN CLUB FOR KIDS.**[155]

It was comparatively rare for cases of assaults against females to receive sustained coverage and, indeed, there were only three cases where at least one newspaper covered the case on three or more separate days. There are two exceptions: one case involving a barrister and an actress received widespread national coverage and were named. The other case which received sustained coverage was mentioned on three consecutive trial days in the local *Lancashire Evening Post*.[156] It shows a different pattern, but is probably much more representative of local coverage where a particular case provokes some general interest. Many people in a locality will follow and talk about such a trial.

The case involved an alleged sexual attack by an 18-year-old young man on a 16-year-old schoolgirl as she was walking home in the early hours after a night out in the town. It was reported that the judge specifically ordered that the girl should not be named. The newspaper complied with this request. The first day's report – headlined **Terror of girl's assault** – described the girl's evidence as "she wept in the witness box". The seriousness of the alleged attack was described: "her clothing was stained with blood, and she suffered grazes, bruises and cuts . . . ". The report concluded with the girl denying suggestions from the defence that "she was a willing sexual partner, and made-up the story because of fears about her parent's reaction".

The next day's headline – **Youth denies sex attack** – told how the teenager maintained that he took the schoolgirl behind a shop for a goodnight kiss, alleging that the girl consented to his advances. He stressed that he never intended to have sex with her and said he never used force or inflicted injury on the girl. The report ended with the defence telling the jury it would be very dangerous to record a conviction on the uncorroborated evidence of the girl.

The third day's headline – **Teenager cleared of sex attack** – provided the news of the outcome of the case. The young man was found not guilty of indecently assaulting the 16-year-old schoolgirl by the jury after a three-hour retirement. The report ended with the information that the judge had told the jury that it would be very dangerous to record a conviction without independent support for the girl's story.

The outcome of many of the contested cases with regard to both rape and sexual assault allegations goes beyond an acquittal of the accused. The verdicts are implicitly defining what is appropriate behaviour for women and suggesting that they do not have much of a safeguard if they stray into areas regarded as 'male territory' whether it be a barracks room or a street late at night. Any hopes that women will eventually feel safe wherever they go is not being helped by the publicity given to such cases. Women's limited space is being clearly marked out.

Females as sexual assailants

There were only two cases mentioned in the media where a charge of indecent assault involved an older female technically assaulting a girl under 16. One was reported in a national newspaper and one in a local newspaper. Both involved lesbian relationships and are fairly cautious. In one case, it was said that "it was the 15-year-old girl who was the dominant partner in the relationship" with a 28-year-old woman separated from her husband,[157] while in the other case "a pretty 15-year-old schoolgirl skipped lessons to have a lesbian love affair";[158] however, the defence counsel said that her mother had told police she thought there was nothing wrong with a lesbian relationship and "if it had not been for the age of the young lady, none of us would be here today".

In contrast, the media enjoyed the opportunity to report cases of mature women being charged with indecent offences against under-age boys. In all six cases it was indicated that sexual intercourse had taken place. In five of the six cases the main focus of the headline was on the woman's marital status: **Church wife's boy lover;**[159] **Young wife's sexy games;**[160] **Sex in Jacuzzi for wife and lover, aged 12;**[161] **A 'sex mad' wife's schoolboy lovers;**[162] **A wife's ten boy lovers.**[163] The *Sun*'s[164] front-page headline of **NURSE HAD SEX WITH A BOY, 14** endorses the respectability of these women. The 24-year-old buxom blonde who "gave her favours freely to young village schoolboys" was told by Mr Justice Sheldon, "If a man had behaved in the same way with girls of this age he would have ended up with a long prison sentence".[165] In another case, the boy's father said:

> She should have been sent to prison. Women have been campaigning for equality for a long time. She should have been treated in the same way that an older man would be dealt with for corrupting a young girl.[166]

Females as teenage temptresses

There were twenty-four cases identified where the main charge was unlawful sexual intercourse with a girl under 16. The cases received quite full reports but, with two exceptions, only one or two of the popular dailies reported a particular case. The first exception was a case extensively reported, probably because of the description of the seduction during a black magic ceremony. On this occasion the 24-year-old occult fanatic was cleared of the charge because he claimed he was misinformed of her age at the time of the offence. (The only other case in this category where the charges were dropped or the defendants acquitted involved a 47-year-old police sergeant accused of having unlawful sex with his babysitter, but the charges were dropped after the prosecution heard that the pair were now married.) The black magic case was the only one where there was a follow-up to the court case. Three other young women involved in his life told of "his bizarre sexual appetites" to a Sunday newspaper.[167] The other case which gained even more extensive coverage, including the front page in some newspapers, involved a headmaster eventually jailed for eighteen months for having sexual intercourse with a pupil aged 14. This case followed a couple of weeks after the extensive coverage given to the case where a teacher was accused of raping a 15-year-old pupil but who was eventually jailed for unlawful sexual intercourse. The amount of coverage given to the sexual transgressions of members of the teaching profession suggests that there was the hidden agenda at work of denigrating the professionalism of teachers at a time when they were in industrial conflict with their employers. However, an interesting feature of this case is how the prosecution likened the girl to a 'Lolita'. Essentially girls under 16 involved in these cases divided into 'Lolitas' or virgins.

The behaviour of 'Lolitas' would be characterised as that of 'whores' among adult women. Because the issue is not one of consent with under-age sex, evidence of their sexual precociousness and previous sexual experience cannot be used to imply consent as happens with adult females. The newspaper reports, however, serve a different function and illustrate the dangers of young teenage temptresses. Men are portrayed as being powerless: **CB LOLITA, 13, HAD SEX ON THE SLIDE** ('A girl of 13 had sex on a kiddies' playground slide with a young man she contacted over CB radio, a court heard yesterday');[168] **Bedtime antics of a 'latter-day Lolita'** ('A 13-year-old girl . . . described as a "latter-day Lolita" went to bed with one man . . . and then swapped him for another in the same room');[169] **Girl, 15, tempted her mother's man** ('She had made propositions to him three times which he resisted before succumbing');[170] **Sex-case man goes to jail** (Defence counsel claimed 'the initiative in the sexual relationship came from the girl');[171] **CABBIE'S TEEN SEX SESSIONS** ('Taxi driver . . . found the cheeky advances of a teenage Lolita hard to resist');[172] **CHOIRMASTER AND GIRL, 15** ('I was tempted and that's all');[173] **Girl gave rapist sex lesson** ('A 14-year-old girl put out a challenge to a convicted rapist . . . . She said she could "show him a thing or two" ').[174] Six months later, the same newspaper produced a similar story from the same magistrates' court: **'COME TO BED' PLEA BY GIRL, 15** ('A saucy schoolgirl sent a sexy message to prisoner [NAME STATED]. She invited him to become her lover').[175]

The spectre of false accusations is another theme that is paraded as another hostage to the deviousness of the female sex:

> Five schoolboys took turns to have sex with a 15-year-old
> girl . . . . But she later told her parents the boys had raped her and
> they were quizzed by police for several days before the girl
> confessed to lying.[176]

RAPE LIE OF LOLITA LOVER ('A father of two . . . was held and questioned for 24 hours before the girl confessed she had lied about being raped').[177] The remaining items tended to be of the titillating variety of which a teenagers' Christmas party is fairly typical: **'8-in-a bed' sex romp.**[178]

In contrast, there was only one case where the seduction of the under-age girl is quite explicit – **A couple seduced virgin, 15**[179] – but even here there was a "blonde wife" aiding and abetting her husband in a kinky sex session.

In conclusion, according to the papers it's women who are the problem, not men. The woman is either the temptress or is lying about her consent. If these claims fail, others who should be protecting her interests will tell her that she contributed to the situation by being in male territory. On the other hand, if a mature woman is sexually assaulted by a stranger in daylight or at home, then she has not been raped by a man but a monster. The media's search for the monster has been completed and the future safety of innocent women can be celebrated.

Anonymity

The Press Council strongly encourages anonymity in sexual assault cases, although unlike rape cases they are not covered by the 1976 Act, and so it is something of a test of the voluntary code. Of the ninety-eight cases, there were only four cases where the victim was named. This is a remarkably small number of cases and needs further examination. In fact, in one of these cases which we discuss below it was not altogether clear whether there was a charge of indecent assault although the sexual connotations were quite apparent. While there a large number of cases where the victims are juveniles, there are many others where the newspapers would be allowed by law to identify the victim. Anyway, the only victims named were a man aged 26 and three women aged 39, 35 and 29 years respectively. With that few number named, one reaction might be to suggest that it is not an area where there needs to be much concern raised. However, the cases where the victim is named tend to be the cases which attract widespread or sustained coverage (or both). In other words, these are the cases where there is the greatest public impact, so, while a small minority, these high-profile cases will tend to be used by the public as indicators of what is normally the outcome. For this reason we need to examine these four cases further.

The named male was the recipient of a homosexual assault. This 26-year-old married businessman was beaten up, burned and sexually assaulted by a torture gang "and the six-man gang tried to tear out their victim's toenails with pliers – then ripped off adhesive tape they had stuck to his genitals . . . ".[180] In another occasion of indecent assault – whereby a drunken soccer fan "put his hand up the British Airway girl's skirt after she tried to subdue him and a group of pals who were on the duty-frees" (*Star*)[181] – both the *Star* and the *Sun*[182] avoided naming the air hostess. However, the *Daily Mail*[183] – which had made a strong point about not naming rape victims, even in civil cases (see Chapter 7) – named the woman on successive days with a large photograph of her on the second day: **I'm jetting away from it all.** She was reported as seeing it as a serious matter and thought the fine by the court was not enough: "I'd have chopped his hand off if I'd had the chance".[184] We do not know whether she was embarrassed at being named – probably not in this case, one suspects – and there is little doubt that her views of this behaviour came over more vividly without the cloak of anonymity. The third named victim was a woman lawyer in a case which was traced in the *Daily Mail* (on three days) and its sister-newspaper, the London *Evening Standard* (once). The offender, a Moroccan international foot-baller, was sentenced to five years' imprisonment for grievous bodily harm. Headlined **Spare my life . . . rape me,**[185] she told the Old Bailey court: "He said 'I'm going to kill you'. I believed him absolutely. I felt I could not breathe and murmured as best I could 'Take me'. I invited him to rape me to try to save my life". Fortunately, a passer-by heard her screams and the attacker fled. She was reported as saying that the trial had taught her one important lesson as a barrister – how the victim feels – and called for changes in the law which would give greater protection to victims. The final case where the victim was named is of a different order from the others. It is one where the clear purpose of extensive coverage was titillation. It was mentioned in all four popular news-papers, but only in the *Star* was the trial mentioned on three separate days. The trial resulted in an acquittal. Not only was the victim named, but also her photograph was shown at least four times. Two of the photos showed her posing in a bikini with the caption, 'Bikini girl' [name stated] . . . she fled half naked from X's [defendant named] flat shouting "rape" '.[186] The outcome was reported thus: 'a wealthy bullion dealer who patiently courted an out-of-work actress for five years with-out having sex was cleared yesterday of molesting her'.[187] There are various nuances in the newspaper reports. The *Daily Mirror*'s report focused on a variation of the false accusation thesis under the headline **FANTASY ROLE OF 'RAPE' ACTRESS.**[188] The defence story was emphasised that she

> had been starved of film parts and wanted to dramatise herself, the Old Bailey was told. So when [named defendant], 41, made sexual overtures for the first time during their five-year friendship she went to a neighbour and cried rape.

The *Star*'s[189] fuller reports gave a vivid illustration of two starkly con-trasting versions of the same incident. The victim claimed that the Canadian bullion dealer had "slapped her, pinned her to the floor and ripped off her trousers".

The *Star*'s report[190] on the day of the verdict – accompanying two photographs of the victim and one of the alleged assailant – indicated the extent of her distress after the case:

WHITE-HOT FURY OF SNOW QUEEN I'm branded a liar, says 'no sex' [name given]. SEXY actress [name given] stormed from a courtroom yesterday after being dubbed 'a cross between the Snow Queen and Greta Garbo. . . . It's a travesty of justice. I have been made out to be a liar but I am determined people will know the truth.

However, the *Sun*'s[191] italicised section in the body of its report – "*he had wooed her five years with champagne and romantic meals, getting just a kiss on the cheek in return*" – provides the clear message of what allegedly out-of-work actresses are expected to give tycoons who take that sort of trouble. Cases of this kind are few indeed, but they are exactly the cases which are read widely by everyone, including future victims of sexual assault. Not only do such cases provide – like other contested cases – public evidence of what is regarded as appropriate behaviour, but also the public humiliation of a named victim will not go unnoticed.

Identification can be made without a name actually being given. Sometimes a judge is noted as intervening in requesting certain kinds of identification not to be made. This happens more often in indecent assault cases than other sex crimes. By intervening in this way, one can reasonably assume that this request can be regarded as making an exception to the general rules – implicit or explicit – of identification. In one case which involved a 'brilliant' public school master from "the top North London school",[192] the judge ordered the school not to be identified. Such an order occurred in another case where the judge again requested that the school should not be identified, and the nature of the school was not clear from the report. In other cases involving schools but where there was no report of any request by the judge, coverage split fairly evenly between occasions when the school was named and those where it was not. Clearly this is an area where guidelines are needed, for it seems unreasonable that certain well-connected institutions can expect to reap the benefits of anonymity in the press, while others have to suffer whatever effects adverse publicity brings.

Conclusion

There are several themes which occur repeatedly in the reporting of the courtroom stage of sex crime processing. Firstly, there is the culpability of the woman. This is expecially pronounced in cases of sex murder and of rape. The woman's sexuality is presented as provoking a violent sexual response in the man. This occurred in those cases of sex murder where the supposed infidelity of the woman was the excuse the man used to justify killing his former wife or lover. It also occurred in the case of the Paratroopers, who were acquitted of the rape charge (though not all were acquitted of all sexual offences) after a woman soldier had entered the men's barracks alone.

The second major issue is that the theme of the sex fiend is much less marked than in the earlier search stage of the criminal investigation. It is present in some cases, most spectacularly in that of The Fox, though even here it is mixed with the sex lives of the women he knew. The major focus has often, but not always, shifted away from the male aggressor to the 'failings' of the woman in protecting herself.

The third major point is that the reporting of the trials marks out the boundaries of 'acceptable' behaviour not only by gender, but also by class, race and age. The media accounts are replete with racialised people, with photographs to lend emphasis to the text where the rapists are black. They make constant reference to the class, location and age of the attacker and victim. The construction of the black man as rapist has a long racist history.

A final point is that the explanatory import of the reporting is such as to back trivial and conservative 'solutions'. For instance, most of the press was more interested in video nasties as a cause of rape than in deeper structural explanations.

Chapter five

Sex offenders after conviction

Only the most notorious sex offenders surface in the papers after the courts have dealt with their crimes. The cases which the papers had made into large media events at the time of pursuit or court hearing do recur from time to time, but those with limited coverage are rarely the subject of press attention again. This means that an even narrower range of cases lingers in the public eye than the restricted sample with which the press started.

When sex offenders are sentenced to terms of imprisonment or locked away in a secure hospital the media generally allows them to be 'out of sight and out of mind'. There are few sex offenders who continue to interest the media during their prison sentence. However, the exceptions are quite exceptional. Some of these are people who will be linked with their crimes throughout their lives and will be followed by the media at their every move. For some the enormity of their crimes has made them well-known throughout the world. These notorious criminals tend to be persons involved in *sex murders* and the trio who most obviously come into this category in our study are Myra Hindley and Ian Brady ("The Moors Murderers"), who were sentenced to life in May 1966, and Peter Sutcliffe ("The Yorkshire Ripper") similarly sentenced to life in May 1981. The Moors Murderers, despite the time since their convictions, figure in the media more than all the rest of the sex criminals currently in custody put together. During the sample year (1985) there were 151 items mentioning the Moors Murderers and 34 items involving the Yorkshire Ripper. In fact, for the Moors Murderers there was not a month in the year when they failed to feature in at least one newspaper. With the more recent massive coverage over the recovery of further bodies in this notorious case, the amount of coverage remains incredible, continuing twenty years after they were first imprisoned for their offences. Similarly there was only two months' respite from a mention of the Yorkshire Ripper in at least one of the newspapers. With the recommendation of a minimum of thirty years' imprisonment for Sutcliffe, there seems little doubt that he will continue to occupy a similar role to that of the Moors Murderers in the coming decades.

Apart from these offenders whose activities did and can still provoke interest throughout the world, there were only three sex criminals serving a prison sentence who were mentioned on more than two occasions during the course of the sample year. All were serving sentences for murder or manslaughter. Two (Colin Evans and Peter Pickering) were child sex killers and the third (Arthur Hutchinson) was a multiple murderer who comes into this sample because he raped the surviving daughter of the murdered couple. Hutchinson had eighteen mentions during the year, while Evans and Pickering were each mentioned eleven times. There were only a further seven cases mentioned involving sex criminals currently serving custodial sentences. Apart from the 'Brixton Gang Rape' men, the rest were individuals. However, before moving on to discuss the kind of coverage these cases attracted, we want to raise the question of whether particular newspapers seem to be interested in this stage of the career of sex criminals.

Table 5.1 shows that over three-quarters of the press coverage of sentenced sex criminals involved either the Moors Murderers or the Yorkshire Ripper. Of the twenty-three so-called 'exclusives' during the year relating to serving prisoners, only three concerned stories unconnected with these cases.

The *Daily Mail*, more than any other newspaper, maintains its focus on convicted sex offenders serving custodial sentences, as is shown in Table 5.1. On average, one can expect such an item in this newspaper about once a week. In contrast, the *Daily Mirror* is likely to feature this kind of item about once a fortnight, with the *Sun* and the *Star* mid-way between these extremes among the more popular dailies. The two quality dailies more rarely mention sex criminals serving custodial sentences. The three local evening papers show that there is likely to be some regional variation; the extra amount of coverage of the Moors Murderers in the *Lancashire Evening Post* is explained by the fact that the crimes took place within or close to this newspaper's catchment area.

This phase of the criminal justice process is of particular interest to Sunday newspapers. Among these, the *Sunday People* (with five major exclusives) has considerable coverage followed closely by the *Sunday Mirror* (with three exclusives), while the *News of the World* features much less prominently.

The types of stories which arise are instructive in appreciating the cascade effect which the major sex criminals engender. A vast range of persons become involved in the media coverage. In contrast, other cases take a different pattern. The crimes of Arthur Hutchinson received fairly even coverage from the national dailies, but this much more recent case

Table 5.1 Sex criminals serving custodial sentences

	Moors Murderers	Yorkshire Ripper	Arthur Hutchinson	Colin Evans	Peter Pickering	All others	Total
Daily Mail	30	8	2	1	5	1	47
Star	28	7	2	1	0	0	38
Sun	22	4	2	1	2	2	33
Daily Mirror	18	3	3	4	0	2	30
The Times	12	2	2	0	0	1	17
Guardian	*	4	3	0	1	0	8
Evening Standard	3	0	0	1	0	2	6
Coventry Evening Telegraph	1	0	1	0	0	0	2
Lancashire Evening PostPost	9	1	1	0	1	0	12
Sunday Mirror	7	3	0	2	0	2	14
Sunday People	12	1	1	0	0	1	15
News of the World	6	1	0	1	0	0	8
Mail on Sunday	2	0	0	0	1	1	4
Observer	1	0	0	0	0	0	1
Lancaster Guardian	0	0	0	0	1	0	1
Middlesex Chronicle	0	0	0	0	0	0	0
Total	151	34	17	11	11	12	236

Note: *Owing to an oversight, the *Guardian* count did not include the coverage of the Moors Murderers' case.

was already fading from the public gaze. The only other two cases which received more than a couple of mentions were largely the focus of attention of particular newspapers. The *Daily Mirror* and *Sunday Mirror* focused on the Colin Evans case and in a similar manner the *Daily Mail* and its stablemate, the *Mail on Sunday*, predominated in the coverage of Peter Pickering. These latter two cases indicate how newspapers do develop their own 'causes' and on occasions focus on particular cases which may not even be thought appropriate for a mention in other newspapers.

Hindley, Brady, and Sutcliffe appear newsworthy in their own right and fascinate the media *all the time*. However, the coverage of these cases may also sometimes be symbolic in the sense that they cover themes which have much more widespread interest. It is often their *normal* activity which provokes interest, while the remaining cases usually need something much more distinctive to trigger media coverage.

The Moors Murderers

While the Moors Murderers received four times as much coverage as any other case, the range of stories was much more limited than the coverage of the Yorkshire Ripper. Firstly, there was the question of the possible parole of the Moors Murderers, and Hindley in particular, which was featured in most newspapers at some point; secondly, there was the *Sunday People* 'world exclusive' from prison cell interviews – **MOORS KILLER BRADY ADMITS TWO MORE MURDERS**[1] – which other popular newspapers could not afford to overlook; finally, at the end of the year the question of Brady's sanity was raised again when he was transferred from prison to a top-security psychiatric hospital – **MOORS KILLER BRADY GOES MAD.**[2] The other substantial coverage was a week-long feature by the *Star*, under the title **The Devil's Disciples,**[3] which was a gruesome detailed re-run of the events twenty years earlier. While these were the main issues and features, other items obtained front-page coverage from time to time, such as that MPs were furious over reports that gory T-shirts featuring Brady and Hindley had become a number one seller.[4] The case still attracted eighteen exclusives (some of the so-called exclusives were also covered by other newspapers on the same day) and at least another dozen occasions when stories were featured on the front page. The *Sun* enthusiastically reported that **MYRA SLAMS SUN**[5] for allegedly leading the campaign to keep her behind bars, while in another newspaper, Lord Longford accused the *Sun* of persecuting Hindley after the publication of an interview with her 65-year-old mother.[6] The *Sun* certainly did maintain a campaign with at least eight aggressive leaders (**The *Sun* says . . .**),[7] arguing vehemently that they should be locked up for life as well as conducting polls on the issue. Earlier in the year, with equal enthusiasm, the *Star* reported how Long Longford felt that the *Star* "has always been vicious towards [Myra Hindley]": **LONGFORD LASHES STAR OVER HINDLEY.**[8]

In May after the announcement of the parole decision, the *Star* boasts **STAR FIRST AGAIN . . . YES, the Star told you first. In an**

**exclusive story on February 19 we said Brady and Hindley would
not be released.**[9] It could be a moral crusade, but the true nature of the
campaign frequently becomes evident. For instance, on 4 December, the
front page of the *Sun* shows **BRADY TODAY: THE FIRST PHOTO
IN 20 YEARS.**[10] The next day the *Star* announced: **IAN BRADY: THE
FIRST PICTURE** 'One of our rivals nearly got it right yesterday . . . Oh dear, it would have been if your way-ahead Star hadn't
published the first picture of Myra Hindley's evil partner two years ago.
It pays to follow the *Star* – everybody else does!'[11]

This one year is just a brief phase in the total press coverage of a saga
lasting now well over two decades. Its fascination for the press and
public is instructive. It simultaneously declares that sex crime is highly
abnormal and an uncommon event, and that long prison sentences are a
successful way of containing the problem.

The Yorkshire Ripper (Peter Sutcliffe)

There is a vast range of news stories and gossip which emerge in a year
(1985) which was four years after his conviction and sentence for
murdering thirteen women. The following chronological summary list
with the headlines and the newspapers illustrate twelve Ripper news
stories emerging in the year:

1 **POLICE DEFEND RIPPER CARD** (*Daily Mail*),[12] where a police
   chief was defending the decision to send an official Christmas card
   to Peter Sutcliffe.

2 **SONIA TAKES TEA WITH THE RIPPER** (*The Star Exclusive*)[13]
   featured Sonia Sutcliffe visiting her husband in the normal way. This
   was repeated in the *Lancashire Evening Post*[14] – **Interval for tea** –
   and followed up again five days later in the *Star*[15] – **Tea for Two
   with the loving monster** – suggesting the abnormality of the loyal
   wife.

3 **RIPPER NOTE JOLTS JURY GIRL** (*News of the World*)[16] refers
   to a letter of congratulations which Sutcliffe sent to a young female
   juror who was imprisoned for four days for refusing to complete jury
   service. The *Sunday People*[17] reports the woman's protest to the
   Home Secretary about receiving a letter from Sutcliffe produced the
   reply that "Sutcliffe is free to write to anyone he cares to". The young
   woman is quoted as saying that "The letter from Sutcliffe horrified
   me. It's even more shocking to learn he can write to a complete
   stranger". The report notes that Sutcliffe obtained the young
   woman's address when he read a newspaper report of her clash with
   the law.

4 **SUTCLIFFE WARRANT** (*Daily Mail*);[18] **SUTCLIFFE HUNT** (*Star*)[19] show how other members of the Sutcliffe family are now news. These items noted that a warrant had been issued for the arrest of Sutcliffe's younger brother, who had failed to answer bail on a drink-drive charge.

5 **BROADMOOR PALS . . . THE RIPPER AND KRAY** (*Daily Mail*)[20] reports that "two of Britain's most notorious killers have struck up a close friendship in Broadmoor . . . through their mutual interest in religion". Notorious inmates who are unconnected prior to their custodial sentence become connected in reality and in the minds of readers.

6 **POISON WATCH ON RIPPER'S ATTACKER** (*Daily Mail*);[21] **MR EVIL POISON PLOT IS FOILED** (*Star*);[22] **RIPPER MAN'S 'POISON PLOT'** (*Sun*).[23] These headlines belie the fact that the news story has nothing to do with Sutcliffe. This inmate has now the notoriety of being the man who slashed the Ripper with a broken bottle two years earlier in Parkhurst Prison. The assailant, now in Rampton, was reported as being involved in a bizarre poison plot allegedly to kill himself and staff.

7 **DORIS'S TRAGIC MISTAKE** (*Sunday Mirror*);[24] **So close to the Ripper** (*Sunday Mirror*)[25] remind readers of the past. The spirit medium, Doris Stokes, maintained that she tragically missed a clue that could have ended Sutcliffe's reign of terror earlier. The *Sunday Mirror* continued to pursue this story, reporting two months later[26] that the mother of the Ripper's youngest victim had turned down the chance to appear as a guest on Yorkshire Jimmy Young programme. The idea had been for the mother to try before a nation-wide audience to have a 'beyond the grave' TV encounter with her daughter.

8 **DISCO GIRLS FOR THE RIPPER! Sutcliffe given run of hospital** (*The Sun Front page exclusive*)[27] tells how Sutcliffe is allowed to attend discos, barn dances and bingo sessions with women patients. It is maintained that this is all part of a "deal" with Broadmoor doctors, which includes having his own colour television, video recorder and stereo. This story produced an outcry from a "furious Tory MP Vivian Bendall [who] attacked the Ripper's easy life as 'farcical' . . . ". Towards the end of the report a nurse indicated that Sutcliffe *had not yet had the chance to attend any of the dances*. Clearly this is the role of the press being used in an anticipatory role rather than on focusing on what has actually happened. The so-called *Sun* exclusive also appeared on the same day on the front page of the *Daily Mail*.[28] Clearly orchestrating the outrage, the *Sun* on the next day[29] – ROW OVER DISCO RIPPER – reported how Tory MP Peter Bruinvels planned to urge the Home Secretary to send Sutcliffe back to Parkhurst Prison, as well as quoting outraged comments by

the mother of one of the victims and a policeman who worked on the case.

9 **RIPPER 'NEGLIGENCE' ACTION CHALLENGED** (*Guardian*)[30] reported that the action for damages against the West Yorkshire police, which had been initiated by Mrs Doreen Hill, mother of the final victim, was being challenged by the solicitors for the police in an application to the High Court. This story was taken up by other papers six months later when a judge in London indicated that the victim's mother must drop her action against the police. Only *The Times*[31] noted that the then Chief Constable had angered the victim's mother when he sold his memoirs to a newspaper for what she described as "blood money".

10 **RIPPER CHIEF DIES A BROKEN MAN** (*Daily Mail*)[32] reported the death of George Oldfield, who had led the five-year investigation into the murders. The *Daily Mail* made clear that Oldfield, for whom the murder hunt became an obsession, was essentially another victim of the Ripper trail of destruction. Oldfield's death was also mentioned in the obituary sections of *The Times*[33] and the *Guardian*,[34] but not by the popular press; however, the *Star* later focused on the **RIPPER COP'S £46,000 WILL.**[35]

11 **RIPPER LAGER STORM** (*Sun*)[36] reported that posters for a Foster's lager – with the word 'ripper' splashed across the front – had been appearing around Bradford in Yorkshire, where Peter Sutcliffe had lived. The justification attempted by the brewers, Watney Mann, was that the word was Australian slang for "super". 'Silly season' items can have unpleasant undertones.

12 **THE 11-YEAR ITCH IS HERE AGAIN** (*Daily Mail*)[37] is an item in the gossip column of the Nigel Dempster Mail Diary. Readers are reminded of the Ripper in hearing of the alleged widening gulf between the Earl of Gowrie, who had just resigned as the Minister of the Arts, and his journalist wife, who "was editor of a German magazine in London but resigned in 1981, after it published a forbidden photograph taken within the Old Bailey of the Yorkshire Ripper". This final story shows how far a case such as the Yorkshire Ripper can continue to be linked with anyone who was remotely connected with it.

These stories which relate to the Yorkshire Ripper show the cascade effect as a result of such a notorious case. Anyone directly or indirectly involved as the Yorkshire Ripper moved through the various stages of the criminal justice process (e.g. the victims' parents, the police, the Earl of Gowrie's wife, and Mrs Sutcliffe) all have established roles in this saga. Others can for a while be drawn into the saga by the actions of Sutcliffe himself (e.g. by the despatch of a congratulatory note to the woman who refused jury service), while others make an active contribution themselves (e.g. the assailant of Sutcliffe in Parkhurst Prison). Some hate to be embroiled in the saga – the woman who received a letter of sympathy from Sutcliffe said "It's . . . shocking to learn he can write to a complete stranger". Others embrace their connection – "I am the man who slashed the Ripper". The media often fail to respect the wishes of the former, who may say, like the parents of the victims, "My family want to try to forget these terrible events". The media also fail to recognise the dangers of giving further publicity to people such as the prison assailant of the Ripper, who now has a new-found reputation for injuring Sutcliffe, or by a silly-season story giving copycat ideas about 'Ripper lager'. The front-page exclusive on Ripper discos, purporting to report on what is happening, shows not only how newspapers can orchestrate stories of outrage. The Ripper coverage shows the immense variety of possible stories, but also some enduring themes, such as the focus on the assumed 'cosiness' of custodial conditions (e.g. discos for the Ripper).

Arthur Hutchinson

Hutchinson had been given three life sentences (with a minimum eighteen-year recommendation) at Durham Crown Court in September 1984 for stabbing to death a solicitor, his wife and son hours after their elder daughter was married. He was also given eight years for the rape of the younger daughter, who was not killed.

Two main issues dominated the seventeen items of coverage of Hutchinson: his request to be let out of prison to attend his father's funeral and the subsequent refusal by the Home office on grounds of being a serious escape risk (six items), and then later in the year the focus was on his unsuccessful appeal (ten items). The one other item mentioning Hutchinson is in the *Sunday People*[38] – KILLER WHO LIVES IN JAIL 'PALACE' – and so links his name with the familiar theme of "cosy prison conditions". This report notes that Hutchinson's mother will be leaving everything in her will to her son and that she "has never stopped loving the 43-year-old son who turned into a monster". Again, the 'abnormality' of loving a 'monster' becomes the focus. It is a relative of Hutchinson who maintains that he is living in a "right little palace". So here the themes of 'cosy conditions' and 'loving a monster' are neatly combined in one report.

Two further points need to be mentioned. Firstly, once a victim's name is identified in the court proceedings, the identification may go on and on. There was identification of the rape victim by name and sometimes a reminder of the unpleasant details in many newspapers months after the conclusion of the trial (*Star* (26 March); *Guardian, Star, The*

Times (all on 26 June); *Daily Mirror*, *Daily Telegraph*, *Daily Mail*, *The Times* (all on 2 July).

The second point is how some newspapers persist with the offender's nickname. For example, the *Coventry Evening Telegraph*[39] headline **'Fox' denied release for funeral** revealed that a letter written to his mother was signed "The fox" – the name he adopted while on the run from the police in 1983. However, Hutchinson's nickname is of only marginal utility in attracting an audience. Unlike Peter Sutcliffe, for whom the nickname 'Ripper' occurs in practically all of the headlines, Hutchinson does not manage to achieve that doubtful accolade. Of the seventeen headlines, only the *Daily Mail*[40] (**The Fox loses murder appeal**) and the *Coventry Evening Telegraph*[41] used the nickname in the headline. Nicknames help to produce and promote heroes and anti-heroes. The persistence in using a nickname helps to perpetuate a notoriety which is unhelpful.

The only other two cases to get mentioned more than twice during the year show how particular newspapers 'adopt' particular cases. Both concern child killers: Colin Evans and Peter Pickering.

The press coverage of incarcerated sex criminals helps to create the impression that sex crime is a narrow band of activity committed by a narrow band of offenders who have been convicted in the past for sex offences and would be a danger in the future if released from prison too soon (or ever). Long sentences are seen as the most appropriate way of dealing with the problem, since this removes the few dangerous men from the streets and acts as a deterrent to others. The focus on imprisoned offenders gives the impression that the strategy is successful, since these men are safely contained. It happily ignores the fact that sex crime is quite common, that the offenders tend not to have abnormal psychological profiles, and that most are never prosecuted, let alone locked up. That is, the focus on imprisoned offenders encourages a sense of security that the evil is being effectively dealt with, which is misplaced since the vast majority of sex offenders are not in prison. Nor, given the pervasive occurrence of these crimes, could imprisonment alone be an adequate solution.

Maintaining a record?

The belief that the tracking and containment of a few men would remove the danger of sexual violence for all women underlies not only these stories of sex monsters in jail, but also a number of stories about keeping track of convicted offenders. In the following set of stories the theme is that if only adequate records of a handful of proven sex offenders could be maintained, then women and children could be protected.

The failure of attempts at record-keeping on sex offenders during the year nearly developed into a mini 'moral panic'. In the following cases new sex crimes committed by convicted offenders were blamed on such failures in record-keeping, while the discovery of convicted offenders working with 'vulnerable' persons was regarded as an unacceptable level of risk, which should have been avoided by keeping better track of such men.

The theme stemmed from the jailing at the end of the previous year of Colin Evans for the murder of Marie Payne, aged 4, when it was disclosed that, although a persistent sex offender against children, Evans had been baby-sitting for families in Reading through a voluntary agency that he had joined. Even more worrying was the fact that he had been recruited for the agency by his probation officer, despite a record of thirteen convictions for child sex offences over a period of eighteen years.

Mr Leon Brittan, the then Home Secretary, told the House of Commons (*The Times*)[42] that he had received a report on the incident from the Berkshire Probation Service and that in the past week he had sent out a Home Office Circular to all chief probation officers reminding them of the guidelines for child sex offenders. The Circular indicated that probation officers should tell prospective employers or others using the services of an offender about any facts which would have a bearing on his work. Also the offender should be told that the probation officer will intervene if unsuitable employment or any activity is to be undertaken. This parliamentary report could be traced only in *The Times* among the sample newspapers and demonstrates a serious gap in the media reporting of the popular press. *In the popular newspapers there is a general absence or lack of information about how topics which had aroused considerable public interest would be dealt with in the future.* There is no serious attempt to inform the public about measures taken to try to rectify a problem. Informative material setting out safeguards to avoid future abuse is not news, while individual examples of abuse are news.

A more specific demand for action arose from another case, which involved a 40-year-old man who had been jailed for seven years for supplying LSD to teenagers – one of whom fell to his death from a block of flats – at a time when the offender was a supply teacher with the Inner London Education Authority. The ILEA Tory schools spokesman, Mr Dudley Fox, called for a national index of drug and sex offenders and a tightening-up of checks into the background of anyone applying to County Hall for a job. Mr Fox said: "It is vital that we come up with a practical checking system. Lives depend on it" (**CALL FOR DRUGS AND SEX INDEX**, London *Evening Standard*).[43] Quite distinct forms of deviance are again being drawn into the same net.

For a 'cause' to be maintained, further evidence needs to be forthcoming. The next related case was in the *Star*[44] under the headline **PARENTS UNMASK SEX PEST**, and the *Daily Mirror* under **SEX**

CASE MAN GIVEN A JOB WITH CHILDREN.[45] There is no explicit link with the earlier demand of the Home Secretary for probation officers to follow certain guidelines. The report opens with the assertion that "A sex offender on probation was given a job working with children. And council officials were criticised yesterday for failing to warn of the man's record". The man, aged 22, was given the job by Cherwell District Council, Oxfordshire, and passed on to a children's charity, the Rainbow Club at Banbury, which has 100 mentally and physically handicapped children. The club organiser was quoted as saying that

> the council took all responsibility for handling the man's references – and knew about his convictions. They are entirely to blame for what happened. We asked to see the references, but the council withheld them. No one at the club knew about his past until some of our parents recognised him and complained.

In the same report the chief probation officer of Oxfordshire said: "This man is still on probation. He has four convictions for gross indecency with young boys and is himself handicapped". There is no evidence that the person employed had committed any further offences. The error of judgment, as the chief probation officer recognised, was the failure to provide the information: "we ought to have written to the club outlining this man's record. I'm sorry about this" (*Star*).[46] The Chief Executive of Cherwell Council refused to comment and ordered all officials connected with the case to say nothing.

The popular press tends to be interested in the individual case, but is not interested in the discussion of any principles underlying any actions taken or not taken. The statutory organisations perhaps feel their duties are done if they can maintain the anonymity of the individuals concerned. The popular press by concentrating on revealing individual cases of abuse clearly sees its task in terms of awakening general concern rather than informing the public whether appropriate action has been taken. The press in such cases is not acting as a public watchdog but simply as annoying yap-dog snapping at the ankles of authority.

The *Sun* ran a headline four days later,[47] CHILD-SEX PEST IS PUT IN CHARGE OF KIDS, proclaiming a new case where "a child-sex pervert has been put in charge of teenage pupils who attend a private school". This was a 56-year-old taxi-driver who had been jailed fifteen months earlier after paying the parents of an educationally subnormal girl of 14 years of age for sex. His minibus firm had won the contract with a school, which was named in the article. The ex-offender declared that "I don't think my previous record makes me ineligible for the job", while the headmaster said "I am not too concerned about his past. We have received no complaints about him". Whereas the previous story had concerned the failure to provide relevant information to the employer, here the employer knew of the man's past. The shift was being made towards arguing for a blanket ban on sex offenders rather than allowing an employer having the opportunity to make an informed decision as to whether or not it would be appropriate to employ someone who in the past had been a sex offender.

The Sunday newspapers kept the general issue alive with brief reports with emotive headlines – SEX FIEND REGISTER (*Sunday People*);[48] WAR ON SEX FIENDS (*News of the World*)[49] – by suggesting that "sex offenders may soon be registered on a central computer", indicating that the Home Secretary "would like bosses to consult the register before employing anyone whose job involves children". The *News of the World* linked this move explicitly with the murder of 4-year-old Marie Payne by Colin Evans. Its tone is anticipatory, giving a clear indication of the supposed direction of the changes and making it appear that such changes were imminent.

However, the next day in *The Times*,[50] their Home Affairs Correspondent, Peter Evans, indicated that "the compilation of a national register of child sex offenders . . . could be used by a review body to be set up by . . . the Home Secretary". *The Times* revealed that the review's terms of reference had not yet been announced, but that the ministers hoped that "the officials will present their recommendations within a year on the possibility of disclosing to prospective employers relevant information about the criminal background of people wanting to work with children". The report also noted that the government felt that the National Criminal Records Office at Scotland Yard did not have the facilities to provide information in the form needed for that type of assessment. In other words, more resources would be needed. Peter Evans also raised the point that the implications of any register "on the technical aspects of the Rehabilitation of Offenders Act, 1974, which wipes the slate clean for certain categories of offenders, would also have to be considered".

Two weeks later the debate at last began to widen. The *Guardian*[51] reported that police officers were pressing for stricter measures to prevent convicted sex offenders from working with children (POLICE WANT CHILD MINDERS TO BE VETTED). It indicated that rank-and-file police officers would be asked at their annual conference in May to approve the extension of criminal record vetting to all child care workers, including volunteers. Referring specifically to the Evans case, Leslie Curtis, Chairman of the Police Federation, said: "There is no need for past offenders to be employed in these posts and I believe that a lot more could be done to prevent it". The focus becomes one of a blanket ban on previous sex offenders.

The *Guardian* report reminded readers that records of violent, indecent, dishonest and drink/drug crimes are automatically available to prospective employers of teachers, medical staff, lawyers and civil servants. The Post Office, British Telecom, the Civil Aviation Authority and the Atomic Energy Authority were said to be the only other employers legally entitled to access when people apply for jobs. However, the Home Office spokeswoman stressed caution in any extension of the vetting process because of the claims of privacy and civil liberties: "it would not be desirable to penalize someone for a minor offence committed many years ago and never repeated". Ms Marie Staunton, legal officer of the National Council for Civil Liberties (NCCL), suggested possible safeguards by stressing that

> Parliament should decide the guidelines for any extension of the vetting, which should be confined to relevant offences. If a candidate was rejected because of a criminal record he or she must be told why and have the right of appeal.

The recognition of the dangers for the ex-offender by the Home Office spokeswoman and the legal officer of the NCCL hidden away in the columns of the *Guardian* provides an important contrast to the war against sex fiends campaign being waged implicitly and explicitly by the popular press.

Little notice was taken by the media of evidence being submitted to the Home Office review. An exception[52] was the submission by the former NCCL legal officer, Harriet Harman, who was now Labour's social services spokesperson. She called for "laws to enforce disclosure of criminal records by applicants for jobs caring for the elderly, handicapped and children". She said that the present system was "a dangerous mess" and that new legislation would need to apply to people seeking paid jobs and to volunteers, but that the disclosure of criminal records should be limited to offences that made people unsuitable to care for the vulnerable and dependent. On the one hand, Harman was proposing extending any changes even further to include the elderly and the handicapped while, on the other hand, there was a recognition that the disclosures of previous offences should be limited. However, no one in the press discussed which offences made people unsuitable to care for the vulnerable and the dependent, whether for instance, this would mean that previous convictions for theft should disqualify someone.

The *Daily Mail* reported that the Prime Minister, Mrs Thatcher, had shown her own interest in the review in a letter she had sent to Mary Whitehouse, president of the National Viewers' and Listeners' Association.[53] The *Daily Mail* maintained that "now it has been decided that a separate national register is not necessary. The National Identification Bureau at Scotland Yard has computerised the previously hand-filed records of 10,000 sex offenders". The *Daily Mail* further suggested that people applying for work in schools or social services departments, for example, will have to complete forms which ask if they have any convictions for sex offences. They will also have to agree in writing to their prospective employer checking with the national police computer.

The following week the *Mail on Sunday*[54] revealed that a blacklist for sex offenders would be announced in the Commons in the coming week. The next day the *Star*[55] similarly announced that "people who work with children will have to be cleared by police in future, *thanks to a Star campaign*" (our italics). The Tory MP, Geoffrey Dickens, was reported as saying: "This is long overdue. Sex offenders always seem to end up working with children. There are countless cases. I would like to pay tribute to the *Star* for highlighting people who prey on children." Curiously, the only two newspapers to report the actual announcement of the change were the *Daily Mirror*[56] and the *Coventry Evening Telegraph*.[57] The *Daily Mirror* indicated that adults seeking work with youngsters will have their names fed into the police national computer.

The final mention of this topic in the sample year appeared in an article nearly three months later in the *Mail on Sunday*,[58] where Barbara Jones, the paper's medical correspondent, when commenting on the proposed massive vetting of health service workers hoped that this would prevent a repeat of the tragedy of Marie Payne.

The concern expressed by the newspapers had throughout been at two levels: firstly, sex offenders getting sensitive posts without disclosing their background and, secondly, the imputed failure of authorities to make 'proper' use of the information by barring former sex offenders from obtaining jobs. The campaign earlier in the year had conflated these two issues on occasions. The amendments to the existing procedure were about ensuring that the appropriate authorities would have the appropriate information. How that information should be used had not been directly faced. The simplistic thrust of the popular newspapers had moved in the direction of suggesting that it was not a discretionary matter and that a ban on former sex offenders in certain employments should be absolute. The following case reported in the *Daily Mirror*[71] begins to bring this issue to more prominence.

TUTOR'S SEX SECRET

A church school teacher's shameful past was revealed yesterday.
French tutor [name revealed], 37, is a convicted sex offender.
Now angry parents are to hold urgent talks over his appointment.
Mr. [name] was jailed in 1982 for inciting 13-year-old boys to commit acts of gross indecency.

He is now in his second year at [Church of England school in the north of England named].

But his secret was only publicly revealed yesterday after the boys' parents heard he was teaching again.

[The School's head also named] said: "This teacher, in seeking the post, made a full and frank disclosure of his circumstances".

Disclosure of other sex offences

The issue of disclosure of previous sex offences for people involved in caring positions produced a particular interest in this area in the year of our study. In addition there are other continuing issues about the extent and appropriateness of the revelation of past offences. The Rehabilitation of Offenders Act 1974 was an attempt to avoid gratuitous disclosures when certain periods of time – which varied with different types of offences – had elapsed with a view to their integration into normal living.

While the numbers of former sex offenders mentioned in any year are few, none the less there is always the possibility that past offences may be revealed. In particular, anyone who tries to enter public – or, more specifically, political – life may have their past disclosed. We include two cases of embryonic political careers in which the disclosure of past offences have quite different implications for sexual politics.

In the first case, the *Sun*[60] reported thus (except for the name which has been changed):

RAPIST FIGHTS FOR SEAT ON A COUNCIL

CONVICTED rapist John Smith is standing as independent candidate in today's county council elections.

And the 32-year-old engineer, who is fighting a Portsmouth ward on Hampshire County Council, says: "I have a perfectly legal right to stand".

Mr Smith was jailed for two years in 1972 after pleading guilty to raping a 20-year-old woman.

* Nearly 10,000 candidates are contesting 3,565 county council seats throughout England and Wales.

In the second case, the sexual politics are quite different, concerning male homosexuality in which the criminal aspect appears to be that the sex did not take place in 'private' but in a 'public' toilet. This parliamentary candidate was also named and the matter received extensive coverage in the *Coventry Evening Telegraph*: front-page news (**Sex-case minister picked by Labour**);[61] again front-page news six weeks later (**Minister quits as Labour choice**);[62] the next day at least one national newspaper showed some interest (**Candidate quits over 'bigots'**, *Guardian*);[63] and a final editorial in the *Coventry Evening Telegraph* (**Indecency his choice**).[64]

This case was of a Methodist minister who had been selected as a Labour parliamentary candidate and who had a conviction for gross indecency. He had been selected overwhelmingly on 20 September, "but at the Labour party conference it was made known to constituency officials that Mr [name] was fined £75 for committing an act of gross indecency with another man in a public toilet near Southampton in 1981"[65]. This revelation was said in the report to be the cause of a split in the constituency party. Nevertheless, a special constituency meeting had decided to ask him to continue as a parliamentary candidate. Within six weeks the front-page news was that the (named) minister was resigning as parliamentary candidate. His decision to resign was said to pre-empt an executive committee, when several resolutions from ward and trade union branches called for the candidate to stand down. The day after his resignation the *Guardian* printed extracts from his letter, in which the minister blamed the "bigoted" view that some party members took of him because he was homosexual, stressing that there had been a whispering campaign against him because he had once been convicted of

> the sort of offence to which gay people are susceptible . . . 'It's mainly the branches, I fear, in the working class end of the constituency who are saying that working class people won't vote for someone who is known to be gay', he said.

He indicated that he "believed he was entitled to put that event behind him".[66] He also disputed the view that a candidate who said publicly that he was gay was unelectable and that his position as Labour candidate was therefore politically untenable.

The different implications of these sex crimes should further caution against simple statements as to the significance of media attention to offenders after conviction.

Conclusion

The treatment of sex offenders after conviction raises important questions on the balance of freedom and control. The coverage of the issue of whether there should be a register of sex offenders could have raised a number of difficult questions. There was a failure to discuss the inherent conflicts between maintaining freedom and extending controls. It is ironic that it was left to the Home Office spokeswoman to point this out.

But most importantly there was the neglect of consideration as to whether this action was likely to have a significant impact on the extent of sex crimes. Such a register may be important if you believe that sex crimes are committed by a limited number of men. However, since all the available evidence runs counter to such an assumption, the keeping of registers of convicted offenders which would massively extend the powers of the state offers little potential for making a serious impact on the real extent of the problem. Such a register together with media interest may act to prevent some instances of sex offenders having the opportunity to re-offend. However, by itself such a policy would have little impact on the much larger number of sex offenders who do not have a criminal record. By focusing on the containment of sex crime by control over convicted sex offenders (which is in fact illusory), the press feeds the political agenda of the law and order lobby.

Chapter six

Informing the public

Introduction

The press reports on discussions of the general issue of sex crime as well as specific cases. This chapter will examine press treatment of official and scholarly publications on sex crime. This is an opportunity for journalists and editors to move beyond the uniqueness of specific cases to the analysis of underlying issues and wider policy matters. In 1985 forty-two such reports were mentioned in the press.

As Table 6.1 indicates, the vast majority of the reports of studies feature in only one or two newspapers in our sample. Only seven (17 per cent) of the reports featured in more than two newspapers. Reports of studies are most likely to be featured in *The Times* (nineteen) which covered nearly one-half of the studies mentioned in the year, while the *Guardian* (fourteen) and the *Daily Mail* (eleven) also featured an appreciable number. At the other end of the scale, the *Daily Mirror* (four) mentioned remarkably few. There seems an almost total absence of such reports from the national Sunday and local weekly newspapers.

Although the women's movement has been influential in this area, there was only one research report of the forty-two mentioned which emanated explicitly from a group of feminists working in this area. This was the Women's Safety Survey conducted by Women Against Rape, written up by Ruth Hall and published under the title, *Ask Any Woman*. The highest number of reports emanated from the voluntary sector (particularly focusing on the sexual abuse of children) and individual experts, such as professional counsellors, academics and police officers writing in an individual capacity. The latter are a motley assortment of items.

Reports emanating from or commissioned by *central government* tended to be mentioned by *The Times* and the *Daily Mail*. For example, the report from the government-backed Women's National

Commission[1] received good coverage in *The Times* and the *Daily Mail* (including a full-length editorial), while two items in *The Times* featured the figures provided by the Home Office in relation to the Lord Chief Justice's sentencing guidelines.[2] The *routine* reports published annually by the Home Office which in the press reports contained a mention of sex crime were reported only in *The Times*, *Daily Mail* or the *Guardian*. *The Times* gave the most amount of coverage to the publication of the official *British Crime Survey 1984*.[3] The *Guardian*, however, showed in relation to the *British Crime Survey* how little attention the government actually paid to its own reports (see pp. 115–16).

Table 6.1 Studies and research reports related to sex crime

| | No. of items in the newspapers referring to a particular study | | | | | | | | | |
	1	2	3	4	7 A	7 B	8	9	13	TOTAL
Daily Mail	5	1	—	1	1	1	1	1	—	11
Daily Mirror	1	—	1	1	—	1	—	—	—	4
Star	2	—	1	1	—	1	—	1	1	7
Sun	2	1	—	1	—	1	1	2	1	9
The Times	7	5	1	—	1	1	1	1	2	19
Guardian	4	1	—	—	2	1	2	2	2	14
Coventry Evening Telegraph	1	2	—	—	—	—	1	—	2	6
Lancashire Evening Post	1	—	—	—	—	—	1	1	1	4
Evening Standard	5	—	—	—	—	1	1	—	1	8
Observer	—	—	—	—	3	—	—	—	—	3
Mail on Sunday	—	—	—	—	—	—	—	1	—	1
Sunday Mirror	1	—	—	—	—	—	—	—	1	2
News of the World	—	—	—	—	—	—	—	—	1	1
Sunday People	—	—	—	—	—	—	—	—	1	1
Lancaster Guardian	—	2	—	—	—	—	—	—	—	2
Middlesex Chronicle	—	—	—	—	—	—	—	—	—	0
Total no. of studies	29	6	1	1	1	1	1	1	1	42

Note: If a report of a study appears on *separate days* in the same newspaper, then this is counted as *two* items in the above table.

Reports emanating from or commissioned by *local government* were, not surprisingly, more likely to be reported in the local evening papers, so the London *Evening Standard* often reported the activities of the then existing Greater London Council. For instance, it gave widespread coverage to the news – **Travel fears of women at night**[4] – that a £25,000 poll had been commissioned by the GLC's Transport Committee at the request of the Women's Committee, which was examining ways of making public transport safer for women. There was a suggestion that on occasions research may make an impact, for Mr Dave Wetzel, chairman of the Transport Committee, was reported as being "surprised" that as many as 75 per cent of women avoided going out alone at night. He suggested that the survey showed that instead of cutting manpower London Transport should be employing more station staff. In contrast, it was rare indeed for mention of local research activity to be traced in a national newspaper.[5]

Among *voluntary organisations* the work of the NSPCC predominates nationally and locally. Other reports, such as *Strong Kids, Safe Kids* by Revd Brian Brown and his staff,[6] produced two items in *The Times* and the *Sun*, while the *Guardian* had a large feature on *KIDS CAN SAY 'NO'!*, a video aimed at children with the object of preventing child sexual abuse. *Child sex abuse dominates the features emanating from the voluntary sector*. The only exception to the emphasis on child sex abuse was the publication of the Howard League's report, *Unlawful Sex*,[7] which was the outcome of the deliberations of a working party set up to consider the problems of sex offending in relation to the criminal justice system of England and to make recommendations. While it got quite widespread coverage, it received perfunctory interest from the government.[8]

Surveys by *university students' unions* on sexual harassment are undoubtedly influenced by the women's movement. This topic raised limited interest in the media, except that such an item from Oxbridge is regarded as nationally newsworthy, while other universities obtained only local coverage. In a neatly provocative double-edged story headlined **Lecturers in love**, emanating from a survey in the previous year by the Women's Committee of the Oxford University Students' Union and described as the *"Dirty Dons"* report, the *Sun* asked,[9] "SO WHAT do the dons get up to when they have all that time on their hands?" A concern about sexual harassment becomes a veiled attack on university education.

Women Against Rape study

The most important book relating directly to rape to be mentioned in the national press during the sample year was *Ask Any Woman*.[10] It was a controversial book, producing some very interesting findings.

The publishers traced forty-five mentions of the book in the media in a twenty-month period.[11] There was an exclusive feature in *Woman* magazine in September 1984 giving some early results from the survey, four months before the book was published; in January 1985, mentions were traced in *eight* national dailies, the London *Evening Standard*, and a variety of other coverage, such as *West Indian World*, *City Limits* and some student newspapers; in February, March and April there were a further twenty mentions in some local dailies, such as *Liverpool Daily Post* and *Western Morning News*, but the main coverage was via book reviews in the informed weeklies, such as *New Statesman*, *Tribune*, and a variety of other journals interested in the topic, such as *Girl About Town*, London's *Alternative Magazine*, *Labour Research*, *Women and Policing in London*, and so on. This book then had wide but brief coverage in the national press. It had a frosty reception by some of the national press and failed to become regarded in any way as an authoritative source for national newspapers, being marginalised in a speedy manner. However, it did have a positive reception in a broad range of the alternative press (using the term in its broadest sense).

The September feature in *Woman*[12] headlined **RAPE The first facts** gave prominence to four of the most striking results or what were described as "some of the shocking statistics to emerge from Britain's first-ever major survey on rape":

* One in six London women say they have been raped
* Almost one in three have been sexually assaulted
* One in seven have been raped by their husbands
* Eight in ten think rape in marriage should be a crime.

The report seemed to give a fair and accurate appraisal of the survey, which was mentioned within the context of its being part of a "campaign for better and safer facilities for women". Clearly it had made an impact. However, this seemed to generate anxiety about the validity of the results. Sue Thomas, the Consumer Editor of *Woman*, concluded the article with a hint of doubt: "*If the figures for rape outside marriage are to be believed*, it is a far more common crime than many of us imagined" (our emphasis).

The reaction of the national press to the published study was varied: the six national dailies featuring the study on the day of publication produced three different slants in their headlines. Two newspapers stressed the figures giving the proportions of London women who had stated they had been raped – e.g. **One in six women are rape victims** (*Daily Mail*);[13] **One in 6 raped** (*Sun*)[14] – while two others shifted the theme slightly by emphasising that rape can no longer be regarded as an abnormal event – **Sex assaults in London 'commonplace'** (*The*

Times);[15] **RAPE 'A COMMON EVENT'** (*Star*)[16]. The other two news-papers focused on an entirely different theme, stressing the apparent demand for weapons: **'Weapons' plea in war on rapists** (*Daily Express*);[17] **90pc 'WANT ANTI-RAPE WEAPONS'** (*Daily Telegraph*).[18] This was a theme that the *Sun*[19] took up two weeks later under the headline **GIRLS ARE GEARING UP TO FIGHT BACK**, which focused on the finding that "90 per cent of women interviewed were so worried about attacks that they want the carrying of weapons to be made legal so that they can fight back without prosecution". This article focused upon comments by Chief Supt Sheila Ward, styled as a Metropolitan Police self-defence expert, who said that self-protection had become a craze and maintained that

> Many people nowadays, especially women, are saying, 'I've got a right to walk the streets and I'm going to do something about it . . . ' We want people to protect themselves but not break the law. *We'd rather they avoided dangerous situations and used self-defence if they can't* (our emphasis).

Clearly this portrays some women as looking for trouble by provocatively going into dangerous situations. In contrast, the respondents to the Women's Safety Survey were not themselves advocating the *unlawful* possession of weapons, while Women Against Rape were essentially campaigning for a *safer* environment and to eliminate the dangerous situations. This is an example of the way that the press select a specific theme and then shift the ground of the debate by getting an 'authority' to comment on the *newspaper*'s selected theme.

The coverage in the *Daily Mirror*[20] came a few days after the initial burst of publicity under the headline **RAPE Why so many victims refuse to talk**. The London survey generally was fairly reported, though with a similar doubt being thrown on the findings, as occurred in the *Woman* article prior to publication: "*if it is accurate*, it sheds a new light on the crime and the criminal" (our emphasis). There was good coverage of some of Ruth Hall's "calls for safeguards like better public transport and tighter security – such as alarms and entryphones – on housing estates". Also mentioned were her proposals that rape in marriage should be made a crime. The Labour MP, Harriet Harman, was reported as agreeing with these various proposals, but stressed her belief that courts treat rapists too lightly. The *Daily Mirror* columnist, Mary Riddell, emphatically asked, '*But what use is it to impose stiffer sentences if most rapists are never reported and never caught?*'

The *Guardian* made no mention of the survey until a fortnight later,[21] and mainly featured a review of Ian Blair's *Investigating Rape*,[22] which was a book by a Metropolitan Police detective inspector who maintained that there are serious shortcomings in Britain's response to rape victims.

Discussion of the Hall book followed. The doubts about the book were raised in two ways. There is an underlying suspicion about the book's claims (e.g. "the book is *said* to have been devised with the aid of academics" – our emphasis), while Deputy Assistant Commissioner Wyn Jones of Scotland Yard's crime department is reported as saying that he found the figures in Ruth Hall's book 'far-fetched'. There was no attempt to say which figures he found puzzling and so in one sweep he cast doubt on all the figures.

Among the more popular dailies with high circulations the largest coverage of the Hall book initially was in the *Daily Mail*, which had a report across three columns and also an editorial on the survey. This newspaper also provided one of the clearest examples of a deliberate attempt to maintain a traditional version of reality. There are, of course, two responses to challenges: ignore them, or demolish them by fair means or foul. The *Daily Mail* clearly chose the latter course. The headline **One in six women are rape victims**[23] had the banner sub-headline in white print on a solid black background: **MP dismisses astonishing claim by feminists**. Ruth Gledhill talked in the text of

> an astonishing series of claims by militant feminists . . . . But the leader of London's Tory MPs, ex-prison governor John Wheeler, said: 'This is a totally absurd proposition. No sensible or intelligent person in the UK could actually regard this as competent or relevant'.

The *Daily Mail* went on, in a scarcely veiled slur on the Greater London Council, that "grants totalling £11,150 helped pay for the report which WAR (Women Against Rape) believes reveals the rape secrets that women try to hide." Gledhill goes on to point to the 'official version' that "the results contrasted sharply with the recent *British Crime Survey* designed to search out unreported crimes. The Home Office questioned 11,000 men and women but all that came to light was one unreported attempted rape." There is no consideration given to the widespread doubts about the way that the *British Crime Survey* handled its survey in relation to eliciting information about sexual assaults. Even the commonsensical notions of the *Daily Mail* would, one have thought, have led to an healthy doubt being expressed about such a low figure in the *British Crime Survey*. The report included statements which either consciously or unconsciously misrepresent the figures contained in the report. For example, the *Daily Mail* report stated specifically that "because rape in marriage is not illegal, it was not included in the open-in-six [sic] figure". In fact, the figure in the study showing that one in six women had been raped did include rape in marriage showing how the *Daily Mail*'s doubts contributed to the mis-reading of the study. This was one of three factually inaccurate assertions in the *Daily Mail*'s report which helped to portray the study as totally unbelievable. Just in case their readers had any lingering doubts about their attempt to discredit the study, the report concluded: "Last year Miss Hall was the subject of a complaint to the House of Commons after she warned that any MP who opposed a Bill to outlaw rape in marriage would 'live to regret it' ".

While Ruth Gledhill's report was critical and inaccurate, in terms of outright dismissal the heavy battalion was reserved for the editorial column, **Dealing with the rape problem**. The full version of the editorial is instructive:

> *Rape is a growing problem in Britain and it is a pity that the survey just published by Women Against Rape was so shoddily conducted as to make it useless as a source of evidence.*
>
> *What is beyond dispute is the fact that rape has increased in recent years. Scotland Yard deserves congratulations on its imaginative new programme to combat it and to handle the victim sensitively.*
>
> *That programme includes the special training of women police officers, the provision of properly designed victim examination suites and the help of victim support volunteers. All this should tend to comfort and reassure rape victims, make them more ready than in the past to report their ordeal and supply evidence on which the police can act.*
>
> *These measures should make it easier than formerly to bring rapists to book.*
>
> *But that is not enough. What is needed in addition is swingeing penalties. There should be exemplary punishments to stamp on the present horrifying trend towards associating burglary with rape.*
>
> *There should also be severe minimum sentences to ensure that no guilty party gets off lightly. Rape is a particularly beastly crime and the law should fully mirror public revulsion.*

The *Daily Mail*'s editorial encapsulates the way that the press focuses on the rape problem. There is a belief that rape is increasing, but there is a complete reluctance to recognise that rape is often much closer to home than simply "the present horrifying trend towards associating burglary with rape". In brief, a particular kind of rape is asserted to be increasing and there is a dismissal of evidence which might suggest there are problems in other areas as well. The police need to be congratulated but the courts could do much more in achieving a 'solution'. These views emerge even more vividly in this newspaper's own features on the rape issue. Certainly, there is no interest in looking towards a wider explanation of rape or indeed in considering environmental changes which could make Britain a safer place for its citizens.

The survey was therefore 'rubbished' in the editorial and misrepresented in the news section of the *Daily Mail*. On the same day as the report appeared in the *Daily Mail*, Judit Kertesz of Women Against Rape wrote a measured letter to the editor of the *Daily Mail*, with a copy to the Press Council, complaining about the coverage and challenging the view that the survey was "shoddily conducted".[24] Kertesz went on to point to the political dimension of considering solutions to the rape problem:

> *It may be inconvenient for John Wheeler to acknowledge the horrifying scale of rape and sexual assault in London. This, however, is the truth which our research uncovered. The Daily Mail too pushes aside what women say, by calling for 'swingeing penalties' as the one and only solution. London women, through the pages of our report, are crying out for far-reaching changes in transport, housing, welfare policies, policing and the law, in order to make them safer. This will require government expenditure, in areas other than the prison system. John Wheeler's and the Mail's dismissal of the Women's Safety Survey findings seems more concerned with defending Conservative Party policy on government spending and on the police than with defending women from rape.*

The report in the *Daily Mail* appeared on 11 January, but a letter signed by Ruth Hall under the headline **Wrong figures** appeared *two months later* with the three corrected figures presented. Nothing of the contents of the above paragraph appeared in the *Daily Mail*.[25]

It may be thought that the *Daily Mail*'s response was exceptional and isolated, but there seems little doubt that the arguments of feminists do continue to be misrepresented in the national press. For instance, more recently, one can identify an interesting nuance in the aftermath of the Ealing Vicarage rape case, which had received widespread interest throughout the country. The *Guardian* leader[26] classed Women Against Rape with "rent-a-quote" politicians looking for "easy headlines" by denouncing lenient rape sentences. "What a shameless slander", retorted Caroline Coleman of Women Against Rape. In a long letter published by the *Guardian*,[27] Coleman pointed out that:

> *In the past week, as often before, we have spent hours patiently explaining to incredulous journalists that rape neither begins nor ends with sentencing. For ten years WAR has been under heavy pressure from the law-and-order lobby to make rape a lever for higher sentences (for all crimes), hanging, castration, sexual repression, state censorship, and worse. We have never obliged . . .*
> *We have always insisted that higher sentences will not stop rape.*

111

> *The rapist knows there is little risk of getting as far as court, let alone a conviction. The racism, misogyny, and priorities of the police are his first line of defence. Ask Any Woman, our London survey, found that only one in 12 survivors report to the police . . .*
>
> *The Guardian has barely noticed Ask Any Woman – Britain's only major survey on rape and sexual assault – when it was published in 1985. Instead of accusing us of the lynch-mob reaction that we spend our lives opposing, the Guardian could well pay close attention to this book, which concludes:*
>
> *'A generalised call for heavier sentencing has traditionally been the way in which politicians have appeared to be 'doing something' about rape, without spending any money on rape prevention or showing any interest in the protection of women. In fact, long sentences are often advocated for reasons which have nothing to do with women's safety.*
>
> *The protection which women are crying out for . . . must not be sidestepped in this way'.*

After the severe strictures on the Women's Safety Survey, the *Daily Mail* seemed to have set itself high standards on what can be regarded as evidence in this area. A headline – **A quarter of rape victims 'are lying'** (*Daily Mail*)[28] – seems an equally 'astonishing' claim as any that the Women Against Rape put forward. The report – culled from a Howard League working party report, *Unlawful Sex*,[29] which is a mammoth exploration of deviant sexual behaviour and the criminal justice system – failed to indicate the real source of this statistic. From well over 250 references contained in the report, the newspaper headlined one sentence from a survey whose results had been published five years earlier in 1980![30] Although in the book it is suggested that "this seems a high proportion" (a comment included in *The Times*[31] report two weeks later), there is no caution expressed in the *Daily Mail* report which also reminds their readers that "the American case where born-again Christian Cathleen Webb confessed she had wrongly accused Gary Dotson and watched him sent to prison, could happen here". The *Daily Mail* had reported on the Dotson case more fully than any other British newspapers. The lying female was a theme which the *Daily Mail* consistently focused upon. Indeed, the *Daily Mail* – rather than expressing caution – suggested that police officers and doctors were backing the report's figures, but gave only one example to add weight to this assertion.

> Dr Harry De La Haye Davies, a leading member of the Association of Police Surgeons . . . said: 'My diary for the last few weeks shows that out of 13 "rapes", only eight were proceeded with. In the other five cases the allegation was withdrawn. As many as 50

per cent in a year can withdraw the allegation. A lot of girls just want to talk to someone. They feel things have gone too far, but they don't want the law to take its course'.

This 'evidence', which does not really probe why the allegation was withdrawn, was obtained by the newspaper by telephone.[32] Many women may not wish to proceed – not because they are lying – but either because they now recognise the ordeal they may have to face or because the police may indicate that it will not be an easy case to prove in court and so may not be particularly encouraging.

Child sex abuse

During the late 1980s child sex abuse has received sustained coverage, largely as a result of the Cleveland inquiry into alleged child sex abuse.[33] This controversy occurred after the year of the present study. Nevertheless, child sex abuse was the other major discussion topic relating to sex crime in the media during 1985. It was sustained almost entirely by news from the voluntary sector, with organisations such as the NSPCC and the National Children's Home dominating the proceedings. During the year there were several major campaigns in which these organisations were essentially trying to educate the public about the scale and nature of child abuse.

This coverage provides an interesting contrast to the coverage on rape, where the 'official' version sustained by the media is that rape is principally a problem of strangers pouncing out of the bushes on to women who are walking in areas which perhaps more wisely they could have avoided. In contrast, the message of the children's charities was that child sex abuse was essentially in the home. This was a message which was increasingly being accepted and not being seriously challenged by the media.

The occasion of the major campaign of the year by the NSPCC – NEW NSPCC CHILD ABUSE FIGURES (press release)[34] – is one illustration of how stories are quickly linked to the sensational. After a press conference for the NSPCC campaign *Trends in Child Abuse*, the story was covered in the majority of the national and regional newspapers and in many of the following Sunday newspapers. Essentially the message was that child abuse by parents is on the increase, with *sexual* abuse showing the biggest proportional rise.

The NSPCC campaign focused on parents who abused their children, while the competing interest was the tragic murder of Leoni Keating. This case subtly shifted the emphasis to *unknown* persons endangering children. In its leader, **Child abuse**, the London *Evening Standard*[35] identified the danger of confusing the two issues commenting that

It is perhaps unfortunate that the NSPCC's report on child abuse should have coincided in its publication yesterday with the news of Leoni Keating's murder. This kind of deranged sexual assault and murder is usually far removed from the banal, terrifying repetition of domestic assaults on children spelled out in the NSPCC's statistics.

Very few newspapers heeded this warning.

The *Sunday People*'s editorial,[36] 'Voice of the People', had a vivid drawing of a child in distress accompanying its headline **HELP!** It opened the leader describing "the sheer horror of what happened to Leoni Keating . . . . Sexually abused. Raped. Tied up and left to drown in a ditch." The leader went on to mention the NSPCC's figures that there had been a *70 per cent* rise in child abuse, most of it sexual, in the past six years and then goes on to note that "*It is estimated that more than ONE MILLION children will be sexually abused before they are sixteen*" (emphasis in the original). Interestingly there is no concern about the authenticity of these quite startling figures. Woodrow Wyatt's column, 'The Voice of Reason', in the *News of the World*,[37] continued the same theme, **EVIL STREAK**, that

> Britain has more child murders and rapes than any other country in Europe. Yet, on the whole, this is a gentle and civilised land.
> Where does this streak of bestial cruelty come from? It's a mystery to which no one knows the answer.

Certainly the popular press do not make any significant attempt to seek an answer. The *Sunday People*[38] was the only newspaper that made a stab in this direction:

> Our society has changed – and not for the better. We live in a country where 'video nasties' and vile magazines are freely available, TV brings violence into our homes almost every night, child drunkenness is rampant and drug-taking has become an epidemic.

In contrast, there is no mention of the NSPCC's views from their research that "marital discord, unemployment and debts were the most common stress factors applying at the time of abuse from 1977–82. All three have remained very prominent, with unemployment playing the larger part" (NSPCC press release).[39]

In sum, the popular press is willing to accept the statistics supplied by the NSPCC without comment or even surprise. The stress factors are given only cursory attention. Indeed, apart from the quick recourse to the television violence and video nasties explanations, there is no serious comment upon what is happening. For the popular press, sex crime, including child sex abuse, is a mystery of which only the dramatic is allowed to be the key.

The quality press is much less ready to focus on such simplistic explanations and gives more credence to the research. The *Guardian*,[40] (**Child sex abuse by parents 'increasing'**) gave the NSPCC figures so that readers could understand the basis of the claims much more clearly than elsewhere: "the number of children sexually abused, usually by natural or substitute father, has risen to 11 per cent of all reported cruelty cases. In 1980, only 1 per cent of reported cases involved sexual abuse". What the figures actually mean is problematic as a NSPCC spokesman quoted only in the *Guardian* acknowledged, saying that "the Society could not tell whether the increase reflected an increase in offences or greater awareness of the need to report incidents". The *Guardian* also went on to mention the factors said to be triggering child cruelty cases: marital discord, unemployment and debt. Only the *Guardian* mentioned that fewer than a third of fathers involved were in paid employment. Further, only the *Guardian* noted the less newsworthy item that "the number of children killed or seriously injured by their parents continued to fall during 1983 and 1984 while the number less seriously injured continued to rise". However, there is no attempt to speculate what this might mean. For example, this could be reasonably interpreted – although nobody did so – as reflecting an increase in awareness of the need to report incidents. When less serious offences increase, this is probably a measure of greater awareness, while when more serious offences rise (which are much more likely to come to the attention of the authorities whatever the general level of awareness) this is probably a measure of an actual increase in offences. However, the subtleties of such an argument to consider whether a shift upwards reflects a rise in awareness or a rise in actual offences does not in general appeal to the media.

Relationship of research to policy

So after reviewing how the major research reports are reported in the newspapers, we can turn briefly to the relationship of research to policy. The impact of carefully constructed research is unlikely to overcome the more pressing demands of the political imperatives. The most dramatic example of this discrepancy emerged in the government's attempt to give the prosecution the right to ask for reviews of alleged over-lenient sentences. A provision allowing the Attorney-General to refer over-lenient sentences to the Court of Appeal had been included in the

Prosecution of Offences Bill, but the proposal had been defeated in the House of Lords and not restored in the Commons. On 16 July Mrs Thatcher told the American Bar Association's convention in London that "the feeling is growing in our country and elsewhere that some of the sentences which have been passed have not measured up to the enormity of the crimes".[41] Mrs Thatcher went on to tell the American lawyers: "Sadly the Bill did not get through. I say sadly because those who so strenuously oppose the Bill appear to ignore the very real anxiety of ordinary people that too many sentences do not fit the crime". Perhaps of equal interest was the way that Mrs Thatcher chose to ignore the findings of the authoritative research of the Home Office Research Unit. As the *Guardian* pointed out,[42] Mrs Thatcher's speech coincided with the publication of the second *British Crime Survey*, which showed that people, including the victims of crime, do not want harsher sentences. As Malcolm Dean commented, "Mrs Thatcher may well have concluded that it will do her no political harm to be seen to be trying to do something about 'soft' sentences".

So we have the situation that there are some authoritative sources, such as the *British Crime Survey*, which are used by the press to challenge the work of feminists, as we saw in the questioning of the figures produced by Women Against Rape. However, the Prime Minister feels no need for the 'authoritative' view of the Home Office's *British Crime Survey*, which explicitly challenges her own version of reality. It is at this point that one can see how closely that Margaret Thatcher and her administration speak the same language as the vast bulk of the popular press – tougher sentencing is seen as the solution.

Newspaper campaigns

Sentencing

Whenever the sentence imposed on a sex offender is reported, then implicitly the newspaper may be making a comment on the sentencing process. The very selection of the types of cases to be included and the prominence given to certain kinds of outcomes are ways that oblique comments are made upon sentencing practice in the courts. Here, however, we are concerned with the situations where the newspaper is explicitly concerned with general sentencing issues.

There was much opportunity for such discussion as at the outset of 1985 it was reported – SEX LAW CRACKDOWN (*Star*)[43] – that the Home Secretary, Leon Brittan, had decided to back proposals recommended by the Criminal Law Revision Committee for an increase in the maximum sentence for certain sex offences. The last mention of the subject of sentencing occurred right at the end of the year in the same newspaper,[44] with an exclusive with an almost identical headline – **CRACKDOWN ON RAPISTS: More to get life sentences** – with the report that "nationwide action follows demands from Mrs Thatcher for a major law and order counter-offensive in which dealing with sex offenders is given top priority".

While the language remains the same, the target shifted quite dramatically during the year. At the start of the year 'the law' was the main focus of attention. In short, if we get the law right, then the problem will go away. By the end of the year, the focus was on the judges. The problem would go away if the judges would only do their jobs properly. In contrast, while the grounds of the debate had shifted, there was no recognition that sentencing alone may not deliver the solution.

In February the *Star*[45] displayed a coupon, **IT'S YOUR VERDICT**. The coupon only gave the option to *support* long sentences for rape and for the prosecution to have the right of appeal against sentences they consider to be too lenient. In contrast to this bogus survey, the *Sun*[46] during the next month asked *ARE YOU THE VICTIM OF OUR SOFT JUDGES?* The appeal to personal experiences was soon followed in May[47] by the screaming headline and a demand for action: **WE WANT JUSTICE! CRIMINALS MUST PAY THE PENALTY . . .** *Today The Sun gives you a chance to add your support to the demand for tougher sentences. Just fill in the petition form on the left and get your friends to do the same . . . .* By July,[48] the *Sun* was announcing: **No.10 GETS SUN PETITION ON KILLERS: 'MAKE LIFE MEAN LIFE'** *The tragic parents of sex murder victim Steven Edmonston yesterday urged Mrs Thatcher to ensure that life sentences for killers MEAN life. . . . The petition signed by more than 50,000 readers urges Mrs Thatcher to insist killers jailed for life should never be set free.* Two weeks later, Mrs Thatcher was speaking to the American Bar Association's convention in London. Her remarks about "the very real anxiety of ordinary people"[49] certainly seem more closely derived from the *Sun* petition than the results in the *British Crime Survey* derived from a systematic sample of the whole country, which was published at the same time.

Apart from bogus surveys and emotional petitions, the coverage of the issues surrounding sex offences was often distorted and rarely was any background information given from which genuine discussion could emerge. The coverage of the Parliamentary debate on rape during which the Labour MP, Gwyneth Dunwoody, made the impassioned plea that "it is not enough to concentrate on the sentencing of rapists" summarises the situation. The headlines almost unanimously focused on one particular contribution and one particular kind of sentence: **"CASTRATE RAPISTS" CALL BY PEERESS** (*Star*);[50] **CUT OUT RAPE, SAYS BARONESS** (*Sun*);[51] **CASTRATE RAPISTS,**

PEERESS DEMANDS *(Daily Mail);*[52] **PEERESS URGES CASTRATION OF RAPISTS** *(The Times).*[53]

Providing information

While the dearth of information on a topical subject – as opposed to propaganda – is evident in most newspapers, there are exceptions. The quality newspapers certainly provide some useful feature articles, but perhaps the surprise is the amount of space that the *Daily Mail* gives to the subject of sexual violence in the women's pages. We have already considered the aggressive stance of the *Daily Mail* towards the study, *Ask Any Woman*, and the particular interest in the supposed false allegations of women in rape cases, but this seems to contrast with the focus of the material in the women's pages. For example in the latter half of the year, the newspaper's *Femail* section had several features specifically on rape. Written by the Woman's Editor, Diana Hutchinson, they focus on the new police reaction to rape: **The hot-line girls out to stop the sex terror on London's streets RAPE SQUAD;**[54] **The revolutionary about-turn in police advice to women STRIKE BACK AT THE RAPIST;**[55] **RAPE: HEALING THE HURT Why the police started their own crisis command.**[56] However, the contrast is largely an illusory one, for, while the features are certainly informative, the message is that the police have now got matters under control and that hence there really is no need for the concern being expressed by feminist groups. The theme of the articles echo an exclusive in the same newspaper in August.[57] Headlined **The gentle touch for sex attack victims**, the article talks of a new police scheme in Northumbria whereby "a unique flying squad of women doctors is helping to ease the distress of rape victims". There is a clear recognition in that article – and is followed in the *Daily Mail* features generally – that the police are making serious attempts to rectify some of their practices following the public outrage over detectives' insensitive treatment of a rape victim filmed during a television documentary in 1981. In that respect the *Daily Mail* is largely concerned in supporting the police efforts and hence dampening down the outrage. In contrast, the popular newspapers – the *Star* and the *Sun* – are concerned in orchestrating a public outrage about the sentencing of rapists.

The concern about sex offences and the information given to the public by the media is a very narrow one. Those who are interested in wider issues often suffer a distorted message reaching the public. When even the quality newspapers, such as the *Guardian* – sometimes seem to think that women's organisations are simply concerned with more sympathetic police questioning of the victims and heavier sentencing for the rapists, there seems little chance that the issues of rape prevention, the causes of rape and the protection of women in the community will get satisfactory coverage. Most of the press either ignores the underlying issues, or vehemently condemns those who produce evidence and argument for deep-rooted change.

Chapter seven

Changing legal practice

Media coverage of attempts to change or challenge the law with respect to sexual offences is the focus of this chapter. Firstly, we examine the media reporting when an existing law is tested. The particular interest in a test case is whether the boundaries of the law will be extended to encompass a new situation. In this respect, the issue of compensation to rape victims came to the fore in the sample year. Although victims of sexual assault are entitled to receive compensation from the Criminal Injuries Compensation Board, rape victims had never before sued their attackers for damages. Secondly, we look at the introduction of new measures which further criminalise certain activities and we take the example of the attempts to reduce the nuisance caused by kerb-crawlers seeking prostitutes.

Compensating raped women

Compensation for victims of sexual assault is an important topic which raises many different kinds of issues. However, our focus must be narrowed to the impact of the media. What was the media response to this challenge in the courts? Is the coverage informative or misleading? Is the material trivialised or does the reader begin to appreciate the broader significance of the issues being reported? In brief, what is the quality of the coverage?

The issue arose when a woman who had been the victim of a sexual assault took a civil action to seek compensation for the mental scars suffered by this attack. The assailant was a minicab driver, Christopher Meah, who had made legal history the previous year when he had been awarded damages (by the same judge trying the current claim) for injuries in a 1978 road accident, which allegedly unleashed his underlying tendencies towards violent sex, thus turning him into a sex attacker. Meah had been awarded £45,750 compensation, but was now serving a life sentence for serious sex offences on three women which

120

had occurred subsequent to this accident (and on which the claim for a personality change had been largely based). The 26-year-old woman was now suing Meah for the effects of the assault during which she was held at knife-point for hours and forced to engage in degrading sexual activity. The judge, Mr Justice Woolf, was also being asked to award damages to another of Meah's victims, "who was trussed up like a chicken, stabbed and raped".

The local evening papers captured the story at the start of the court hearing and on front-page headlines – **VICTIMS SUE SEX ATTACKER** – the London *Evening Standard*[1] gave an account of the first day's hearing. The *Standard* announced that "the outcome of the case is being awaited by rape victims throughout the country". Except for readers of the *Observer*,[2] who may have noticed a very brief item in the previous day's paper, this was the first news of the case. The claim that "the outcome of the case is being awaited by rape victims throughout the country" is an example of media hyperbole. Nevertheless, the case did raise important issues which lawyers regarded as a test case.

This story not only quickly became more than media hyperbole but also became seriously misleading in terms of its importance. The newspapers failed to indicate the likely limited scope of even a favourable outcome of the case for the victims. The limitation is that most rapists do not have the money to hand over. In this "unique test case against a rapist", the women won their case, but something heralded as a major battle proved to be only a minor skirmish. For all the fulsome words the outcome meant very little to most survivors of sexual assault, but this was not the message which was provided by the media.

The limited coverage of previous compensation awards for victims of sexual assault and the extensive coverage of this "test case" is both curious and instructive. Prior to the test case, the *Sunday Mirror*[3] had featured an article on protests over an award (**A PALTRY £10,000 FOR FOX'S VICTIM**) by the Criminal Injuries Compensation Board. This had been the award to a teenager who had been raped twice at gunpoint – in front of her brother and boyfriend – by Malcolm Fairley, the rapist nicknamed The Fox. Despite extensive coverage of this case, no other newspaper in the study took up the story about compensation. The *Sunday Mirror* itself did not express a direct reaction but reported that of others. A spokeswoman for Women Against Rape said: "We are disgusted that such a paltry sum was awarded to the young woman – disgusted but not surprised. For far too long rape has not been treated as the serious crime it is". The victim's mother said: "She is going to get on with her life. We thought the amount might have been more, but it is not really important."

In contrast to the one article on the compensation claim in The Fox case, the coverage on the Meah compensation case produced thirty-five items in less than a three-week period, including three days' coverage in all the national dailies and front-page treatment in *The Times*, the *Guardian*, the *Daily Mirror* and the *Daily Mail*, and with leaders on the topic in the *Star*, the *Guardian* and the *Daily Mirror*. The local evening papers also followed the case; it was mentioned briefly in the *Observer* and the *Mail on Sunday*.

Naming of the victims

This civil case shows how newspapers deal with the issue of anonymity when they are not covered by the restrictions of the 1976 Act, for the legislation forbidding the identification of rape victims did not apply to civil cases. All the newspapers, except the *Daily Mail*, took the opportunity of naming this victim of serious sexual offences (although it should be noted that her counsel did not request anonymity). The *Daily Mail* stated that "it believes that it is not in the women's interest to give their names and that the principle of anonymity for the victims of rape should be preserved"[4]. In fact, the first claimant was a victim of serious sexual offences which – while horrendous – were not technically rape and hence would not have been covered by the 1976 Act in a criminal court. The decision of the *Daily Mail* with respect to preserving the anonymity of the first victim shows that it was not a decision of the whole newspaper group, for the London *Evening Standard* continued to reveal the name throughout the hearing; such discretionary decisions are presumably ones for the individual newspapers rather than the publishing group.

In the second claim the judge specifically pointed out that the legislation forbidding the identification of rape victims did not apply to civil actions but asked, however, for this victim's request for anonymity to be respected. The second victim was identified as "Miss D" and as aged 37, but no newspaper revealed her full name. In this civil court case the women had to describe their ordeals in court in detail. The first woman told how she knew Meah as a friend of her husband at the time of the attack. She also told how she felt "degraded and humiliated" by the assault. The assailant had arrived at her home in East London at about midnight, wielding a knife; she had been alone with her son. She was forced to carry out degrading sex acts in the presence of her son. "It was horrible," she said. "I felt extremely frightened. I was crying and shaking and thought he was going to stab me. I was very scared". She told how she could not bear to return to the flat after she escaped; her marriage had broken up and "as a result of what happened men in general became repugnant to her".[5]

The other woman

told Mr Justice Woolf how she was threatened with a knife,
'trussed like a chicken' with electric cord, sexually abused and
raped. . . . The woman said she had not had sex since the attack in
September 1982. She kept a hammer by her front door and was
frightened when the doorbell rang. "I feel dirty and guilty", she
said. "I have nightmares. He's sitting on me and stabbing me. It's a
clear face, it's Chris Meah's face – it's just staring at me".[6]

The reports initially stated that this rape victim had already received
£3,500 from the Criminal Injuries Compensation Board. The other
woman had received nothing. The next day this information had
changed to receiving £3,600 and £1,000 respectively from the Criminal
Injuries Compensation Board. The front-page headlines proclaimed in
the evening newspapers **£17,560 FOR SEX ATTACK VICTIMS**
(London *Evening Standard*).[7] The first woman received £7,080, while
the second woman was awarded £10,480.

The judge said "the damages in each case were aggravated because
both women knew their attacker, the assault took place in their own
homes, a knife was used and because of the particular circumstances of
each assault" (London *Evening Standard*).[8] The judge stressed that there
was no direct precedent for awarding damages in such a case and "it was
only too easy to recognise that any sum of money the court can award is
not going to compensate these ladies for what they have undergone".

Outside the courtroom the rape survivor was reported as saying that
' "Bringing the case was worth it definitely. Of course it's not just the
money". . . . The important thing, she thought, was that it was a moral
and psychological victory, and she hoped it would encourage other
women to follow her example'. Her counsel said that while the unique
claim by the women had set a legal precedent that would be followed in
future cases, he did not expect a flood of similar actions. He also pointed
out that the award by the Criminal Injuries Compensation Board would
now have to be repaid.

The next morning the newspapers largely focused in their front-page
headlines on the growing storm over the amount of damages paid:
Storm over 'paltry' £17,560 for rapist's victims (*The Times*);[9] **Fury
over award to rape victims** (*Daily Mirror*);[10] **MP's anger over
judge's award to two women WHAT PRICE RAPE?** (*Daily Mail*).[11]
The Times highlighted the issues:

* Why did the victims of rape receive far less compensation than did
  the offender for the car crash that affected his personality and turned
  him into a rapist?

* Where should rape stand in the scale of damages for injuries?
* Will the decision encourage more women to report rapes?
* Will the awards lead to more such claims?

The *Daily Mail* gave considerable coverage to the case and featured on the front page an account of the way that the rape had destroyed the second woman's life:

'I WAKE UP SHAKING AND CRYING . . . I JUST LIVE FROM DAY TO DAY'

The woman raped, stabbed and left to die by Meah still suffers nightmares about the attack. She has visions of his 'puffy eyes' staring at her virtually every night.

'I wake up shaking and shivering and crying. I have a lot of trouble sleeping', she said at her smart London maisonette last night.

'Like any woman, I wanted to get married and have children – I love kids. but now I just live from day to day. I don't even think about next week'.

Surrounded by family and friends celebrating her unique triumph, she confided that she would never recover from her ordeal at Meah's hands.

Her nine knife wounds healed remarkably quickly, keeping her in hospital for only five days, but the mental scars left by the attack will probably always be with her, despite the help of psychiatrists.

Three years on, a man has only to brush against her arm to make her flinch with fear.

The brutal attack in her home by a neighbour she thought was a friend has turned the 36-year-old from a vivacious socialite into a virtual recluse.

'I feel cut off socially,' she said. 'It's self-inflicted but I just can't help it. I used to have boyfriends but nowadays I never plan to go out. Most people have given up asking me.

'I can't see myself with a man for years. I'm nearly 37 so what chance have I got of having my own family before it's too late?'

The size of her award did not worry her. 'What matters is that this is a moral victory. If I'd got £1 I would have been happy', she said.

The Labour MP, Jack Ashley, argued[12] that "yesterday's awards were a 'judicial scandal'", saying in a letter to the Lord Chancellor that he was "sick to death" of judges who failed "to appreciate that rape scars a woman for life". He was demanding a public rebuke for the judge. Two Tory MPs, Terry Dicks and Derek Coaway, considered the payouts to the two women as "miserly" and the judge of "very bad inconsistency".[13] In contrast, another Tory MP, Geoffrey Dickens, claimed it was a great advance for women (*Daily Mirror*).[14] Most of the morning newspapers noted that the judge had pointed out that it was important to relate the damages to awards made in more conventional actions for injury compensation: "although these ladies underwent terrible experiences, sadly, as a result of traffic accidents, others undergo experiences which are every bit as cataclysmic".[15] This observation reflects the direct conflict between the view that serious sexual offences must not be regarded as a special case and the view of many women's organisations involved in dealing with rape who think otherwise.

The Times[16] noted that the awards were considerably larger than those already obtained by the women from the Criminal Injuries Compensation Board, which was said to use £2,750 as its starting figure for awards in rape cases. The reporting of the comments of Women Against Rape was limited to the observation that "it was unjust that the women received much smaller sums than the man who attacked them". Clues as to what enters into a damage assessment were only available with the judge's comments, reported in *The Times*, that the 37-year-old woman "is an attractive person and if she was able she could undoubtedly resume relationships with members of the opposite sex with comparative ease". The *Guardian*[17] was the only paper to mention the psychiatrist's description of the 37-year-old woman as a "tough and determined coper". There were no reports which focused on the appropriateness of the basis or evidence by which the level of assessment of the damages was reached.

Two regular women columnists – Lynda Lee-Potter of the *Daily Mail*[18] and Alix Palmer of the *Star*[19] – made the case the main story in their feature page, while Rosemary Collins had a full-page report in the *Daily Mirror*[20] on **The shocking price of rape**. Each focused on a different aspect of the case. Collins, while reminding readers that one price to pay was the loss of anonymity in a civil action, concentrated on the continuing ordeal of the victims of sexual assault. She also noted the apparent discrepancy of the award to the assailant compared with what was received by the women. Her report concluded by recording the various views on the importance of the case. The rape victim's lawyer saw it as a legal precedent. This was a view shared by the National Council for Civil Liberties: "We hope this award will give courage to rape victims to pursue remedies through the courts and that the Criminal Injuries Compensation Board will now start making more realistic awards". Collins herself introduced an important note of caution. Perhaps for the first time in the coverage someone focused on the crucial point that there was unlikely to be a flood of claims from women because in most cases their attackers would not have the money to pay out damages.

Lynda Lee-Potter (**A judgment adding insult to injury**) commented fiercely in the *Daily Mail* on the judge's award to the two raped women. She suggested that

> the judge has inflicted another burden on these two women and called it justice. He has implied to the outside world that the suffering of Meah was more horrendous than that of his victims. The jubilation and euphoria amongst imprisoned rapists today must be immense and I don't say that lightly.

With an understanding of what tends to count in court she noted that

> if those women had been facially scarred they would have got lavish compensation, Mr Justice Woolf may well have felt more compassion. Their suffering can't be seen but it's probably forever. I've interviewed many rape victims and again and again they talk of how defiled they feel, how dirty, how rotten. . . . Male judges live in a rarefied world and increasingly seem to be making unrealistic judgments. Rape victims have long feared the nudge nudge you must have asked for it jocularity of some sections of the police. . . . Understandably many victims for the rest of their lives see men and all men as the enemy.

This forceful piece of journalism is on a page which probably attracts mostly women readers. It contrasts strongly with the editorial which the report *Ask Any Woman* attracted (see Chapter 6). Similarly Alix Palmer of the *Star*, *The woman writer people really read*, had a similarly hard-hitting piece. **No wonder women are still victims** suggested "there are only two places a man can really be hurt. One of them is his pocket." The following day several newspapers reported a rare defence of a judicial decision when the judge answered criticisms from MPs and women's groups that the amount he awarded to the two women was 'miserly' compared with what he awarded to Meah. The judge maintained that it was not true that Meah's award was excessive: "but for his injuries, he would not have consequently been sentenced to life imprisonment for his crimes".[21] The neurologist, who had given evidence about Meah, suggested that "as a man who received a very serious injury in 1978, he was entitled to that award like anyone else".

The coverage raises several issues. The energies of the press were largely engaged in perpetrating facile comparisons between rapist and raped. By continuing to accentuate this comparison, more meaningful comparisons were being overlooked, namely, the awards routinely being made by the Criminal Injuries Compensation Board (CICB). The CICB went largely undiscussed, despite the fact that a report on the work of the Board could have a much greater impact on the rape victim's receiving reasonable financial compensation than encouraging the suing of the assailant through the civil courts. The leader in the *Guardian*[22] suggested that interest in the disparity between the award to the rapist and the much lower sums awarded to his victims "has found the women's movement in bed with the Fleet Street tabloids". The *Guardian* argued that "the real issue is not so much the inadequacy of the High Court settlement. It is the inadequacy of the arrangements for compensating victims of crime in general, and not even victims of rape in particular." The *Guardian* went on to argue that

> the neglect of victims in the criminal justice system has long been one of its dark failings. . . . The Government has been loud in its concern for victims, but the deeds have not yet matched either its own words or the sense of urgency which emerged from the Home Affairs Select Committee report on victims of crime, published a year ago today.

The *Daily Mirror*[23] took this wider focus, suggesting that "the award of £10,000 to a rape victim is insulting to women. But the kind of payment made by the Criminal Injuries Compensation Board is worse. With the board, rape starts at £2,750, when even losing two teeth is worth £1,200 . . . . " The *Mirror* 'Comment' concentrated on the point that

> This Government lavishly promised to reduce crime. Perhaps the promises shouldn't have been made. Perhaps no Government can put a brake on violence. . . . Money cannot erase the effect of violence. But it can ease the problems which flow from it for the victims. And the sooner it is given the better.

In contrast, the *Star* leader[24] continued on the theme that the courts had opened up a new pathway and focused on its supposed value in tackling the problem of "sex molesters and rapists". This new departure provided scope so that "his house, his car, his savings and any other assets could be taken away". It argues that "it is not just the culprit who is set to suffer as a result of the crime. The future comfort of his entire family is also at risk." The leader regretted that Mr Justice Woolf "took cold feet and only tip-toed down [this new path]". The leader in the *Star* totally failed to relate the award to the normal pathways of criminal injuries compensation. The contrast of emphasis is stark between the two popular dailies. The *Star* focused on the usually impossible task of getting the money back from the offender and his family, while the *Daily Mirror* stressed the shortcomings of the state's compensation scheme.

The *Daily Mirror* implicitly challenged the new scenario being presented by the *Star* of the whole family of the rapist suffering as a result of the crime. The *Daily Mirror* featured an exclusive[25] by Rosemary Collins (**MY LIFE SENTENCE BY WIFE**) in which the wife of the rapist Meah spoke of the life sentence she is effectively serving for her husband's crimes. She revealed that she is seeking a divorce to give her three children a new name and a new start. She stated, "He committed the crimes but we're paying. Chrissie is behind bars, but I'm serving a life sentence too". She told of the public revenge on her and the three children, aged 4, 5 and 10, and talked of men urinating through the letter-box, the children being roughed up at school, her washing being slashed and receiving obscene phone calls night and day: "from the public reaction you'd think I was alongside helping him", she said. She stressed that she did not begrudge a penny paid to the victims: "nothing will ever compensate those two. But one of them is talking about having a holiday and I'm worried about buying tomorrow's bread". This provides an interesting contrast to the *Star*'s editorial, when it would quite happily make inroads into the life of the offender's wife and family. There is little doubt that the offenders' wives often have a difficult time from the press: they are portrayed either as crazy to stay married to their husbands or as disloyal to break away. Indeed, it is by no means unknown for wives of rapists to be implicitly blamed for their husbands' crimes. In contrast, this feature in the *Daily Mirror* usefully portrayed another side to the issue.

Nevertheless, the issue of the routine payments of the Compensation Board had received sufficient airing for the Chairman of the Board, Mr Michael Ogden QC, to feel obliged to explain the level of awards given by the CICB to the two women, saying that they had received far lower awards from the Board because its rules prevented it from awarding "aggravated" damages above the level appropriate for the injury itself, as Mr Justice Woolf had done in this case. No newspaper took up the point that the Board may be unnecessarily constrained in such matters.

The Labour MP, Harriet Harman, had earlier pointed to the maleness of the Criminal Injuries Compensation Board, so it was perhaps stage-managed for one of the two women lawyers on the Board, Miss Shirley Ritchie, to defend the guideline payment of £2,750 to rape victims, arguing that it was right that the guideline for rape was lower than for a facial scar, the loss of an eye or hearing. The brief report of her statement in the *Daily Mirror*[26] concluded with her terse view that "some people get over rape quite well". The defence of maintaining the status quo continued to be reported in the quality newspapers, with the Chairman again rejecting criticism of the amounts paid to rape victims saying that "of course, rapes which cause serious injuries result in higher awards" (*Guardian*).[27] Again, nobody challenged the limited scope of how the Board regarded 'serious injuries'. He went on to suggest that the £2,750 sum attracted little adverse comment when first published in 1984 but he said it was now being criticised as "chauvinistic" and "an insult to women". In a letter to *The Times*,[28] he continued to defend the guideline of the Board for rape victims:

Our figure was the result of an assessment exercise in which 41
judges and lawyers experienced in personal injuries cases
participated, in addition to 20 board members. There were women
participants; the highest figure suggested by any woman was
£3,000. In earlier assessment exercises the figures suggested by
women were also in line with those suggested by men. In view of
the fact that female and male participants were in agreement it is
plain that the board must adhere to its starting figure.

The utilisation of the consent of token women to legitimise the CICB
stance is an interesting development.

Most newspapers lost interest in the issues a few days after the case
had been decided. The *Guardian*[29] published a letter from the Strath-
clyde Rape Crisis Centre, which stressed the damaging way in which the
press readily adopted the view that the rapist's accident "changed his
personality and turned him into a rapist". It was argued that this served
to falsify the reasons why rape occurs, which reinforces the myth that
rapists are all psychologically disturbed. The fading interest of the
Guardian can always be measured by the speed with which a stylish
letter appears as a 'Miscellany' item on the letters page. On Christmas
Eve, Joy Ogden, in the light of a recently successful libel action,
commented

> a moral for rapists from the judgment on Charlotte Cornwell's libel
> action: if you're worried about the size of damages which may be
> awarded against you, go ahead and rape the woman; but for
> heaven's sake don't add insult to injury by telling her she has "a
> big bum"; it will cost you more than the rape.[30]

So what do we learn from the media coverage of a *successful* compensation claim, which filled several front pages and had several vigorous
features by women journalists? The crucial point is that the issue had
faded within a month without making any serious impact on routine
questions of compensation for victims of sexual assault. What had been
headlined from the outset as a "unique test case" failed to generate any
serious and sustained discussions of the underlying issues. The headlines demonstrated some brief and passing concern, but the coverage
was essentially misleading. The headlines by challenging the 'paltry'
sum of £17,560 for these two victims of sexual assault had the effect of
implicitly suggesting that this was the usual scale of payment for victims
of sexual assault. Newspapers generally supportive of the Conservative
government – and particularly the *Star* – began to highlight this case as
a way of punishing the offender and his family, and removing some of
the burden of meeting compensation claims from the state system embodied in the Criminal Injuries Compensation Board. The *Daily Mirror*,

in contrast and almost alone, indicated the very special circumstances of this case in that most sexual assailants would not have the money to pay out damages. Indeed, the *Sunday Mirror* – part of the Mirror Group – was also the only newspaper to highlight the earlier concern about the amount paid out to one of The Fox's victims, indicating how limited the genuine concern about the plight of rape victims was among the media. Nevertheless, when the occasion came, of course, the focus was on the amount of compensation. The quality dailies, particularly the *Guardian*, helped to focus the discussion on the normal amounts paid out to victims of sexual assault by the Criminal Injuries Compensation Board. By some adroit moves, implicitly supported by some of the popular press and more fully reported in *The Times*, the spokespersons for the Board quelled any hints that the issues should be fundamentally reconsidered. The two victims who had been portrayed as receiving 'paltry' sums would not, therefore, become the flag-bearers of larger amounts of compensation for other victims. Within a few days almost all the newspapers had switched from proclaiming the iniquities of the system for victims of sexual assault, to implicitly and explicitly upholding the status quo by narrowing the terms of the debate or ignoring the issues raised.

In contrast to this brief furore over money, the various rape survivors themselves involved in these cases were reported as saying that the amount of money was not *really* important. If these sentiments were accurately reported, no newspaper took the trouble to find out what *was* really important to raped women. All we have are fragmentary comments suggesting that the most important thing was having the attacks recognised as serious.

Curbing kerb-crawling

In any year there are discussions about changing the law with a view to modifying sexual behaviour. One legislative innovation in the criminal law on which we will focus is the introduction of measures to attempt to reduce the nuisance caused by kerb-crawlers. These measures were embodied in the Sexual Offences Act 1985 and our interest is in the media coverage leading up to this change in the law, as well as the immediate aftermath.

The Bill, which had government backing, aimed to create three new offences: kerb-crawling, persistently soliciting women for prostitution, and soliciting women for sexual purposes in a manner likely to cause fear. It also proposed to increase the maximum penalty for attempted rape from seven years to life imprisonment and that for indecent assault on a female to ten years. At the time the maximum penalty was five years for assaulting a girl aged under 13 and two years in other cases.

Under the Bill there would be fines of up to £400 for kerb-crawling and for persistently soliciting a woman in the street. It was proposed that a man who persistently solicited a woman for sexual purposes in a manner likely to cause fear could receive a fine of up to £2,000. Only magistrates would be able to try the new offences. The interest is to see which aspects of the Bill specifically interested the press during its passage through Parliament. In fact, while there were several issues which could have been the main focus of interest, the kerb-crawling provisions almost totally monopolised the coverage of the Bill in the press. At the start of the year there was already on the table a proposal from the Criminal Law Revision Committee to try to tackle what had been identified as a kerb-crawling problem. The first relevant item appeared in the *Coventry Evening Telegraph*.[31] A news story, headlined **Group calls for curfew on men**, reported that a women's pressure group was calling for men to be banned after dark to stop kerb-crawlers bothering women at night. The suggestion came from Rose Dangerfield, Conservative councillor for Dudley, at a forum backed by West Midland County Council. Cllr Dangerfield said the problem of women being safe on the streets was a drastic one and so called for drastic measures and "if this brings the problem to the fore in the public eye I am very pleased." Cllr Trudy Bowen, who seconded the motion at the forum, said that if men were subjected to a curfew, they would get an idea of how a woman felt about not being safe on the streets at night. Cllr Bowen went on to say, "Of course we couldn't enforce this, but it does highlight the situation in a light-hearted way". While this suggestion was initially reported sympathetically, explicitly feminist initiatives were treated very differently.

The county council's initiatives on women's issues were criticised under the headline, **Women's committees 'a waste of money'**. The main focus of the criticism, emanating from three female Councillors, one Conservative and two Labour, was that all it had done was to criticise 'nude girl calendars' and to campaign against the use of the word 'chairman'. An editorial in the *Coventry Evening Telegraph*[32] took up a critical stance with considerable vigour:

LET'S BAN MEN!

Ban men from the streets after dark – that would stop women being bothered by kerb crawlers.

No, the suggestion did not come from a music hall comic. It was seriously proposed at the West Midlands council's forum yesterday and will go to the women's sub-committee on Friday.

And how would the proposer have such a ban enforced? Simple, she said. Just make a law saying men with no business in the street after curfew time, shouldn't be out!

To allow this sort of nonsense to be aired the council is spending some £20,000 a year, mostly on councillors' allowances.

When the women members aren't talking pointlessly about a non-sexist alternative for the title "chairman", or the degradation of girlie calendars, they fill in time fixing the date of the next meeting.

Coventry can be thankful its women councillors have the common sense to see it all for what it is. A total waste of time and money.

So ended an effort to raise people's consciousness on the serious issue of women's safety on the streets. There is both a clear dilemma and a paradox for women raising a matter of this kind. If they do so in a serious manner, then their views are not treated seriously. If they do so in a light-hearted manner to focus attention, their views are then taken seriously.

The *Guardian*[33] was the only newspaper to mention that Janet Fookes would be seeking a second reading for her Bill to make "kerb-crawling" and harassment of women an offence, but both quality dailies (*The Times*[34] and the *Guardian*[35]) gave full coverage to the Bill when it was given an unopposed second reading in the Commons. The only other newspaper to mention it at this stage was the *Star*:[36] – **Curb on Crawlers**. This brief item on the second page followed the front-page headline **We name saucy VIP** in which the feature – taken from the debate on the Bill – focused on the story related by the former Solicitor-General for Scotland that Mrs Thatcher had been propositioned by a Scottish lord. The Conservative MP, Nicholas Fairbairn, focused his concern on the section of the Bill which made it an offence for a man to solicit a woman for sexual purposes in a manner likely to cause her fear. He went on to say that he had always been attracted to Miss Fookes (the sponsor of the Bill), but had never dared to ask her to go to bed with him. He would now have to ask her without causing her fear. He went on to describe the propositioning of the Prime Minister when she was the guest of the Lord High Commissioner of the Church of Scotland, to which she had replied: "Quite right. You have very good taste but I just do not think you would make it at the moment". He maintained that interaction would have been an offence under that section. The *Star* gave great emphasis to Fairbairn's two tales of thwarted courtship but did not mention what Fookes wanted to achieve in her Bill. While not giving it the benefit of a headline, *The Times*[37] gave full coverage to Fairbairn's tale telling. In contrast, the *Guardian*'s[38] report mentioned Fookes's remark but did not include anything on the Fairbairn intervention. The problem, of course, is that readers would be at a complete loss as to what the debate was really about.

At this unopposed reading, Janet Fookes maintained that it was intolerable that kerb-crawlers had made certain parts of British cities 'no-go' areas for women who were afraid to go out alone and that a modern law was needed to replace the medieval breach of the peace laws used by the police. She further hoped that women

> would be prepared to give evidence themselves and not rely on agent provocateur action by the police. *One is not looking to find prosecutions for all, but a few solitary examples would have a deterrent effect.* (our emphasis)[39]

Clearly the sponsor of the Bill was trying to counter the suggestion that the new law would be used in a draconian fashion in a wide number of contexts which would threaten the excesses of all men. Nevertheless, Clive Soley, Labour home affairs spokesman, said that while he did not oppose the Bill he had several anxieties about it, including the fear that it could become another "sus" law with a conviction that could be secured on police evidence alone. He suggested that decriminalisation, which would allow prostitution without impinging on other people, might be the long-term way forward. From the government side of the House, Matthew Parris, then a Conservative MP, expressed his misgivings about the Bill, calling for a general revision of prostitution laws and also raising the spectre of police officers acting as *agents provocateurs*.

David Mellor, the junior Home Office Minister, stressed that the present laws were inadequate and the problem could not wait for a general review of legislation on prostitution. He maintained that, while it was desirable that an accosted woman should give evidence in court, to insist upon it as a requirement for a conviction would undermine the effectiveness of the measure. Senior police officers should ensure that entrapment did not take place. In contrast, *The Times* alone focused more specifically on Mellor's remarks that the government attached great importance to increasing the maximum penalties for attempted rape to life imprisonment and the other proposed sentence increases.

Within a week the popular newspapers demonstrated the kind of interest that they often displayed in developments of this kind. Both the *Star* and the *Sun*[40] reported on the detective chief inspector, head of a county vice and drugs squad, who had retired with an ill-health pension – a year after a magistrates' court had bound him over for kerb-crawling in Nottingham's red-light district. This brief report is interesting coming two weeks after the unopposed second reading of a Bill of which one of the proclaimed tasks was to protect women from kerb-crawlers and whose main sponsor, Fookes, had proclaimed that "one is not looking to find prosecutions for all, but a few solitary examples would have a deterrent effect". This case which came to court under the then existing legislation – with its mention in popular dailies – certainly had all the ingredients of an example to deter the others. However, no one took up the issue that the existing legislation already seemed to be adequate for the stated purposes of Miss Fookes. In fact, we have here some of the paradoxes of press reporting in Britain. The popular newspapers include titillating cases, which implicitly show the shortcomings of some of the arguments being used to buttress impending changes in the law, but the popular press is not interested in the general arguments being put forward. In contrast, the quality press whose readers may be interested in a challenge to the rationale for legislative change are not usually provided with the day-to-day cases which illustrate such inconsistencies.

Later in the same month (London *Evening Standard*)[41] Fenton Bresler in his feature, 'London's Law', noted how a visiting police officer from Qatar had approached a woman in the Earls Court area and made indecent suggestions to her. The local police charged the indecently minded Arab policeman with "behaviour likely to cause a breach of the peace", which is contrary to the Justices of the Peace Act 1361. Bresler remarked that "progress and legal reform are wonderful, but there is still some life in the old law yet".

However, the momentum for the new legislation had begun to build up in February. The London *Evening Standard*[42] reported that Janet Fookes was visiting a South London red-light district and then would attend a meeting of residents, police chiefs and Wandsworth councillors to discuss the problem. Meanwhile, *The Times*[43] was indicating (**Kerb protest**) the beginnings of serious opposition to the Bill. Concerned how the Bill "may bring about the wrongful conviction of innocent men", a paper by the Law Society suggested that a man might stop his car to ask a woman walking in a red-light area if she knows the time. If she has no watch, she may well shake her head in reply. In fact, the newspaper was published on the day that the Sexual Offences Bill started its committee stage in the Commons.

On the same day as *The Times* report, the *Star*[44] mentioned briefly that "a group of MPs will claim . . . the Bill could land innocent men in the dock", so suggesting that the report had already gained ground in the thinking of some MPs. In contrast, the *Mail on Sunday* (**Lone Tory may kill off kerb crawl Bill**)[45] implied that the opposition to a Bill which had government support was very limited indeed and reported on how Matthew Parris had tabled more than thirty amendments to the Bill; the newspaper suggested that the Bill, "which has wide support, may never become law". The identification of Parris as vice-president of the Conservative Group for Homosexual Equality seems a further mechanism to question the motives of this 'lone Tory'. The next day the *Star*[46] reported how the Home Office minister, David Mellor, had challenged Parris's opposition to the Bill. Mellor told Parris, whose constituency included Bakewell: "You are in the happy position that the only tarts in Bakewell are consumable". Such was the level of debate.

The Times[47] and the *Guardian*[48] reported that the first clause to the Sexual Offences Bill, making it an offence for a man to "kerb-crawl" in search of sexual intercourse from prostitutes, had been passed by ten votes to seven in the Commons Standing Committee. The *Guardian* mentioned how the Labour members of the committee had argued that the Bill, as drafted, could lead to innocent drivers being arrested and prosecuted for asking women questions in the street. In contrast, there was no evidence of the popular newspapers mentioning what was happening in the committee stages of the Bill.

The interest in kerb-crawling was maintained in the popular press in the familiar fashion. Both the *Star*[49] and the *Sun*[50] had a new, titillating story under the headline **Parson accused**. A Church of the Nazarene clergyman (who was named) had been charged with kerb-crawling in Nottingham's red-light district. He had denied the charge. The *Sun*'s report, on the notorious page three, noted that he was one of twenty-eight men arrested in a December clamp-down on kerb-crawling. He was arrested after allegedly kerb-crawling alongside a woman police constable. After an adjournment this case received extensive coverage in the London *Evening Standard*[51] and the popular dailies. The details of the case were clearly appealing to the popular newspapers when the clergyman accused of kerb-crawling maintained that he had wanted to preach the Gospel to prostitutes. He initially refused but later agreed to be bound over in the sum of £100 to keep the peace. The Chairman of the Bench said the court accepted that the pastor did not seek a vice girl for sex but said his actions were "unwise". Nevertheless, the Chairman was reported in the *Star*[52] as saying that "the manner in which he approached and talked to the policewoman was not only unwise, but likely to cause a very serious offence if the woman police officer was a resident of the area". There was no mention in any of the reports that the clergyman was one of a large number who had been picked up during a police swoop, as mentioned in the original hearing. More pertinently, there was no reference in the popular newspapers to the kerb-crawling legislation being considered by Parliament. Again, this is interesting in so far as many of the fears being expressed in Parliament by the Labour Opposition about police entrapment could have been raised regarding this case.

In the *Guardian*,[53] however, the case was mentioned and placed in a wider context. The barrister, Geoffrey Robertson, was at pains to point out that the proposed legislation "poses grave threats to civil liberties". He pointed to the anomalies of the case "where recently the bench, in a blaze of publicity, bound a clergyman to be of good behaviour in spite of its finding that he had 'no immoral intent' in approaching prostitutes in a Gladstonian effort to save their souls". Robertson's concern was that Parliament, in failing to tackle the decriminalisation of prostitution, was trying to deal with kerb-crawling "as an inconvenient symptom of a demand which the law does not allow to be satisfied in any rational way". His main concern, however, was how the law would be enforced on the streets and in the courts. He maintained that "the danger of the conviction of the innocent is considerable, but the damage will be almost as great to the reputation of innocent men *whose acquittals are accompanied by sensational publicity in their local newspapers*" (our emphasis). The spectre of publicity is the major issue of concern. This is particularly relevant in so far as the sponsor of the Bill, Janet Fookes, had stressed that in her view "a few solitary examples would have a deterrent effect". As an aside, Robertson felt that it was perhaps too much to hope that the first person prosecuted under the new law would be an MP who had stopped his car to ask a young woman the way to a constituency function. Some of the fears raised in Parliament had, of course, already shown that this was a major concern of the largely male MPs. The potential danger to their reputation is always a concern close to the hearts of many of our elected members.

The next day all the headlines gave very similar messages: **Tories talk out kerb crawl Bill** (*The Times*);[54], **Tory MPs blamed for failure of kerb-crawling bill** (*Guardian*);[55] **ANGER AS MPs DITCH KERB CRAWLING BILL Janet slams fellow Tories** (*Sun*);[56] **Storm as kerb-crawling Bill fails** (*Star*);[57] **Anger as Tories kill kerb-crawling Bill** (*Daily Mail*);[58] **KERB CRAWL FURY** (*Daily Mirror*).[59] The reports indicated that the Bill had been unexpectedly talked out after a filibuster by two Conservatives, Matthew Parris and Antony Marlow.

Three days later the counter-attack started, with the popular newspapers all relating the account of Emma Nicholson, a vice-chairman [sic] of the Conservative Party, who told of her twenty-minute ordeal being pursued by a car-load of foul-mouthed kerb-crawlers. There was, however, no indication as to when the incident had actually taken place. She said it was "very sad indeed" that two male Tory MPs last week killed off a Bill aimed at making kerb-crawling illegal. The *Daily Mail*'s[60] account suggested that her ordeal involved being stalked by a middle-aged man in a black limousine and gave very full details of a most unpleasant episode of kerb-crawling harassment in London's West End. Next day in Peter Tory's gossip diary in the *Star*,[61] there was an attack by innuendo on Emma Nicholson, suggesting that she was a most unlikely person to be shaken by such an ordeal: "So what a great hoo-ha some might conclude, over being asked by a stranger to 'come for a little drink'". Nevertheless, the intervention of well-placed Tory women in the debate, with stories such as these being placed in the media, became a useful element in fighting for the survival of the Bill.

Four days later the London *Evening Standard*[62] announced that "kerb-crawling is likely to be outlawed later this year after all, thanks to a Commons deal struck today". It was reported that intense pressure from the government and Tory grassroots had enabled the Home Office minister David Mellor, to persuade Matthew Parris and Antony Marlow to drop their opposition. Mellor promised them that their anxiety about 'innocent men' being subjected to embarrassing court cases would be fully considered when the Bill was debated in the Lords. The outcome of the negotiation was that the Bill was given an unopposed third reading in the Commons. Apparently the Bill's re-emergence was so unexpected that the original sponsor, Janet Fookes, was not at Westminster and in her place. The Home Office minister, David Mellor, regarded the saving of the Bill as "one of the greatest revivals since Lazarus", managing to resurrect the Bill certainly came as a relief to the government because of its proclaimed wide range of support. The possible loss of the Bill was beginning to attract attention, particularly in newspapers which expected a 'tough' stance on law and order from a Conservative administration.

Only the *Guardian*[63] noted that Labour MPs had voiced opposition to the Bill, saying it would give the police new powers that could easily be abused. In none of the other newspapers was there a serious attempt to present the range of opposition to the Bill. The government was presented as coming to the rescue of an uncontentious Bill, which was in danger of being lost by the filibustering of two men who were blocking the cause of women. In fact, in some quarters there was a deep concern about elements of this Bill, which was being portrayed as being essentially non-controversial and as obviously helpful to women and other residents in certain inner-city areas. It was only in the *Guardian*[64] that the curtain to another side of the debate was momentarily lifted. In a letter to the *Guardian*, representatives of four organisations (Bristol Rape Crisis Line, Women Against Rape, South London Women's Hospital Occupation Campaign and the Tyneside Rape Crisis Centre) objected "to women being used as an excuse for repressive legislation", arguing that "in addition, it would make us more vulnerable to assault, rather than less". The argument was that prostitute women would have less time to check out potential clients before going with them, because men talking to them would risk arrest and so the corollary to this was that women would be in greater danger.

Using the results of the Policy Studies Institute authoritative report on the Metropolitan Police,[65] where sexual assaults on women were the public's highest priority for police time, while prostitution was rated the second lowest, these correspondents maintained that the proposed Bill reversed the public's priorities and directed police time and resources into arresting prostitutes and kerb-crawlers rather than on catching rapists and other violent men. The specific concern – which was shared by some Labour MPs – was that the Bill was "designed to give increased and arbitrary powers to the same police who refuse to take seriously cases of actual physical assault where women have asked for their help".

This letter brought into the public domain a critical concern about this legislation which was not heard elsewhere in either the popular or quality newspaper's coverage of this Bill:

There is a long tradition of using women's safety as a pretext for racist and repressive legislation and activities. Lynchings in the USA and white race riots, immigration controls, and the clamour for the return of capital punishment in Britain, have all used this appeal. The Sexual Offences Bill is the latest example.

The National Council for Civil Liberties was reported by *The Times*[66] as writing to all members in the Lords, urging them to oppose the Bill to outlaw kerb-crawling when it reached its second reading in the Lords. The NCCL felt that the proposed Bill would exacerbate the problems of kerb-crawling and street prostitution. It focused on the point that under the Bill convictions could be obtained on the evidence of a single person, namely the police officer, and believed that it would lead to wrongful arrests, particularly of young black and working-class men in red-light areas. So beyond the concern that white middle-class men might be arrested, there was now developing the concern of the dangers for black and working-class men living in these areas. The NCCL further pointed out that the Bill gave no protection for women when giving evidence to the police, and they could face humiliating cross-examinations in court when convictions were brought. Corinne Sweet, the women's rights officer for the NCCL, noted that women could have adverse publicity in the press. So the hazard of innocent women being challenged in court was the concern of the NCCL as much as that of the dangers for innocent men.

The *Guardian*[67] had a letter signed by representatives of several black women's and related organisations (Black Women for Wages for Housework; Croydon Black Women's Group; Sikh Women's Group; Campaign Against Police Violence; African Refugee Action Group; Newham Defence Campaign; Peckham Labour Party Black Section; Afro-Caribbean Organisation; Hackney Police Monitoring Group) who spelt out their concern: "as black people we oppose the Bill because it will give the police increased power and thereby put black, immigrant, and other working-class communities at further risk". The letter noted that "although some Labour MPs have acknowledged that it would in effect be a new 'sus' law, they have offered only token opposition, and have refused to take responsibility for its effects on black communities".

Again the report by the Policy Studies Institute on the Metropolitan Police was quoted in support of their concern, but it went further and expressed the political dimension:

> The Bill is being presented by a member of the party that passed the Police Act, which codifies unprecedented police powers of stop, search, and detention; and the Immigration Act which is breaking up black families. The same party, by cutting wages, welfare, and social services is forcing more women, black and white, into prostitution.
>
> The Bill is presented as achieving equality by proposing to arrest both prostitute women and their clients. Equalising men down to women's low level extends rather than does away with racism and sexism.

This letter was published on the same day as the government spokesman was presenting the Bill in the Lords. In terms of opposition to the Bill in the House, the concern had now shifted from innocent MPs going about their business to innocent peers. The Labour peer, Lord Mishcon, stressed that if they were not careful in the way that they legislated, peers might find themselves being accused in a magistrates' court and it would be of little consolation to them or their families when the court said there was insufficient evidence to convict. Reputations could be killed in a moment by things of that kind. Any discussion about the wider implications for black working-class communities was either non-existent or not reported upon.

How were the public informed of the passage of the legislation by the British press? On 6 July the following is the totality of the reporting in the four popular newspapers in the study:

CRAWLERS CURBED

TORY MP Janet Fookes won final Commons approval for her new law against kerb crawlers.

(Daily Mail)[68]

No further material on kerb-crawling was traced until the following report in the *Star*.[69] It again illustrates how the serious concerns of the opposition which had been muted in the press about the use of entrapment was not questioned in this report. It revealed how the more limited existing legislation was being used:

KERB-CRAWLERS LAND IN POLICE SEX TRAP
Decoy WPc Lynn nets 14 drivers

PRETTY Lynn Palmer had motorists queuing up to chat her up for sex in a red-light district.

But the randy men got more than they bargained for.

For dark-haired Lynn, a woman police constable, was the decoy in a major crackdown on kerb-crawlers.

And 14 drivers who approached her appeared in court yesterday.

For two weeks Lynn posed as a prostitute in Bournemouth's notorious Knyveton Road . . . and detectives swooped as, one after another, the men aged 19 to 56 and from al! over the country, pulled up to ask Lynn for sexual services.

Police acted . . . after at least a dozen complaints from women residents in the area about kerb-crawlers making sexual suggestions to them.

The 14 men, most of them dressed in smart suits, were bound over to be of good behaviour for 12 months.

They were summoned under a 600-year-old Act for "disturbing a passer-by".

The new Sexual Offences Act does not come into force for another month . . . and he warned that more clampdowns could be on the way.

"If people persist in kerb-crawling in that area they run the risk of approaching a policewoman", he said.

And Mr Smith revealed that officers had noted the registration numbers of more than 120 cars whose drivers had shown 'abnormal interest' in women in Knyveton Road during the two-week operation.

It would be interesting to know what reaction a report of this kind would have brought forth if this news story had appeared in the *Guardian*, but few real cases are brought to the notice of *Guardian* readers. In contrast, real cases are brought to the notice of readers of popular newspapers but without the background of the general issues which cases of this kind actually raise.

A local evening newspaper may often be a half-way house between a popular national daily and a quality national daily, in the sense that while its style and news coverage is usually more akin to popular newspapers, its readership may have a wider range, including those who may be concerned about the implications of the coverage of certain topics. In August, for example, the *Coventry Evening Telegraph*[70] produced several issues specifically focusing on some of the vice problems of the local area. A reader noted that a report on the court appearance of a 19-year-old prostitute featured a large photograph of the woman:

apart from pandering to the prurient interest of some of your readers, what other justifications can there be for such a grotesque report? Why don't you photograph and publish the kerb crawlers? Why don't you reveal their identities? Why do newspapers like the EVENING TELEGRAPH make the woman the subject of their spotlight? . . . I should imagine, as a result of your publicity, potential kerb crawlers must be driving to Coventry from all over the place.

On this occasion the newspaper could hardly make derisory remarks about women's pressure groups as the plea had come from a male reader.

No more was heard of kerb-crawling in the popular press until 16 September, when it was announced that the kerb-crawling law came into force that day. In fact, the *Coventry Evening Telegraph* had anticipated the event by focusing on the Act a few days earlier:[71] **Red light law aims to halt kerb crawlers**. It was portrayed as coming to the rescue of Hillfield's streets, where men in cars looking for prostitutes often proposition non-prostitute women. It also outlined the other provisions in the Act relating to the rise in maximum sentences for attempted rape and indecent assault. Senior Coventry police officers were said to be currently studying the new Act and deciding how best to implement it in the city. A spokesman said: "We want to ensure we are making full use of the new powers".

The national newspapers briefly mentioned the new law on the day that it came into force. The only popular newspaper which focused on the new Act as a full-page feature was the *Star*[72] where, headlined *STAR GIRLS TEST THE NEW SEX PEST LAW:* **KERB CRAWLERS . . . YOUR NUMBER'S UP**, it had two reporters taking a walk along the streets of Bayswater in West London just prior to the new Act coming into force. They maintained that "most curb [sic] crawlers thought the new Sexual Offences Act 1985 was nothing to worry about". In their article they quoted a Home Office spokeswoman, who said: "Some people's lives have been made a misery by kerb crawlers. We hope this much stronger law and the publicity from papers like the *Star* will cut down their numbers". However, the only other item traced in the *Star* mentioning this offence during the rest of the year occurred in the gossip column of the 'Peter Tory Diary' in November,[73] where the interest in the woman involved in promoting the Bill continued. The Diary noted that "Janet Fookes, the scourge of kerb-crawlers, and a lady not always approving the ways of men, tells us with apparent pleasure how she spent two nights sleeping in a tent with seven marines in the Arctic Circle . . . . " This piece demonstrates how Miss Fookes will now remain with the stereotype of "scourge of the kerb-crawlers". No serious attempt was made by any of the newspapers to investigate how this new Act was working in the residential areas of concern. Indeed, the only comment on the effectiveness of the law or otherwise came in a letter in the London *Evening Standard*[74] from Gigi Turner of the English Collective of Prostitutes in the aftermath of the murder of the prostitute, Jackie Murray (see Chapter 4), where she stressed that they had pointed out

> how kerb-crawling legislation has endangered prostitute women by cutting the time they have to check out who the client is. We have said in our campaign against this legislation that it could lead to murder and unfortunately this is what has happened.

A week later,[75] a correspondent responded that the point of kerb-crawling legislation

> was not brought in for the benefit of prostitutes but so that people going about their business generally, not touting for sexual trade, would not be harassed. Quite obviously prostitutes would be only too pleased to have men kerb-crawling, it is one of the ways they get their trade.

Another letter took a less pleasant stance by pointing out that the English Collective of Prostitutes

> and some other rather odd groups such as Wages Due Lesbians and Housewives in Dialogue, are all housed at a place called The King's Cross Women's Centre, and they are all maintained at the ratepayers' expense by the GLC and Labour-controlled Camden council.

This correspondent felt that no more need be said about the argument put forward by Gigi Turner. So this dismissive letter ended this brief discussion of the effectiveness of the Act.

In fact, the London *Evening Standard* was the only newspaper to comment further on kerb-crawling during the year. The headline **Kerb crawlers curbed**[76] may have encouraged informed readers to believe that the new law was actually working effectively. However, the text shows that effective results could be achieved in rather less dramatic ways than the new legislation.

KERB CRAWLERS CURBED

An experimental traffic scheme aimed at reducing the nuisance caused by kerb crawlers seeking prostitutes has been voted a success.

Finsbury Park residents who took part in a Hackney council

opinion survey have told councillors they wish to retain the
Brownswood ward scheme.

It was introduced on an experimental basis in January to "reduce
circulating traffic associated with prostitution".

Hackney council's public services committee has agreed to make
the scheme permanent subject to minor amendments.

(London *Evening Standard*)

Such a success story remained of only local interest, for it has none of
the ingredients to attract national coverage. Solving a problem without
drama is not news. Perhaps more surprising is that during the rest of the
year there was only one court case which directly mentioned the new
Act. This seemed to have all the features which tend to fascinate the
popular papers, but at the outset it was identified only by the *Guardian*.[77]
Barrister faces kerb-crawl charge involved a named part-time Crown
Court judge being prosecuted under section one of the Sexual Offences
Act 1985. While the details of the alleged offence were not released, the
full public career of the named barrister was. The media become
interested only in individual transgressions of the law, particularly when
professional people are involved. Examining the effectiveness of the
law against the objectives set remains a very low priority.

This brief incursion into the coverage of a law change illustrates that
the public are poorly served by the media in general. There is very little
information provided which focuses on the issues raised by a possible
change in legislation. What is perhaps even more surprising is that when
the law is passed there is virtually no proclamation to the public that a
new law is now in place. The Home Office spokeswoman who hoped
that "this much stronger law and publicity from papers like the *Star* will
cut down [the] numbers [of kerb-crawlers]"[78] had little initial help from
the source of the popular press. In fact, this 'stronger law' creeps on to
the statute books almost unnoticed by the general public and the publicity must await 'a few solitary examples' of the famous or near-famous
to provide news of this law change. If it is a significant change in the law
and part of the general process of the strengthening of police powers –
and, after all, the police spokesman suggested, "We want to ensure we
are making full use of the new powers"[79] – the public heard very little
about it through the media.

Conclusion

The cases of kerb-crawling and compensation for victims of sexual
assault show that the law on sex crimes is under constant review and
revision at the margins. However, the press reporting of attempts to
change the law on kerb-crawling by statute and that on compensation to

victims of sexual assault by reforming case law is very limited. The issue we have been concerned to raise is partly that the reports prioritise salacious details at the expense of the serious issues. But more seriously, the reports provide a very biased account of the possible effectiveness of these forms of change.

In the case of compensation, the papers drew greater attention to the development of the legal possibility of suing the attacker than to that of the defective conduct of the Criminal Injuries Compensation Board. This was problematic, since the attacker is rarely going to have the money to hand over to the woman he attacked. Hence this procedure is irrelevant as far as most women are concerned. In those circumstances where the attacker does have some resources this may well be in the form of the house that he shares with his wife, who would then be penalised for her husband's crimes. Far less attention was paid to the option open to all, rather than some, of the survivors of these attacks, namely an appeal to the Criminal Injuries Compensation Board. Interest in state compensation to such women as compared to private compensation by the criminal was much less marked in the press. This was despite the fact that the sums dispensed by the CICB were significantly lower than the ones declared by the press to be too low when won by private suit.

The press reporting of the introduction of the law on kerb-crawling was again limited, salacious and biased. The opposition to the Bill was reported only if it came from middle-class white men and not when it came from black or working-class communities. This was a case in which there were complex divisions between women and also in issues about racialised policing, neither of which were adequately explored. The views of prostitute women who wanted the opportunity to check out their potential customers were given space only in letters, while concerns about giving the police powers which they might use as a new form of the old discredited 'sus' law, which had allowed the police to stop and search on suspicion of an offence being committed, and which had been shown to be used disproportionately against black male youth, were largely ignored by the press.

In short, even when the issue being reported is that of changes in the law, rather than a sensational instance of sexual violence, the press were not able to provide space for the views of the various constituencies affected. It is not only that the issues were trivialised and sensationalised, but also that the only reasoned account reported was that of white middle-class men.

Chapter eight

Conclusion

Rape and other forms of sexual assault are now matters of public debate. Most newspapers today, unlike most of those in the 1950s and 1960s, publish reports of these crimes and of the issues around them. Popular daily newspapers, in particular, have dramatically increased their coverage over the years since 1951, with the largest increase coming in the mid-1970s. It is no longer a subject read by only a small and very specific audience in the pages of the *News of the World*, but is a regular topic in the mass circulation dailies.

Why is this happening? We have pointed to the increased politicisation of sexual violence, and in particular the challenge to the police and judicial response to this violence. Feminists have argued forcefully that these issues should be taken seriously and have been successful in placing them on the political agenda. Demands have included the reform of the treatment of women who have suffered sexual assault, but more importantly have included demands for wider structural change in order to eliminate the circumstances under which considerable numbers of men want and feel entitled to be violent towards women. These demands have met with a varied response. For instance, the police improved their practices in relation to women who have suffered sexual assault, though the extent and importance of these changes have yet to be sufficiently evaluated. However, the response has not been a simple one of agreeing to feminist demands, but has entailed the assertion of an alternative perspective on sex crime. In this latter view sex crimes are dreadful, but rare, and are best dealt with by an increased law and order effort, rather than wider social reform. The newspapers in our study exemplify this latter response. They clearly state how dreadful such crimes are, while casting doubt on the pervasiveness of such attacks. Indeed they call upon public revulsion of such crimes with their sensational headlines. Yet most attacks are not considered to merit front-page treatment, and reports which suggest that sex crime is widespread are mercilessly trashed. The popular press cultivates a belief that a stronger law and order response is the best way to beat such crime, despite evidence from rape survivors and official crime surveys that this is not what most women (or men) want. Indeed the nature of the press reports, which are supposed to be sympathetic to the plight of such 'victims' is such as to render them still further distressed.

The problems with the press reports can be summarised under four headings: seeking the sensational, producing a cascade effect, embracing a narrow definition of sex crime, and information and explanation.

Seeking the sensational

The major theme in the coverage of sex crime is the construction of the sex beast, the sex fiend or the sex monster. We have indicated that the manifestation of the sex beast in florid form does not happen that often in the media, but the endeavour is consistently geared up to sponsoring the arrival of the sex fiend on the national scene. In this respect the national press differs substantially from the local press. The local press is dealing much more closely with the everyday reality of rape, while the popular dailies coalesce the fantasy of the video nasty with real life.

Only a few major sex offenders dominate at every juncture, whether it be the search, the arrest, the trial, the aftermath of the trial, the prison sentence, or the parole decision. A few get massive coverage at only certain points of the process. Nevertheless, a pattern becomes clear.

In focusing upon the search, the emphasis is on serious sexual attacks and sexual murders by unknown assailants. The sex beast imagery is widespread and the popular press generate the excitement of 'the chase'. The man is an animal who must be trapped and caught. In contrast, there is rarely the need to search for assailants who are known to the victim, so the media rarely follows in these types of assaults, at least until the public trial, compounding the general neglect of attackers known to the woman.

Only a few court cases each year get massive coverage across most newspapers. But for the survivor, of course, painful exposure in one newspaper may be more than enough. Nevertheless, the widespread coverage of a few cases provide the messages of the court arena for all those who have not personally experienced the court interaction. The interest in the court arena is largely built upon contested cases. The woman's behaviour is often challenged and all women, whether they are 'chaste' or not, have to endure a distressing experience in the witness box. Curiously the 'sex beast' imagery of the search stage largely disappears in the reports of the court interaction. In fact, the 'sex beast' often pleads guilty on account of the overwhelming evidence; the court proceedings are often minimal, or, in a contested case, the defence counsel will re-direct the focus upon the survivors of the sexual assault. Even the prosecution at times seems reluctant to emphasise that the victim is a free agent who is entitled to participate fully in life without the fear of being sexually assaulted.

From the widespread media reporting of the spectacular rape trials, women seem to have only two roles imposed upon them to play in a trial – a whore or a virgin – and yet, whether experienced or inexperienced in sexual activity, women are portrayed as "asking for it". Contested cases may well be where the boundaries of "acceptable" behaviour are being tested – acceptable to the male-defined courts, that is. Whether women can enter certain territories generally inhabited by males without being regarded as available to any man is a classic question. Whether young girls can return from a disco late in the evening without being accompanied by a 'safe' male is another. In seeking justice the 'virgin' tag is still an important one. The message of these trials, as represented in the press, is that women may well be culpable. There is little room for alternative readings of such reports.

After the sentence has been imposed, a different pattern emerges. The 'sex beast' is resurrected. The focus of the popular newspapers on the sensational story which they have helped to create during the search is perhaps inevitable, but we need to recognise that there are at least two serious consequences. The massive concentration on a few cases where the person has been sexually assaulted by a total stranger has a cascade effect on all those connected with the sensational cases and provides for the public a dangerously narrow version of sex crime.

Producing a cascade effect

The lives of everyone even remotely connected with a case which is made the focus of massive newspaper coverage are 'at risk'. Distortion, exaggeration and bias are all used to maintain the momentum of a secondary 'trial'.

The 'sex beast' often pleads guilty and this may lead to further distortions. The Member of Parliament for Ealing raised an interesting point in the House[1] in relation to the atrocity of the Ealing Vicarage case, which caused widespread outrage:

> reflect on the victim's position. . . . because the rapist pleads guilty, the full details of the case are not brought before the judge, the victim's evidence is not heard and the case is thus not open to full assessment by the judge.

The danger is that in making a speech in mitigation, the defence counsel may reflect adversely on the character of the rape survivor and others connected with the case and they have no chance of rebuttal.

Extensive coverage in the immediate aftermath of the trial provides another set of victims who may suffer the consequences of publicity. There seem to be no limits to the extent that the popular press will seek to provide background material to titillate their readership. Previous wives, lovers and mistresses, who may be settled in new relationships, are probed about all aspects of their earlier existence with a notorious sex fiend.

Embracing a narrow definition of sex crime

The problems for those involved in any sensational case reported in the media may be immense, but such cases have even more serious consequences. The media coverage provides the definition of the 'normal sexual assault'. Sex crime for the media is essentially when a woman or girl is sexually assaulted by a total stranger. In contrast, the importance of other kinds of sexual assaults is subtly undermined in various ways by the focused reporting of the media. Most seriously, contested cases in the courts, which attract considerable media coverage, tend to be those where the defendants try to construct some kind of claim from their previous knowledge of the victim that she consented to what happened. The media contribute to the notion that such sexual assaults are 'abnormal' and less damaging. In fact, it can be cogently argued that rapes and sexual assaults by men known to the victim are potentially more psychologically damaging than the serious sexual assaults of the stranger. The former involves the breach of trust, which may be more traumatic. This is why the sexual abuse of children by their fathers may be particularly deeply disturbing for the child in the long term. If one cannot trust one's parents, then whom can one trust? In the two compensation claims for sexual assault discussed in Chapter 7, the judge recognised this argument and said one of the reasons that the damages in each case were aggravated was because both women knew their attacker. In contrast, in considering the media coverage of sexual assault, the message consistently comes across that the only 'real' rape or 'real' sexual assault is committed by a stranger. This is a serious distortion perpetrated by the media and has widespread effect.

A further narrowing of the image of the sex criminal is achieved by the reporting of an even smaller number of offenders after conviction and imprisonment.

Information and explanation

The coverage of serious academic work in the general area of sexual violence is poorly reported in the media. This may, of course, be partly the fault of the academic community in failing to present its findings in a coherent manner for inclusion in newspapers read by the general public. Hence, the burden for explaining the general lack of serious interest in such material should perhaps not fall entirely on the media. However, the 'authoritative' material which was included in newspapers was extraordinarily selective and certainly not always presented in a considered and dispassionate manner. In particular, it was quite apparent how some serious work carried out by feminists was cursorily dismissed and, on occasion, ridiculed. While this was perhaps not an unexpected outcome in relation to some of the more popular newspapers, it was also quite evident that what are regarded as the 'quality' newspapers sometimes failed to understand the general arguments of the women's movement in relation to sex crime. If a newspaper, such as the *Guardian*, sometimes seems to think that feminists are simply concerned with more sympathetic police questioning of raped women and that they readily embrace tougher sentencing for rapists as the most appropriate solution for the sex crime problem, their message has clearly not yet been taken on board. Such concerns about the protection of women in the community are rarely addressed in a serious manner by any newspaper. The issue of rape prevention is either trivialised or expressed in terms of women avoiding potentially dangerous situations rather than providing an environment in which women can move about without fear.

The popular newspapers – particularly the *Sun* and the *Star* – are primarily concerned with orchestrating public outrage regarding the sentencing of rapists and are just not interested in focusing on the wider issues of the causes of sex crime. There is a lack of analysis beyond the most simplistic observations. For example, the judge's pronouncements in The Fox case, where he maintained that the viewing of pornographic films provided the explanation for this ghastly series of crimes, were embraced enthusiastically by all the newspapers. A detached, considered, let alone critical, analysis of such a narrow and simplistic explanation is totally lacking. Instead of a pornographic film or 'video nasty', the popular newspapers themselves provided a 'printed nasty', displaying all the unpleasant accoutrements of this notorious offender. Ironically if these newspapers actually reflected on the type of explanation offered by the judge and which they so readily espoused, then they would recognise that the explicit illustrations on the pages of these newspapers would provide the very fodder required for the 'sons' of The Fox.

When law changes on sex crime are being proposed in Parliament, we found that the general approach of the media is essentially of two kinds – trivialise or ignore the debate. Only by the occasional letter to the *Guardian* could at least some of the public begin to grasp some of the wider political dimensions of the proposed sexual offences legislation which occurred in 1985. Apart from these letters there was no recognition in the popular newspapers that a link could be drawn between the Sexual Offences Bill and the more overtly repressive legislation of the Thatcher government. However, it is perhaps not surprising that what would be characterised as a left-wing critique should remain missing from the pages of all but one newspaper. However, even the modest concern about the Bill expressed by the official Opposition received very poor coverage. In fact, the law on kerb-crawling crept on to the statute books almost unnoticed by the general public. What was more surprising was the lack of information – apart from one or two newspapers – when the new law came into place. It would not be unreasonable for any member of the public, on being arrested for the new sex offences, to plead – undoubtedly to no avail – ignorance of the law.

For a brief moment the issue of compensation for the victims of sexual crime came into prominence when two women sued their assailant for damages in the civil court. Again the public could only patch together the issues involved. The interest in this successful compensation claim – proclaimed in a sensational way by newspapers – faded within a month without making any serious impact on routine questions of compensation for victims of sexual assault. However, it did poignantly illustrate the underlying political dimensions of questions of this kind. Newspapers generally supportive of the Conservative government – and particularly the *Star* – began to highlight the damages claim as a way of punishing the offender and 'his' family, and so removing some of the burden of meeting compensation claims from the state system embodied in the Criminal Injuries Compensation Board. The *Daily Mirror*, in contrast and almost alone, indicated the very special circumstances of this case, in that most sexual assailants would not have the money to pay out damages. The *Daily Mirror* and the *Guardian* addressed their concern towards the level of payments made routinely by the Criminal Injuries Compensation Board.

Forms of regulation of press reporting

The three main forms of regulation of the press are, firstly, those embodied in the Sexual Offences Amendment 1976 Act, secondly, the Press Council administered Code of Practice, and thirdly, the libel laws. In the first, the press is expressly refused permission to print the name of the raped woman. The 1976 Act also sought to restrict the extent to which a woman's prior sexual history could be used as admissible evidence in court, thus indirectly affecting the material available to the press to publish. In the second, the press is restrained by its own professional Code of Practice not to misrepresent or mislead the public. In the third, the press faces financial penalties if anyone successfully sues a newspaper through the civil courts for defamation of character.

What are the implications for the media reporting of rape? Firstly, there is the issue of whether the raped woman is able to maintain her anonymity as intended under the 1976 Act. The letter of this law was strictly kept in both the 1978 and 1985 sample of newspapers. In 1978 we found only one reported case where the judge used his discretion to revoke the anonymity on the application of the defence. In that case Judge Miskin agreed with counsel that the defence was entitled to seek to attempt to prove that the victim was a prostitute. In 1982, a woman named during a rape trial accused the judge of ruining her life ("**I thought my secret was safe**", says woman named by court, *Daily Mail*[2]), so demonstrating that rape survivors are not always reconciled when exceptions are made. However, during 1985 there were no rape victims named during the court proceedings or, indeed, afterwards. The exception was the continued blatant naming of the young woman raped by Arthur Hutchinson in the Wedding Party massacre, when Hutchinson's appeal was being considered. This had been allowed by the judge during the original court proceedings, but it was evident that the practice of naming the victim in the subsequent discussion of the case continued quite unnecessarily.

However, the spirit of the law is broken by the publication of details which may well lead to the victim's identification. This is especially the case where there is sustained coverage (a minority of cases) and where there is local reporting (very common). The details may well involve age, town, occupation, marital status and number of children which, in any but the largest of cities will enable many who know the rape victim to identify her. For instance, one brief report of the first rape reported in 1985 named the town and hospital where the raped woman worked as a doctor. Later reports gave her age and marital status. This information was sufficient to identify her to those who worked in that hospital. In the example of the Ealing Vicarage case, the intrusive reporting by the media prior to the trial ensured that Parliament maintained its interest in extending the anonymity provision backwards to the time that an offence was alleged to have taken place to prevent reoccurrences. The Criminal Justice Act 1988 now protects a woman from being named or photographed from the time of her making the complaint, not merely during and after the court hearing.

Interestingly the press follows a voluntary code of keeping the names of survivors of sexual assaults confidential, although the Act does not actually cover this type of violence, only rape, though again the press may print identifying details.

A growing feature is the identification of many others in some way associated with the case being revealed in the press, exposing them to abuse and humiliation. This is often the case in relation to the women associated with a rapist, such as his wife, ex-wife, ex-lovers, mother, sisters and so on. These women are then linked to the rapist in such a way that they also can become the subject of abuse. So while some women have undoubtedly benefited from the non-publication of their names as rape survivors – although this provision is not as comprehensive a protection as was intended by the legislation – the ripples of the media coverage of a celebrated rapist nowadays disturb more and more women's lives.

It is difficult to estimate the effect of the recent change removing the anonymity of the rape defendant until conviction. The discussion has largely centred on why the accused should have this special provision in contrast to other defendants. We have shown that, prior to the trial, the relatives of some defendants were being harassed and in effect identified. The wife of The Fox was in a psychiatric hospital owing to the shock of the impending trial. Further misery by being identified by name to a national audience could only have added to her misery without any good reason. It is quite evident that some newspapers, such as the *Star*, have the view – expressed in relation to possible compensation to rape victims – that the offenders' families should suffer the consequences as well. It might be considered that, since wives are not guilty of their husbands' crimes, they have enough to cope with without suffering the additional burden of publicity prior to trial.

The 1976 Act tried to restrict the gratuitous and quite unnecessary display of women's sexual histories. Adler [3] has forcefully demonstrated how the 1976 Act has failed to live up to the expressed hopes in this respect. Yet against Parliament's intentions, sexual histories are revealed in court and sexual innuendoes abound in the court interaction. Inevitably the media coverage reflects this continuing problem. As Adler showed, while the subtleties of the court interaction, which are often so upsetting to the victim, may not be routinely captured by the media, the vividness of how the victim may be seriously disadvantaged in the court proceedings will not have escaped the notice of the general reader.

In the mid-1970s over one-half of the rape reports in newspapers named the victim of rape. Now that practice has been almost totally eliminated. Where the name is publicised it is the result of a specific court decision, which then results in reporting by the media.

The second restraint on the media is that of their own Code of Practice. This is supposed to ensure a degree of honesty and accuracy in the newspapers. It is administered by the Press Council and is essentially voluntary. So, for example, there are very few cases where the victim of an indecent assault is named in the press reports, despite the absence of statutory requirement for this. This voluntary practice is encouraged by the Press Council. However, the very few occasions where this reticence was not observed involved sensational cases which had a considerable blaze of publicity; this undermines the recognition by potential victims that the rather more savoury practice of withholding the names of victims in cases of sexual assault has grown up. It would need very little effort by the press to ensure that this practice was observed as a general rule. The current exceptions seem quite unnecessary and, with goodwill, could easily be avoided without statutory control.

The majority of complaints to the Press Council do not lead to a successful conclusion for the complainant. The case has to be extreme for the council to intervene, and even then little is won except a small statement of apology printed in the newspaper. In the year following our study (1986), of the 1,158 complaints made to the Press Council only 118 came to adjudication, of which 47 were upheld, that is, only 4 per cent were finally upheld.[4] The need for a committee[5] into the intrusion of the press suggests that concerns are much more widespread than these figures suggest. However, there are some instances where the making of a complaint does have an effect but it is beyond the scope of the present study to provide a definitive evaluation of their role.

Our study suggested that there was a disproportionate use of photographs when black offenders were convicted of rape. The use of photographs seemed to assist a subliminal message that rapists are disproportionately black men. It is impossible to be definitive about this, for we did not have the information about the race of all offenders convicted of rape, or even of those where there was a report in a newspaper. The Press Council has stressed that a person's race should be included in newspaper reports only where it has some bearing on the story being told; recently the Press Council upheld a complaint that it was improper of the *Daily Telegraph* to report the colour of a rape gang when this had no relevance to the report. The newspaper

carried a court report saying that a man, who was forced to watch his wife being raped and then made to have sexual intercourse with her himself, saw one of the black rapists jailed for a total of 12 years.[6]

The Press Council "said that an irrelevant and prejudicial description tends to exacerbate hostility against minority groups".[7] Similarly, in reporting the multiple rape of two 16-year-old girls by a gang of youths in Brixton, the council ruled that the race of the gang and its victims was irrelevant on the basis that no evidence was given to the council that the colour of the gang or its victims was relevant to the crime. There have been several Press Council judgments with regard to the irrelevance of race in court reports.

In a complaint that was upheld, the *Daily Mirror* was accused of not identifying the colour either of defendants or victims while the case was continuing but that it did so in its final report. In defence, the editor of the *Daily Mirror* "said that after conviction the paper was entitled to identify the accused, including the publication of their pictures". The Press Council, following previous judgments, ruled that "people's race or colour should only be introduced in prejudicial contexts where it was relevant to the story."[8]

The Press Council is geared up to examining the blatant individual excesses of newspapers, but the steady drip or gradual erosion in which more subliminal messages are being put across does not easily fall within its remit. The more general concern which is being raised here is that there is no mechanism to examine whether a disproportionate number of photographs of black rapists are being used more routinely and not simply in blatantly prejudicial contexts where complaints of abuse may quickly arise. In other words, while sensational abuse can be captured by current methods, the more systematic, low-key, routinised, institutionalised abuse is unlikely to be exposed to serious regulation.

The success or otherwise of the Press Council is beyond the scope of our study. Certainly the previous Chair of the Press Council – set up to preserve the freedom of the British press but also to act as the conscience of the press and to uphold the legitimate expectations of the public – warned that newspapers that "treat [Press Council] rulings cynically, [or] disregard it or abuse it, put at risk the continuance of a system of voluntary regulation". Castigating in particular the reaction of the *Sun* to an adverse ruling, Sir Zelman Cowen stressed that this struck at the very heart of the Press Council's role and functions and that if newspapers persisted in such behaviour "they will surely jeopardize what the Council characterised as 'the future of self control by British newspapers'. If this goes, it cannot be imagined that nothing will be put in its place." [9]

The third restraint on the press is that of the libel laws. If a newspaper defames a person's character it can be sued for damages through the civil courts. If the complaint is upheld the courts can provide a significant punishment on the newspaper in the form of a very substantial payment of damages to the complainant. One recent case is that in which Jeffrey Archer won several hundred thousand pounds for being accused of having sex with a prostitute woman. However, the high cost of legal fees means that few people can afford to challenge newspaper reports through the courts.

Do then sufficient mechanisms exist to restrain the media's reporting of rape? We have identified three: one legal, where the Crown would prosecute; a second which is a voluntary Code of Practice, where the injured party takes the initiative; the third is another legal device, where the injured party takes the action. The first, the legal restraint on publishing the names of rape victims, is the most successful. It could be extended to cover related assaults and associated parties, and to include specified identifying detail. The issue of the anonymity of the injured party in court cases is already established where it can be maintained that they would suffer significantly from publicity. Interestingly this is not usually called censorship, although this is quite clearly what it is. It is a state-maintained blackout on certain information.

The Press Council's Code of Practice is somewhat feeble. This is not surprising, given the composition of the Press Council and the lack of teeth given to it. However, other professions do have tight and effective codes of practice (e.g. doctors) which are strictly adhered to, so it is not inherent in a profession's code of practice that it must be so feeble. However, it is not clear that journalism would ever constitute a profession in a similar way, so that a code of practice could be effective. However, we must return an open verdict on the Press Council, since this was not a major focus of our study.

The third restraint, that of the libel laws, does have some degree of effectivity for those who can afford the legal fees. This barrier is not insuperable if either legal aid were made available for such cases (though that is unlikely), or if solicitors took cases on a payment-by-results basis (which is more likely in these days of enterprise culture).

Conclusion

Censorship or no censorship is not the issue. Rape reports are already subject to constraints. The question which already exists is that of how much restraint, not whether there should be any.

However, all these three mechanisms deal only with individual cases, and not with the most serious problem, that of the selection of only a few unusual cases for media treatment, together with the selection of a limited number of themes through which the story is told. For the more significant issue then, these mechanisms are unlikely, even if further reformed, to provide a solution. That could happen only if either the goals of newspaper reporting were changed towards genuine information away from cheap sensation for readers, or if the nature of rape discourse were to be changed for other reasons.

To an optimistic observer there are, within the newspapers themselves, different voices. They are not uniformly insensitive and sensationalist. They contain within their own pages their own contradictions. Some are better informed as to the implications of the processing of sexual assault for women than others. As we have seen, the better informed accounts often come from women columnists. They tend to understand the difficulties and complexities facing women who have suffered male violence in gaining justice better than the (male) writers of the headlines or the leaders. However, they do not usually write in the places of most impact on the front pages and in the leader columns.

Why do newspapers represent sexual assault in such an unrealistic manner? The imperatives of journalism in a 'free market' might appear to explain the creation of such a myth. However, this is not sufficient for three reasons. Firstly, not all newspapers treat sex crime as a front-page soap opera; in particular the local papers have a more restrained and factual mode of reporting, despite facing just as intense pressures for survival. Secondly, it does not explain why such a bizarre notion of sex crime has such a popular resonance, given that it is so out of line with any recorded data. Thirdly, it does not explain why the search for the sex fiend took off as a regular headline news story in the popular press at this particular historical juncture, and not before.

It is this last point which is particularly important. Newspapers did not always portray such a view of rape, nor to such an extent. The regular presence of the sex fiend on the front pages is a phenomenon of the 1970s and 1980s.

The reporting deals in a particularly conservative way with the debate on the policy response to rape, systematically hyping the significance of longer prison sentences within a law and order framework, despite the fact that this is not the preferred solution of either the general public or the survivors of such attacks themselves. The press highlights the race of the rapists in those instances in which they are black, feeding the classic law and order thesis that black and working-class men pose a threat to the social fabric through their criminality. While it was feminists who put sexual violence on to the political agenda of the 1970s and 1980s, leading sections of the press are backing a conservative reinterpretation of both the nature of the problem and its solution. While for feminists male sexual violence is quite common, and a wide social solution is necessary to give women real security, the conservative response suggests that it is the product of a few sex fiends, and that the solution is to lock them away for a long time. The evidence does not support the view that sex crime is a rare phenomenon caused by a handful of sex monsters, nor is the preferred solution of most rape victims that of long prison sentences. But such evidence is not welcome in the press.

Rape and other forms of sexual assault have become politicised over the last few years. It is now an issue for public debate as well as private pain. This is better than the previous silence, when even the word 'rape' was not used in newspapers. But the nature of the reporting obscures the real nature of sexual violence: it underestimates the extent of these crimes, and reports on unusual cases, for instance those in which the rapist is a stranger, and serial rapists.

The increase of such press reporting illustrates the increasing controversy of official means of dealing with sexual violence, even as it attempts to hold back the tide.

Notes

1 Introduction

1 *Criminal Statistics, England and Wales 1987* (Cm. 498) London, HMSO.
2 *Criminal Statistics, England and Wales 1977* (Cmnd. 7289) London, HMSO; *Criminal Statistics, England and Wales 1987* (Cm. 498) London, HMSO.
3 ibid.
4 ibid.
5 ibid.
6 See Chapter 4.
7 For an account of popular conceptions of rape see S. Klemmack, H. Klemmack and L. David (1976) 'The social definition of rape', in M.J. Walker, J. Walker and S.L. Brodsky (eds) *Sexual Assault: The Victim and the Rapist*, Lexington, Mass., Lexington Books.
8 For discussions of women's fear of male violence see E.A. Stanko (1987) 'Typical violence, normal precaution: men, women and interpersonal violence in England, Wales, Scotland and the USA', in J. Hanmer and M. Maynard (eds) *Women, Violence and Social Control*, London, Macmillan; J. Hanmer and S. Saunders (1984) *Well-Founded Fear: A Community Study of Violence To Women*, London, Hutchinson.
9 For a discussion on the possible relationship between pornography and rape see A. Dworkin (1981) *Pornography*, London, Women's Press; S. Kappeller (1987) *The Pornography of Representation*, Cambridge, Polity Press; N.M. Malamuth and J.V.P. Check (1981) 'The effects of mass media exposure on acceptance of violence against women: a field experiment', *Journal of Research in Personality* 15, 436–46.
10 G. Geis (1978) 'The case of rape: legal restrictions on media coverage of deviance in England and America', in C. Winick (ed.) *Deviance and the Mass Media*, London, Sage.
11 Personal communication (Orjan Landelius, Swedish Embassy) 8 December 1987.

12 A. Hay, K. Soothill and S. Walby (1980) 'Seducing the public by rape reports', *New Society* 53, 924: 214–15.
13 Z. Adler (1987) *Rape on Trial*, London, Routledge & Kegan Paul.
14 D.J. West, C. Roy and F.L. Nichols (1978) *Understanding Sexual Attacks*, London, Heinemann.
15 M. Amir (1971) *Patterns in Forcible Rape*, Chicago, Ill., Chicago University Press; E. Wilson (1983) *What is To Be Done About Violence Against Women?*, Harmondsworth, Penguin.
16 L. Kelly (1989) *Surviving Social Violence*, London, Virago.
17 S. Brownmiller (1976) *Against Our Will: Men, Women and Rape*, Harmondsworth, Penguin; Hanmer and Saunders op. cit.; S. Jackson (1978) 'The social context of rape: sexual scripts and motivation', *Women's Studies International Quarterly* 1, 1, 27–38; Kelly, op. cit.; B. Toner (1977) *The Facts of Rape*, London, Hutchinson, pp. 9–37.
18 Kelly, op. cit.
19 N. Jouve Ward (1988) *The Street Cleaner*, London, Marion Boyars.
20 D. Cameron and E. Frazer (1988) *The Lust to Kill: A Feminist Investigation of Sexual Murder*, Cambridge, Polity Press.
21 See among others D. Rhodes and S. McNeil (eds) (1985) *Women Against Violence Against Women*, London, Onlywomen Press; London Rape Crisis Centre, *Sexual Violence: The Reality for Women*, London, Women's Press; V. Binney, G. Harkell and J. Nixon (1981) *Leaving Violent Men*, London, Women's Aid Federation England; Kelly, op. cit.
22 B. Campbell (1987) *Iron Ladies: Why Do Women Vote Tory?*, London, Virago.
23 ibid.
24 *DPP* v. *Morgan and others* (1975), 61 Cr.App.R.136.
25 (Criminal Law Revision Committee) p. 5 footnote 1:

Morgan and three other men spent the evening together. Morgan then invited the others to come home with him and have sexual intercourse with his wife, to whom they were unknown. They asserted, but he denied, that he told them she might struggle a bit because she was 'kinky' – but she would welcome intercourse with them. When they arrived at the house she was asleep in a bedroom with one of her sons, aged 11. Despite her violent struggles and shouts to her sons to call the police, she was forcibly subjected to sexual intercourse by all four men without her consent. When the case came to trial the defence of the three strangers was that the wife had actually consented to and enjoyed the sexual intercourse; alternatively, if she did not consent, that they genuinely believed that she did. The trial judge directed the jury that they were entitled to be acquitted only if their belief was genuine and it was based on reasonable grounds. All were convicted and appealed to the Court of Appeal and thence to the House of Lords on the ground that the belief did not have to be based on reasonable grounds.

26 Toner B., op. cit.

27 Geis seems to conflate these two separate cases in his text G. Geis
   (1978) 'The case of rape: legal restrictions on media coverage of
   deviance in England and America', in C. Winick (ed.) *Deviance and
   Mass Media*, Beverly Hills, Sage.
28 *Report of the Advisory Group on the Law on Rape* (known as 'The
   Heilbron Committee') Cmnd. 6352, London, HMSO.
29 H.C. Debates, vol. 875, col. 39 (17 June 1974, written answer to Mr
   Kilroy-Silk); col. 219 (20 June 1974, written answer to Mr Trotter; col.
   322 (24 June 1974, written answer to Mr Rose).
30 H.C. Debates, vol. 878, cols. 498–500 (30 July 1974).
31 *Report of the Advisory Group on the Law on Rape* (known as 'The
   Heilbron Committee') Cmnd. 6352, London, HMSO.
32 H.C. Debates, vol. 905, cols. 845–6 (13 February 1976).
33 H.C. Debates, vol. 911, col. 1,930.
34 H.C. Debates, vol. 917, cols. 887.
35 See for instance S. Edwards (1984) *Women on Trial*, Manchester
   University Press, p. 170.
36 J. Radford (1989) 'Police response to rape', *Rights of Women Bulletin*,
   Spring, 6–8.
37 ibid.
38 Radford, op. cit.; T. Gillespie (1989) 'Rape crisis workers and local
   agencies', Paper presented to BSA Violence Against Women Study
   Group, June, London.
39 ibid.
40 Radford, op. cit.
41 Gillespie, op. cit.
42 See for instance: Rhodes and McNeil, op. cit.; Kappeller, op. cit.; G.
   Chester and J. Dickey (eds) (1988) *Feminism and Censorship: The
   Current Debate*, London, Prism Press.
43 Chester and Dickey, op. cit.
44 There have been official government commissions examining this issue
   in both the USA and the UK. For academic work see for instance N.M.
   Malamuth and E. Donnerstein (eds) (1984) *Pornography and Sexual
   Aggression*, New York, Academic Press; Dworkin, op. cit.
45 Malamuth and Check, op. cit.
46 See for instance R. Coward (1982) 'Sexual violence and sexuality',
   Feminist Review, 11, 9–22.
47 Kappeller, op. cit.
48 ibid.
49 Chester and Dickey op. cit.
50 Mary Whitehouse has long called for controls on pornography.
51 P. Wagner (1982) 'The pornographer in the courtroom: trial reports
   about cases of sexual crimes and delinquencies as a genre of
   eighteenth-century erotica', in P.-G. Bouce (ed.) *Sexuality in
   Eighteenth-Century Britain*, Manchester University Press.
52 ibid., p. 131.
53 C. Pelham (1886) *The Chronicles of Crime; or The New Newgate
   Calendar*, London, Reeves & Turner (vols I and II).

54 ibid., p. v.
55 J. Goodman (1971) *Bloody Versicles*, Newton Abbot, David & Charles, p. 10.
56 A. Gamble (1988) *The Free Economy and the Strong State*, London, Macmillan.
57 S. Walby, A. Hay and K. Soothill (1983) 'The social construction of rape', *Theory, Culture and Society*, 2, 1, 86–98.
58 Coward, op. cit.; A. Kuhn (1982) *Women's Pictures: Feminism and Cinema*, London, Routledge.
59 D. McQuail (1977) 'The influence and effects of the mass media', in J. Curran *et al.* (eds) *Mass Communications and Society*, London, Edward Arnold.
60 Coward, op. cit.; Kuhn, op. cit.; Kappeller, op. cit.

2 The newspaper studies

1 K. Soothill and A. Jack (1975) 'How rape is reported', *New Society* 32, 663: 702–70; A. Hay, K. Soothill and S. Walby (1980) 'Seducing the public by rape reports', *New Society* 53, 924: 214–15; S. Walby, A. Hay and K. Soothill (1983) 'The social construction of rape', *Theory, Culture and Society* 2, 1: 86–98.

2 The number of copies examined of each newspaper were as follows: *Daily Mail* (309), *Daily Mirror* (300), *Star* (309), *Sun* (303), *The Times* (309), *Guardian* (306), *Observer* (52), *Mail on Sunday* (52), *Sunday Mirror* (52), *News of the World* (52), *Sunday People* (52), *Coventry Evening Telegraph* (307), *Lancashire Evening Post* (253), the London *Evening Standard* (255), *Lancaster Guardian* (52) and *Middlesex Chronicle* (52). In total the study comprised examining 3,015 newspapers. The discrepancy within categories is the outcome of the non-appearance of newspapers owing to an industrial dispute or distribution problems in the North of England. Of the local evening papers, the *Coventry Evening Telegraph* was the only one where we also considered the Saturday editions; until too late, we were not aware of a Saturday edition of the *Lancashire Evening Post*, but in fact it is of a totally different format from the weekday paper. Other newspapers were consulted in 1985, particularly when the sample newspapers did not appear, but this additional material was not collected on a systematic basis.

In the study of 1985 the previous neglect of local newspapers was partially overcome by including two other local evenings, so that we now had a local evening predominantly circulating in the south of England (the London *Evening Standard*), one circulating in the Midlands (*Coventry Evening Telegraph*) and one circulating in the north-west (*Lancashire Evening Post*). The two local weeklies from the north and south of England (*Lancaster Guardian* and *Middlesex Chronicle*) were included as examples of another kind of local coverage. The *Star* was included to ensure that we had all the popular dailies, while the *Daily Mail* was felt to be representative of the range of newspapers appealing more to the staid middle class, which had been missing from our previous studies. It was thought useful to supplement the quality dailies by adding the *Guardian* to provide a comparison for *The Times*, which we had suggested in our earlier study had begun to change the style and nature of its coverage of sex crime in the late 1970s. Finally, among the Sundays we added for the first time a quality Sunday newspaper, the *Observer*, as well as increasing the range of Sunday newspapers which appealed to other readerships by adding the *Mail on Sunday* and *Sunday Mirror* to our collection. The only two significant national dailies omitted from the study in 1985 and which had comparatively high circulation and readership figures were the *Daily Telegraph* and the *Daily Express*.

3 K. Soothill and A. Jack (1975) 'How rape is reported', *New Society* 32, 663: 702–4.

4 ibid., p. 703.

5 ibid.

6 ibid. Interestingly the words of this case taken from the earlier study are almost identical to one of the major rape trials in 1985; see Chapter 4 concerning the paratroopers' case.

7 A. Hay, K. Soothill and S. Walby (1980) 'Seducing the public by rape reports', *New Society* 53, 924: 214–15.

8 ibid.

9 Z. Adler (1987) *Rape on Trial*, London, Routledge & Kegan Paul.

10 *The Times*, 10 October 1978.

11 *News of the World*, 5 February 1978.

12 *The Times*, 14 October 1978.

13 Hay, Soothill and Walby, op. cit.

14 *New Society* (letters) 7 August 1980. The whole text of this letter is instructive:

Your tame sociologists from Lancaster may or may not have got their figures right, but their conclusions, as far as this company is concerned, are absurd.

Neither the *Sun* nor the *News of the World* has anything so grand as a 'marketing strategy' – whatever that is. Far from being sold 'as a package' they are encouraged to compete.

A glance at any of the mass of available statistics would have shown your contributors that the markets are very different, and the circulation overlap in no way significant.

At no time in the past ten years have the respective editors of these two newspapers been advised of any 'policy' – joint or otherwise – on the reporting of rape cases.

At no time in the past ten years have the editors ever even discussed between themselves which cases the other planned to cover.

No pressures have ever been brought to bear upon News Group's editors to operate other than instinctively, as good journalists should, in all matters of selection and presentation.

15 Hay, Soothill and Walby, op. cit.
16 However, we regarded a case which was reported in the evening newspapers and then also the next day in the national dailies as 'one day', for almost invariably the same set of facts were being rehearsed.
17 There was only one case where there was wide coverage on just *one* day. Here a three-man gang brutally raped a 21-year-old woman in St James's Park, London, while her 21-year-old boyfriend was forced to look on.
18 *Daily Mirror*, 10 January 1985.
19 *Sun*, 13 February 1985.
20 *Sun*, 28 March 1985.
21 *Sunday People*, 10 November 1985.
22 *Daily Mail*, 21 November 1985.
23 London *Evening Standard*, 29 November 1985.
24 *Middlesex Chronicle*, 9 May 1985.
25 ibid.
26 *Middlesex Chronicle*, 31 October 1985.
27 *Middlesex Chronicle*, 24 December 1985.
28 ibid.
29 *Daily Mirror*, 10 January 1985.
30 *Sunday Mirror*, 20 October 1985.

3 Seeking out the sex fiend

1 The discrepancies between media images and other evidence are explored more fully in S. Walby, A. Hay, K. Soothill (1983) 'The social construction of rape', *Theory, Culture and Society*, 2, 1, 89–94.
2 See S. Chibnall (1977) *Law-and-Order News*, London, Tavistock, especially pp. 146–54 and pp. 172–205 for an account of the relationship between crime reporters and police sources on other crimes.
3 During 1985 there was much made of the assertion that Malcolm Fairley, dubbed 'The Fox', was the first sex criminal caught by a computer. The development of computer techniques in investigating crime is increasingly evident. For example, after the brutal rape of an 18-year-old girl, the report noted that the man's description and the words he used during the attack were being checked through a computer at a special Rape HQ in Hendon, which was set up to catch two men who have carried out a total of twenty-seven rapes in London (*Daily Mail*, 2 December 1985).
4 *Daily Mail*, 15 February 1985.
5 *Daily Telegraph*, 2 July 1985 (this newspaper replaced the *Guardian* on this day owing to its non-appearance in the North of England).
6 *Mail on Sunday*, 27 October 1985.
7 *Star*, 21 and 22 August 1985.
8 London *Evening Standard*, 21 August 1985.
9 *Star*, 22 August 1985.
10 *Star*, 25 July 1985.

11 *Star*, 3 May 1985.
12 *Daily Mail*, 13 August 1985.
13 *Star*, 23 November 1985.
14 *Star*, 17 May 1985.
15 *Daily Mirror*, 16 October 1985.
16 *Sun*, 16 October 1985.
17 *Star*, 19 October 1985.
18 *Sun*, 19 October 1985.
19 *Star*, 20 February 1985.
20 See J.H. Brunvand (1983) *The Vanishing Hitchhiker: American Urban Legends and Their Meanings*, London, Picador, on 'Urban belief tales' and 'Urban legends'.
21 *Daily Mail*, 9 August 1985.
22 *Sunday Mirror*, 20 January 1985.
23 *Star*, 26 January 1985.
24 *Sun*, 28 November 1985.
25 *Star*, 23 November 1985.
26 *Sun*, 19 October 1985.
27 *Sun*, 13 May 1985.
28 D. Daiches (ed.) (1971) *The Penguin Companion to Literature*, Harmondsworth, Penguin.
29 *Star*, 25 July 1985.
30 *Star*, 26 July 1985.
31 *Daily Mail*, 1 March 1985.
32 *Sun*, 1 March 1985.
33 *Star*, 1 March 1985.
34 London *Evening Standard*, 8 March 1985.
35 *Sun*, 4 June 1985.
36 *The Times*, 4 June 1985.
37 *Sun*, 21 August 1985.
38 *Star*, 22 August 1985.
39 *Star*, 7 September 1985.
40 *Sunday People*, 29 September 1985.
41 *Sun*, 8 November 1985.
42 *Sun*, 27 February 1985.
43 BBC television *North-West Regional News*, 2 November 1987.

4 Sex crime in court

1 J. Radford (1984) ' "Womanslaughter": A licence to kill? The killing of Jane Asher', in P. Scraton and P. Gordon (eds) *Causes for Concern*, Harmondsworth, Penguin. It is a point also raised in D. Cameron and E. Frazer (1987) *The Lust to Kill: A Feminist Investigation of Sexual Murder*, Cambridge, Polity Press.
2 S. Lees (1989) 'Naggers, whores and libbers: provoking men to murder', mimeo, North London Polytechnic.
3 *Daily Mirror*, 31 October 1985.
4 *Daily Mirror*, 12 July 1985.

5 *Sun*, 24 January 1985.
6 *Coventry Evening Telegraph*, 26 June 1985.
7 *Star*, 27 July 1985.
8 ibid.
9 *Daily Mail*, 5 December 1985.
10 *Sun*, 3 December 1985.
11 *Daily Mirror*, 3 December 1985.
12 *Daily Mail*, 5 December 1985.
13 *Sun*, 5 December 1985.
14 ibid.
15 *Star*, 5 December 1985.
16 *Daily Mirror*, 5 December 1985.
17 *Lancashire Evening Post*, 10 December 1985.
18 *Sun*, 26 November 1985.
19 *Sun*, 6 December 1985.
20 London *Evening Standard*, 25 July 1985.
21 *Daily Mail*, 25 July 1985.
22 *Sun*, 25 July 1985.
23 *Daily Mail*, 27 July 1985.
24 *Daily Mail*, 20 July 1985.
25 *Daily Mirror*, 6 February 1985.
26 *Daily Mail*, 7 February 1985.
27 *Star*, 7 February 1985.
28 *Daily Mirror*, 9 February 1985.
29 *Daily Mail*, 9 February 1985.
30 *Sunday People*, 8 September 1985.
31 *Sunday People*, 28 April 1985.
32 *Sunday People*, 28 April 1985.
33 London *Evening Standard*, 5 September 1985.
34 *Sun*, 18 June 1985.
35 *Sun*, 20 June 1985.
36 *Middlesex Chronicle*, 8 August 1985.
37 *Daily Mirror*, 1 November 1985.
38 *Sun*, 26 November 1985.
39 *Star*, 26 November 1985.
40 *Daily Mirror*, 26 November 1985.
41 *Daily Mail*, 20 December 1985.
42 *Sun*, 20 December 1985.
43 London *Evening Standard*, 19 December 1985.
44 *Daily Mirror*, 20 December 1985.
45 *Star*, 20 December 1985.
46 *Sun*, 20 December 1985.
47 ibid.
48 *Sun*, 19 September 1985.
49 London *Evening Standard*, 3 December 1985.
50 *Star*, 4 December 1985.
51 The headings of these nine cases are an amalgam of various newspaper headlines relating to each case.

52 *Sun*, 27 February 1985.
53 ibid.
54 *Sun*, 2 February 1985.
55 *Star*, 2 February 1985.
56 *Coventry Evening Telegraph*, 26 February 1985.
57 *Sun*, 27 February 1985.
58 *Star*, 27 February 1985.
59 *Sun*, 27 February 1985.
60 *Star*, 27 February 1985.
61 *Daily Mail*, 27 February 1985.
62 *Star*, 2 March 1985.
63 *Sunday Mirror*, 3 March 1985.
64 *Sunday People*, 3 March 1985.
65 *News of the World*, 3 March 1985.
66 *Daily Mail*, 27 February 1985.
67 *Lancashire Evening Post*, 26 February 1985.
68 *Sun*, 27 February 1985.
69 ibid.
70 *Star*, 27 February 1985.
71 *The Times*, 27 February 1985.
72 *Daily Mail*, 27 February 1985.
73 *Sunday People*, 3 March 1985.
74 *Sun*, 2 March 1985.
75 *Daily Mirror*, 2 March 1985.
76 *Star*, 2 March 1985.
77 S. Hall, C. Critcher, T. Jefferson, J. Clarke and B. Roberts (1978) *Policing the Crisis*, London, Macmillan.
78 London *Evening Standard*, 18 November 1985.
79 ibid.
80 *Star*, 20 November 1985.
81 *Sunday People*, 24 November 1985.
82 *Star*, 12 October 1985.
83 *Sun*, 11 October 1985.
84 *Daily Mirror*, 11 October 1985.
85 *Daily Mirror*, 6 November 1985.
86 London *Evening Standard*, 18 November 1985.
87 33rd Annual Report of the Press Council (1986), *The Press and The People*, London, The Press Council.
88 *Daily Mail*, 18 December 1985.
89 S.M. Edwards (1981) *Female Sexuality and the Law*, Oxford, Martin Robertson; Z. Adler (1987) *Rape on Trial*, London, Routledge & Kegan Paul; J. Temkin (1987) *Rape and the Legal Process*, London, Sweet & Maxwell.
90 *The Times*, 14 November 1985.
91 *Daily Mirror*, 14 November 1985.
92 *Sun*, 14 November 1985.
93 *Star*, 15 November 1985.
94 *Daily Mirror*, 16 November 1985.

95 *The Times*, 7 December 1985.
96 *Star*, 13 November 1985.
97 *Daily Mail*, 18 December 1985.
98 *Daily Mirror*, 18 December 1985.
99 *Sunday Mirror*, 22 December 1985.
100 *Star*, 9 January 1985.
101 *Daily Mirror*, 26 February 1985.
102 *Sun*, 4 May 1985.
103 *Middlesex Chronicle*, 9 May 1985.
104 *Sun*, 15 June 1985.
105 *Star*, 21 September 1985.
106 *Star*, 14 December 1985.
107 *Daily Mail*, 20 April 1985.
108 *Sun*, 4 June 1985.
109 *Star*, 25 October 1985.
110 *Daily Mail*, 22 June 1985.
111 *Star*, 9 February 1985.
112 *Daily Mail*, 16 February 1985.
113 *Star*, 9 May 1985.
114 *Sun*, 18 May 1985.
115 *Star*, 18 November 1985.
116 *Daily Mirror*, 24 September 1985.
117 *Star*, 2 November 1985.
118 *Daily Mirror*, 18 May 1985.
119 *Sun*, 16 October 1985.
120 *Star*, 14 August 1985.
121 *Sun*, 24 January 1985.
122 *Sun*, 10 October 1985.
123 *Sun*, 19 October 1985.
124 *Sun*, 16 March 1985.
125 *Sun*, 18 October 1985.
126 London *Evening Standard*, 22 November 1985.
127 *Star*, 23 November 1985.
128 *Sun*, 23 November 1985.
129 *Daily Mirror*, 23 November 1985.
130 *Daily Mail*, 2 July 1985.
131 *Daily Mirror*, 2 July 1985.
132 *Coventry Evening Telegraph*, 18 March 1985.
133 *Coventry Evening Telegraph*, 24 September 1985.
134 *Sun*, 18 July 1985.
135 *Sun*, 15 March 1985.
136 *Daily Mirror*, 14 May 1985.
137 *Sun*, 25 May 1985.
138 *Daily Mirror*, 14 November 1985.
139 *Star*, 23 July 1985.
140 *Lancashire Evening Post*, 27 May 1985.
141 *Daily Mirror*, 29 October 1985.
142 *Star*, 31 May 1985.

143 *Sun*, 21 December 1985.
144 *Lancashire Evening Post*, 21 November 1985.
145 London *Evening Standard*, 26 April 1985.
146 *Sun*, 20 April 1985.
147 *Sun*, 27 November 1985.
148 *Middlesex Chronicle*, 19 December 1985.
149 *Sun*, 3 May 1985.
150 *Daily Mirror*, 19 December 1985.
151 *Sun*, 20 July 1985.
152 *Sunday People*, 6 October 1985.
153 *Lancashire Evening Post*, 1 November 1985.
154 *Daily Mirror*, 9 November 1985.
155 *Sun*, 21 December 1985.
156 *Lancashire Evening Post*, 9,10,11 January 1985.
157 *Lancashire Evening Post*, 1 March 1985.
158 *Sun*, 18 July 1985.
159 *Daily Mail*, 16 October 1985.
160 *Daily Mirror*, 9 August 1985.
161 *Daily Mail*, 19 October 1985.
162 *Daily Mail*, 24 July 1985.
163 *Daily Mirror*, 8 March 1985.
164 *Sun*, 19 January 1985.
165 *Star*, 8 March 1985.
166 *Daily Mail*, 19 October 1985.
167 *Sunday People*, 27 October 1985.
168 *Sun*, 16 January 1985.
169 *Daily Mirror*, 7 February 1985.
170 *Lancashire Evening Post*, 21 March 1985.
171 *Daily Mirror*, 3 April 1985.
172 *Daily Mirror*, 7 August 1985.
173 *Star*, 4 December 1985.
174 *Daily Mirror*, 26 June 1985.
175 *Daily Mirror*, 7 December 1985.
176 *Daily Mirror*, 15 March 1985.
177 *Daily Mirror*, 26 July 1985.
178 *Daily Mirror*, 16 October 1985.
179 *Sun*, 26 October 1985.
180 *Daily Mirror*, 26 July 1985.
181 *Star*, 26 February 1985.
182 *Sun*, 26 February 1985.
183 *Daily Mail*, 26 February 1985.
184 *Daily Mail*, 27 February 1985
185 *Daily Mail*, 23 April 1985.
186 *Star*, 2 August 1985.
187 *Daily Mail*, 2 August 1985.
188 *Daily Mirror*, 2 August 1985.
189 *Star*, 1 August 1985.
190 *Star*, 2 August 1985.

191 *Sun*, 2 August 1985.
192 *Sun*, 4 May 1985.

5 Sex-offenders after conviction

1 *Sunday People*, 30 June 1985.
2 *Daily Mail*, 30 November 1985.
3 *Star*, 7-11 October 1985.
4 *Sun*, 9 December 1985; *Daily Mirror*, 9 December 1985.
5 *Sun*, 10 June 1985.
6 *Lancashire Evening Post*, 10 June 1985.
7 *Sun*, 2 March, 15 April, 29 April, 10 June, 14 June, 2 July, 2 December
  and 4 December 1985.
8 *Star*, 15 April 1985.
9 *Star*, 24 May 1985.
10 *Sun*, 4 December 1985.
11 *Star*, 5 December 1985.
12 *Daily Mail*, 17 January 1985.
13 *Star*, 25 January 1985.
14 *Lancashire Evening Post*, 25 January 1985.
15 *Star*, 30 January 1985.
16 *News of the World*, 10 February 1985.
17 *Sunday People*, 28 April 1985.
18 *Daily Mail*, 16 March 1985.
19 *Star*, 16 March 1985.
20 *Daily Mail*, 22 March 1985.
21 *Daily Mail*, 20 April 1985.
22 *Star*, 20 April 1985.
23 *Sun*, 20 April 1985.
24 *Sunday Mirror*, 21 April 1985.
25 *Sunday Mirror*, 28 April 1985.
26 *Sunday Mirror*, 16 June 1985.
27 *Sun*, 10 June 1985.
28 *Daily Mail*, 10 June 1985.
29 *Sun*, 11 June 1985.
30 *Guardian*, 12 June 1985.
31 *The Times*, 20 December 1985.
32 *Daily Mail*, 6 July 1985.
33 *The Times*, 6 July 1985.
34 *Guardian*, 6 July 1985.
35 *Star*, 12 September 1985.
36 *Sun*, 1 August 1985.
37 *Daily Mail*, 25 September 1985.
38 *Sunday People*, 30 August 1985.
39 *Coventry Evening Telegraph*, 27 March 1985.
40 *Daily Mail*, 2 July 1985.
41 *Coventry Evening Telegraph*, 27 March 1985.
42 *The Times*, 25 January 1985.

43 London *Evening Standard*, 4 February 1985.
44 *Star*, 8 February 1985.
45 *Daily Mirror*, 8 February 1985.
46 *Star*, 8 February 1985.
47 *Sun*, 12 February 1985.
48 *Sunday People*, 3 March 1985.
49 *News of the World*, 3 March 1985.
50 *The Times*, 4 March 1985.
51 *Guardian*, 19 March 1985.
52 *The Times*, 3 June 1985.
53 *Daily Mail*, 15 July 1985.
54 *Mail on Sunday*, 21 July 1985.
55 *Star*, 22 July 1985.
56 *Daily Mirror*, 24 July 1985.
57 *Coventry Evening Telegraph*, 24 July 1985.
58 *Mail on Sunday*, 6 October 1985.
59 *Daily Mirror*, 19 October 1985.
60 *Sun*, 2 May 1985.
61 *Coventry Evening Telegraph*, 1 November 1985.
62 *Coventry Evening Telegraph*, 11 December 1985.
63 *Guardian*, 12 December 1985.
64 *Coventry Evening Telegraph*, 13 December 1985.
65 *Coventry Evening Telegraph*, 1 November 1985.
66 *Guardian*, 12 December 1985.

6 Informing the public

1 Women's National Commission (1985) *Violence Against Women*, London, Cabinet Office. It is of interest that this was the only report where it was clearly stated that the government was considering its recommendations (H.C. Debates, vol. 90, col. 268; H.C. Debates, vol. 96, col. 422).
2 *The Times*, 20 and 21 November 1985.
3 M. Hough and P. Mayhew (1985) *Taking Account of Crime: Key Findings from the Second British Crime Survey*, London, HMSO.
4 London *Evening Standard*, 25 April 1985.
5 *The Times* (1 November 1985), however, mentioned a report by a criminologist, Richard Kinsey, commissioned by the Merseyside County Council.
6 *The Times*, 11 June 1985; *Sun*, 11 June 1985 (*Strong Kids, Safe Kids*, CIC Videos).
7 *Guardian*, 15 October 1985 (*KIDS CAN SAY 'NO'!*, Rolf House Video).
8 H.C. Debates, vol. 87, col. 612 (28 November 1985, written answer to Mr Soley).
9 *Sun*, 11 February 1985.
10 R.E. Hall (1985) *Ask Any Woman*, Falling Wall Press.
11 Personal communication (Falling Wall Press).
12 *Woman*, 29 September 1984.

13 *Daily Mail*, 11 January 1985.
14 *Sun*, 11 January 1985.
15 *The Times*, 11 January 1985.
16 *Star*, 11 January 1985.
17 *Daily Express*, 11 January 1985.
18 *Daily Telegraph*, 11 January 1985.
19 *Sun*, 25 January 1985.
20 *Daily Mirror*, 14 January 1985.
21 *Guardian*, 25 January 1985.
22 I. Blair (1985) *Investigating Rape*, London, Croom Helm in association with Police Foundation.
23 *Daily Mail*, 11 January 1985.
24 Personal communication (Falling Wall Press).
25 *Daily Mail*, 12 March 1985.
26 *Guardian*, 4 February 1987.
27 *Guardian*, 9 February 1987.
28 *Daily Mail*, 17 June 1985.
29 Report of a Howard League Working Party (1985), *Unlawful Sex*, London, Waterlow.
30 In continuing their quest for something new, it is rare for newspapers to acknowledge the date of earlier work they sometimes quote.
31 *The Times*, 29 April 1985.
32 Personal communication (30 September 1986).
33 The Cleveland child abuse controversy had a great deal of media coverage in 1987. The diagnosis by two Middlesbrough General Hospital paediatricians that 121 children had suffered child abuse led eventually to an inquiry conducted by Mrs Justice Butler-Sloss. The seventy-one days of public hearings produced an unprecedented media coverage on the issue. See B. Campbell (1988) *Unofficial Secrets: Child Sexual Abuse – The Cleveland Case*, London, Virago, for a fuller account of the crisis.
34 NSPCC Press Release, 18 September 1985. It was stated that 'the latest figures update and reinforce the findings in the Society's report *Trends in Child Abuse* published last year. This research is the largest, continuing survey of child abuse being carried out in England and Wales'.
35 London *Evening Standard*, 19 September 1985.
36 *Sunday People*, 22 September 1985.
37 *News of the World*, 22 September 1985.
38 *Sunday People*, 22 September 1985.
39 NSPCC, op. cit.
40 *Guardian*, 19 September 1985.
41 *Guardian*, 16 July 1985.
42 *Guardian*, 17 July 1985.
43 *Star*, 5 January 1985.
44 *Star*, 28 December 1985.
45 *Star*, 14, 18 February 1985.
46 *Sun*, 27 March 1985.

47 *Sun*, 22 May 1985.
48 *Sun*, 5 July 1985.
49 *Guardian*, 17 July 1985.
50 *Star*, 5 December 1985.
51 *Sun*, 5 December 1985.
52 *Daily Mail*, 5 December 1985.
53 *The Times*, 5 December 1985.
54 *Daily Mail*, 4 October 1985.
55 *Daily Mail*, 5 October 1985.
56 *Daily Mail*, 11 October 1985.
57 *Daily Mail*, 20 August 1985.

7 Changing legal practice

1 London *Evening Standard*, 9 December 1985.
2 *Observer*, 8 December 1985.
3 *Sunday Mirror*, 6 October 1985.
4 *Daily Mail*, 10 December 1985.
5 London *Evening Standard*, 9 December 1985.
6 *Daily Mail*, 10 December 1985.
7 London *Evening Standard*, 10 December 1985.
8 London *Evening Standard*, 10 December 1985.
9 *The Times*, 11 December 1985.
10 *Daily Mirror*, 11 December 1985.
11 *Daily Mail*, 11 December 1985.
12 *The Times*, 11 December 1985.
13 *Sun*, 11 December 1985.
14 *Daily Mirror*, 11 December 1985.
15 *Guardian*, 11 December 1985.
16 *The Times*, 11 December 1985.
17 *Guardian*, 11 December 1985.
18 *Daily Mail*, 11 December 1985.
19 *Star*, 11 December 1985.
20 *Daily Mirror*, 11 December 1985.
21 *The Times*, 12 December 1985.
22 *Guardian*, 12 December 1985.
23 *Daily Mirror*, 12 December 1985.
24 *Star*, 12 December 1985.
25 *Daily Mirror*, 12 December 1985.
26 *Daily Mirror*, 13 December 1985.
27 *Guardian*, 17 December 1985.
28 *The Times*, 28 December 1985.
29 *Guardian*, 19 December 1985.
30 *Guardian*, 24 December 1985.
31 *Coventry Evening Telegraph*, 9 January 1985.
32 *Coventry Evening Telegraph*, 9 January 1985.
33 *Guardian*, 18 January 1985.

34 *The Times*, 26 January 1985.
35 *Guardian*, 26 January 1985.
36 *Star*, 26 January 1985.
37 *The Times*, 26 January 1985.
38 *Guardian*, 26 January 1985.
39 ibid.
40 *Sun*, 6 February 1985.
41 London *Evening Standard*, 27 February 1985.
42 London *Evening Standard*, 18 February 1985.
43 *The Times*, 20 February 1985.
44 *Star*, 20 February 1985.
45 *Mail on Sunday*, 24 February 1985.
46 *Star*, 25 February 1985.
47 *The Times*, 28 February 1985.
48 *Guardian*, 28 February 1985.
49 *Star*, 2 March 1985.
50 *Sun*, 2 March 1985.
51 London *Evening Standard*, 25 April 1985.
52 *Star*, 26 April 1985.
53 *Guardian*, 10 May 1985.
54 *The Times*, 11 May 1985.
55 *Guardian*, 11 May 1985.
56 *Sun*, 11 May 1985.
57 *Star*, 11 May 1985.
58 *Daily Mail*, 11 May 1985.
59 *Daily Mirror*, 11 May 1985.
60 *Daily Mail*, 14 May 1985.
61 *Star*, 15 May 1985.
62 London *Evening Standard*, 17 May 1985.
63 *Guardian*, 18 May 1985.
64 *Guardian*, 28 May 1985.
65 D.J. Smith and J. Gray (1985) *Police and People in London: The PSI Report*, Aldershot, Gower.
66 *The Times*, 7 June 1985.
67 *Guardian*, 7 June 1985.
68 *Daily Mail*, 6 July 1985.
69 *Star*, 8 August 1985.
70 *Coventry Evening Telegraph*, 14 August 1985.
71 *Coventry Evening Telegraph*, 13 September 1985.
72 *Star*, 16 September 1985.
73 *Star*, 4 November 1985.
74 London *Evening Standard*, 11 November 1985.
75 London *Evening Standard*, 18 November 1985.
76 London *Evening Standard*, 6 December 1985.
77 *Guardian*, 23 December 1985.
78 *Star*, 16 September 1985.
79 *Coventry Evening Telegraph*, 13 September 1985.

8 Conclusion

1 H.C. Debates, vol. 111, col. 15 (23 February 1987).
2 *Dail Mail*, 29 October 1982.
3 Z. Adler (1987) *Rape on Trial*, London, Routledge & Kegan Paul.
4 33rd Annual Report of the Press Council (1986) *The Press and the People*.
5 Committee on Privacy and Related Matters.
6 Press Council, op. cit., p. 120.
7 Press Council, op. cit., p. 121.
8 Press Council, op. cit., p. 136.
9 Press Council, op. cit., pp. 9–10.

Name index

Subject index